CONVERSATIONS WITH MILOŠEVIĆ

Conversations with
Milošević

Ivor Roberts

The University of Georgia Press
Athens

Paperback edition, 2018
Published by the University of Georgia Press
Athens, Georgia 30602
www.ugapress.org
© 2016 by Sir Ivor Roberts
All rights reserved
Set in Minion Pro by Graphic Composition, Inc

Most University of Georgia Press titles are
available from popular e-book vendors.

Printed digitally

The Library of Congress has cataloged the hardcover edition of this book as follows:
Names: Roberts, Ivor, 1946–
Title: Conversations with Milošević / Ivor Roberts.
Description: Athens : The University of Georgia Press, 2016. | Includes bibliographical references and index.
Identifiers: LCCN 2015043961 | ISBN 9780820349435 (hardcover : alkaline paper) | ISBN 9780820349428 (ebook)
Subjects: LCSH: Roberts, Ivor, 1946– | Yugoslav War, 1991–1995—Diplomatic history. | Milošević, Slobodan, 1941–2006. | Serbia—Politics and government—1992–2006. | Balkan Peninsula—Politics and government—1989– | Ambassadors—Great Britain—Biography. | Great Britain—Foreign relations—Balkan Peninsula. | Balkan Peninsula—Foreign relations—Great Britain. | Western countries—Foreign relations—Balkan Peninsula. | Balkan Peninsula—Foreign relations—Western countries.
Classification: LCC DR1313.7.D58 R63 2016 | DDC 949.703—dc23 LC record available at http://lccn.loc.gov/2015043961

Paperback ISBN 978-0-8203-5471-2

This work was originally published in Serbian in 2012.

For Elizabeth
and for Huw, David, and Hannah

CONTENTS

List of Abbreviations   ix

Preface   xi

Acknowledgments   xiii

Dramatis Personae   xv

Chronology   xxiii

Maps   xxviii

Introduction   1

CHAPTER 1. The Pyromaniac Fireman   24

CHAPTER 2. Early Belgrade Days   33

CHAPTER 3. Close Encounter with the Bosnian Serbs: The Three Ks   39

CHAPTER 4. A First Private Meeting with Milošević   46

CHAPTER 5. Meeting General Mladić   52

CHAPTER 6. Point Man for the Contact Group   58

CHAPTER 7. The UN Hostage Crisis   65

CHAPTER 8. Srebrenica   70

CHAPTER 9. The End of the Krajina Serbs and NATO Bombing   75

CHAPTER 10. Dayton from the Sidelines   79

CHAPTER 11. Independent Media and the Opposition   82

CHAPTER 12. The High Representative's Delegate   91

CHAPTER 13. The Winter of Discontent   98

CHAPTER 14. Bildt's Farewell and the B92 Saga   109

CHAPTER 15. Kosovo   113

[viii] CONTENTS

CHAPTER 16. Final Days   127

CHAPTER 17. Secret Emissary   136

CHAPTER 18. Aftermath   146

Conclusions   152

Notes   157

Suggested Further Reading   165

Index   167

ABBREVIATIONS

BH	Bosnia and Herzegovina
CINCSOUTH	Commander-in-Chief, Allied Forces Southern Europe
DS	Democratic Party
DSS	Democratic Party of Serbia
ECMM	European Community Monitoring Mission. European organization with observers throughout former Yugoslavia
EC	European Community, which under the Maastricht Treaty became EU in 1993
EU	European Union
FRY	Federal Republic of Yugoslavia. Rump Yugoslavia established after breakup, comprising Serbia and Montenegro.
FYROM	Former Yugoslav Republic of Macedonia
HDZ	Hrvatska Demokratska Zajednica. Croatian Democratic Union (Croat nationalist party)
HV	Hrvatska Vojska. Croatian army
HVO	Hrvatsko Vijeće Obrane. Bosnian-Croat forces
ICFY	International Conference on the Former Yugoslavia. Organization established by the EC and UN in 1992 to mediate in the conflict in Yugoslavia
ICJ	International Court of Justice
ICRC	International Committee of the Red Cross
ICTY	International Criminal Tribunal for the Former Yugoslavia
IEBL	Inter-Entity Boundary Line. Boundary between the Muslim-Croat Federation and the Republika Srpska established under the Dayton peace accord
IFOR	Implementation Force. NATO force leading military operations in Bosnia in 1996
IMF	International Monetary Fund
JNA	Jugoslovenska Narodna Armija. Pre-breakup Yugoslav army.
JUL	Yugoslav United Left
KFOR	Kosovo Force. Nato international peacekeeping force in Kosovo
KLA	Kosovo Liberation Army
LCY	League of Communists of Yugoslavia

LDK	Democratic League of Kosovo
NATO	North Atlantic Treaty Organization
NSC	National Security Council. Foreign and security policy staff at the White House, Washington
OHR	Office of the High Representative
OSCE	Organization for Security and Cooperation in Europe (previously Conference on Security and Cooperation in Europe [CSCE])
PIC	Peace Implementation Conference
RRF	Rapid Reaction Force. Military force under UN command during summer of 1995
RS	Republika Srpska. Bosnian Serb entity
RSK	Republika Srpska Krajina. Croatian Serb statelet
SACEUR	Supreme Allied Commander Europe (NATO)
SANU	Serbian Academy of Sciences and Arts
SDA	Stranka Demokratske Akcije. Party for Democratic Action (Muslim nationalist party in Bosnia)
SDS	Srpska Demokratska Stranka. Serbian Democratic Party (Serb nationalist party in Bosnia)
SFOR	Stabilization Force. NATO force leading military operations in Bosnia in 1997
SFRY	Socialist Federal Republic of Yugoslavia. Tito's Yugoslavia, which outlived him until the breakup in 1992
SHAPE	Supreme Headquarters Allied Powers Europe NATO's headquarters in Europe
SPO	Serbian Renewal Movement
UN	United Nations
UNHCR	United Nations High Commissioner for Refugees
UNPROFOR	United Nations Protection Force. UN forces in Bosnia 1992–95
VJ	Yugoslav Army. Army of the post-breakup FRY
VOPP	Vance-Owen Peace Plan
VRS	Vojska Republike Srpske. Army of "Republika Srpska." Bosnian Serb army

PREFACE

This book has been a long time in gestation. Shortly after I left Belgrade as British ambassador at the end of 1997 after four very long years in the middle of the Yugoslav wars, I was allowed a sabbatical year before my next posting as ambassador at Dublin. I'd been encouraged by senior colleagues in the Foreign Office to commit to writing my experiences in the former Yugoslavia, and a year at St Antony's College, Oxford, presented itself as the perfect opportunity.

I wrote a first draft quickly, while the memories and impressions were still fresh, supplemented by the notes I had taken of the conversations with the protagonist of the book. By the end of that year, I'd completed a manuscript, which, following normal procedures, I submitted for authorization before publication. The initial reaction was encouraging. "There shouldn't be a difficulty . . . expect it will all go through quite painlessly," and so on, but days turned to weeks with an ominous silence, and then a final verdict emerged: even with amendments, the book could not be published. The undesirability of creating a precedent in publishing exchanges between an ambassador and a head of government or state, even when the latter was regarded as a war criminal, was the reason given for the ban. Perhaps this was true up to a point, but was the more compelling reality anxiety over offending various friendly countries? I was, to put it at its most restrained, disappointed. I also pointed out that Richard Holbrooke, the U.S. negotiator who had brought the negotiations over the Dayton Agreement to a successful conclusion, had just published his own version of his time as lead negotiator. I thought it right that the UK story, and mine in particular, should be fairly aired. Holbrooke's vivid account had little to say about most of the European actors, and there was a tendency to underplay their role. Holbrooke, I was told, was in a different category: someone who transferred between his law firm and government service seamlessly. Not an option in British government service then and none too easy now.

And so, the manuscript went, as it were, onto the shelf where it remained for many years until finally, after I'd retired from the diplomatic service, I was told that I could publish if I wished. By then I was back at Oxford, running one of its colleges, and had another book project, namely editing a standard work on diplomatic practice, its first revision for thirty years. This project took some years to realize, so it was not until relatively recently that my thoughts turned again to the Milošević book. I have now revised and updated the book to take in the Kosovo crisis and the Rambouillet conference and, of course, the bombing of Serbia. The text benefits rightly from the historical perspective that was not always clear in the heat of the aftermath of the Bosnian and Kosovo crises. The essentials of my exchanges with Milošević and the other motley crew of criminals, opposition leaders, negotiators, and even some of the ordinary and perforce less colorful people in Bosnia, Serbia, and Montenegro remain largely untouched, which I hope will convey something of the immediacy.

The title of the book borrows from the famous book by Milovan Djilas, the legendary first dissident in the communist world, whose "Conversations with Stalin" remains unsurpassed in its chilling account of dealing with a ruthless autocrat and its evocation of the nightmarish world of Stalin's Moscow and the Kremlin in the mid-1940s. It was an inspiration to me, and although, of course, the parallels are not exact, there were striking similarities. Which brings me to one of the reasons for writing this book. Dealing with dictators and autocrats is never easy, but there are lessons to be learned from the experience of negotiating with those who are answerable to nobody and who allow no disagreement from their peers. Otherwise one might be tempted to ask why we need another book on Milošević. Well, however much has been written already, not much has been written from the perspective of someone living in Belgrade who had sustained interaction on more than forty occasions with Milošević, negotiating texts, drafting treaties, exchanging communications from capitals in a joint attempt to corral him into a pattern of improved behavior. As often as not this involved persuading him to be rough and tough with his Frankenstein's monsters, the Bosnian Serb leadership.

Sometimes over a nearly four-year period the contacts with him were intensive, several times a day; at other times weeks went by without any exchange. My hope is that this account will provide some useful insights into the workings of a highly unusual, complex figure who played a prominent but consistently negative and baleful role throughout the last decade of the last millennium. He effectively provided one of the most demanding diplomatic and military challenges to diplomats, statesmen, and generals. More often than not we failed to read him correctly. If nothing else, I hope this book will serve to provide some helpful appreciation of the problems likely to be encountered in dealing with ruthless autocrats like Milošević in the future and to assist others to rise to such challenges more successfully.

Milovan Djilas's son, Aleksa, who has read this text, was kind and overgenerous enough to say of it that his father now had a worthy rival. This book is very far from being in that category, but I hope it will nevertheless shed some light on why the former Yugoslavia died in agony.

Ivor Roberts
Trinity College
Oxford
July 2015

ACKNOWLEDGMENTS

Over the long incubation period of this book, I've incurred many debts. Rather than enumerate all creditors (some may have forgotten that they ever read the manuscript!), let me single out the most egregious, who include my former colleagues in Belgrade, George Busby and David Austin (they ensured that my memory didn't stray). In Oxford, Hermione Lee at Wolfson College and Othon Anastasakis at St Antony's both made comments that, I believe, enhanced the text, and Earle Scarlett, formerly of the State Department, and Philip McDonagh, Irish Ambassador to the OSCE, put forward a range of constructive suggestions. Aleksa Djilas's help from Belgrade was priceless and was the single most important source of encouragement.

The organizational skills of my long-suffering PA, Ulli Parkinson, have proved more than a match for my perverse attraction for the chaotic, while Trinity College's librarian, Sharon Cure, has made heroic and virtually instantaneous efforts to obtain books from the most distant of libraries.

Lastly the contribution of my wife, Elizabeth—her meticulous reading of the text and frank criticism, not to mention her patience—has as usual been the gold standard.

DRAMATIS PERSONAE

ABDIĆ, FIKRET. Muslim leader of the breakaway "Autonomous Province of Western Bosnia." Allied with Bosnian Serb army before his ministate collapsed in August 1995.

AKASHI, YASUSHI. Japanese diplomat. Special representative of the UN secretary-general in former Yugoslavia, head of UNPROFOR Mission (December 1993–October 1995).

ALBRIGHT, MADELEINE. U.S. ambassador to the United Nations (1993–97) and U.S. secretary of state (1997–2001).

ANNAN, KOFI. UN under-secretary-general heading the Department of Peace-Keeping Operations in New York until he became UN secretary-general in January 1997. Served as special representative of the secretary-general in former Yugoslavia in October 1995.

ARKAN (NOM DE GUERRE); REAL NAME, ŽELJKO RAŽNATOVIĆ. Commander of feared paramilitary unit, international criminal, and briefly MP. Worked for Serbia's secret police. Accused of war crimes in Bosnia and Croatia. Assassinated in 2000.

AUSTIN, DAVID. First Secretary, British Embassy, Belgrade.

AVRAMOVIĆ, DRAGOSLAV. Governor of National Bank of Yugoslavia (1994–96). Briefly leader of (Zajedno) coalition of opposition parties, 1996.

BABIĆ, MILAN. A central figure in the self-styled Republika Srpska Krajina in Croatia (1990–95). Held a number of positions, including foreign minister at the time of Croatian offensive in August 1995.

BADINTER, ROBERT. French constitutional court judge, chairman of the EC Arbitration Committee on Yugoslavia (1991).

BAKER, JAMES. U.S. secretary of state (1989–92).

BILDT, CARL. European Union peace envoy, replaced Lord David Owen (spring 1995). Former Swedish prime minister. Appointed High Representative in charge of civilian aspects of Dayton Agreement.

BLOT, JACQUES. Political director at the French Foreign Ministry.

BOUTROS-GHALI, BOUTROS. Secretary-general of the United Nations (1990–97).

BRAITHWAITE, JULIAN. First Secretary, British Embassy, Belgrade.

BUGARČIĆ, BOJAN. Yugoslav diplomat and foreign policy adviser to Milošević.

BUHA, ALEKSA. Bosnian Serb foreign affairs minister in the Republika Srpska.

BULATOVIĆ, MOMIR. President of Montenegro until 1997. Protégé of Slobodan Milošević.

BUSBY, GEORGE. First Secretary (Political), British Embassy, Belgrade.

ČANAK, NENAD. Colorful and charismatic Serb politician. Cofounder (1990) and leader of the then opposition center-left League of Social Democrats of Vojvodina. Later president of Vojvodina Assembly.

CARRINGTON, LORD PETER. Former British Foreign Secretary. First EC peace envoy (1991–92).

CHERNOMYRDIN, VIKTOR. Prime minister of the Russian Federation (1992–98).

CHRISTOPHER, WARREN. U.S. secretary of state (1993–97).

CHURKIN, VITALY. Russia's special envoy to former Yugoslavia (1993–94).

CLARK, WESLEY. U.S. general. Supreme allied commander Europe (SACEUR).

CLINTON, BILL. U.S. president (1993–2001).

COOK, ROBIN. British Foreign Secretary (1997–2001).

ČOSIĆ, DOBRICA. Influential Serbian nationalist writer. Seen by some as spiritual leader of Serbs. President of FRY (1992–93).

CROMBIE, TONY. Deputy head of mission, British Embassy, Belgrade.

DE LA PRESLE, BERTRAND. French general. UNPROFOR force commander (1994–95).

DEMAQI, ADEM. Kosovo Albanian politician. Long-term political prisoner. Dubbed the "Kosovo Mandela." Political head of the Kosovo Liberation Army (KLA).

DJINDJIĆ, ZORAN. Opposition leader, mayor of Belgrade. Later prime minister (2001 until assassinated in 2003).

DJUKANOVIĆ, MILO. Montenegrin leader. Came to power on Milošević's coat tails (youngest prime minister in Europe at the age of twenty-nine) in 1991, but turned against him in 1996. Variously, prime minister and president of Montenegro. Oversaw its independence in 2006. Controlling figure in the ruling party (DPS) in Montenegro, which has been in power continuously since the first multiparty elections in 1990.

DRAŠKOVIĆ, VUK. Charismatic Serbian opposition leader. Jailed briefly by Milošević in 1991 and 1993, but in 1999 became deputy prime minister of FRY under Milošević. Foreign minister of Serbia and Montenegro, later just Serbia (2003–7). Survived several assassination attempts. Married to **Danica Drašković**, a power in her own right.

FRASURE, ROBERT. U.S. Contact Group member. Key player in the U.S. peace initiative in 1995 until he was tragically killed in a road accident on Mount Igman in August 1995.

FROWICK, ROBERT. U.S. ambassador, OSCE head of mission in Bosnia-Herzegovina until December 1997.
GALBRAITH, PETER. U.S. ambassador to Croatia until February 1998.
GANIĆ, EJUP. Bosnian Muslim politician, vice president of the Federation. "Yugoslav" representative to the prewar Presidency of Bosnia, but later joined SDA party and in 1992 became Bosnian de facto vice president.
GELBARD, ROBERT. U.S. special representative for the implementation of the Dayton Agreement; later special envoy for the Balkans.
GENSCHER, HANS-DIETRICH. German foreign minister. Bulldozed EC into Croatian recognition in 1991.
GLIGOROV, KIRO. Veteran Yugoslav politician. President of Macedonia from 1991 and guided the republic through to independence. Seriously injured in assassination attempt in October 1995.
GONZÁLEZ, FELIPE. Spanish prime minister (1982–96).
GRANIĆ, MATE. Foreign minister of Croatia since 1993.
GREENSTOCK, JEREMY. Political director, British Foreign Office (1996–98).
GVERO, MILAN. JNA spokesman and later deputy commander of the Bosnian Serb army.
HOGG, DOUGLAS. British junior Foreign Office minister dealing with Balkans (until 1995).
HOLBROOKE, RICHARD. U.S. assistant secretary of state for European and Canadian affairs until his departure in early 1996 to private business. U.S. chief negotiator at the Dayton conference.
HOXHA, ENVER. Stalinist communist leader of Albania (1944–85).
HURD, DOUGLAS. British Foreign Secretary (until July 1995).
ILIĆ, MILE. Milošević stooge. Mayor of Niš (1990–96). While mayor, attempted to falsify election results in 1996.
ISCHINGER, WOLFGANG. Political director of the Foreign Ministry in Bonn. German representative at the Dayton conference.
IVANOV, IGOR. First deputy foreign minister of the Russian Federation and Russian representative at the Dayton conference.
IZETBEGOVIĆ, ALIJA. President and founder of the SDA Muslim Party in Bosnia. Member of the Presidency of Bosnia and Herzegovina from September 1996. President of the Presidency of Bosnia-Herzegovina after the elections in 1990. Presided over Bosnia's declaration of independence and war.
JANVIER, BERNARD. Lieutenant-general of France. Commander of UN forces in former Yugoslavia (from February 1995). Uneasy relationship with the United States over reluctance to use NATO air power.
JEKNIĆ, JANKO. Montenegrin foreign minister (1994–97).
JEREMIĆ, VUK. Serbian foreign minister (2007–12).
JOVANOVIĆ, VLADISLAV. Serbian foreign minister (until summer 1995).

JOVIĆ, BORISLAV. Serbia's representative on the Federal Presidency. Held a host of party and political posts. A close associate of Slobodan Milošević.

JUPPÉ, ALAIN. French foreign minister (until appointed prime minister in 1995).

KARADŽIĆ, RADOVAN. President of the SDS party and "president" of the "Republika Srpska" until July 1996. Indicted for war crimes.

KARDELJ, EDVARD. Leading partisan during World War II. Later major economic and political figure in Tito's Yugoslavia.

KINKEL, KLAUS. Minister of foreign affairs of Germany (1992–98).

KOHL, HELMUT. Chancellor of Germany (1982–98).

KOLJEVIĆ, NIKOLA. "Vice president" of "Republika Srpska" until September 1996. Previously lecturer in English literature at the University of Sarajevo. Committed suicide in Pale in January 1997.

KORNBLUM, JOHN. Succeeded Richard Holbrooke as assistant secretary of state for European affairs.

KOŠTUNICA, VOJISLAV. Opposition leader. Instrumental in downfall of Milošević and subsequently last president of the FRY and prime minister of Serbia after dissolution of FRY in 1996. Strong nationalist with emotional attachment to Kosovo.

KRAJIŠNIK, MOMČILO. Prominent SDS leader. Member of the Presidency of Bosnia and Herzegovina from September 1996. Speaker of the Bosnian and Herzegovina Parliament before the war.

KUČAN, MILAN. Slovene Communist Party leader who became the first president of independent Slovenia.

LEKIĆ, MIODRAG. Montenegrin Foreign Minister (1992–95) later FRY ambassador in Rome.

LILIĆ, ZORAN. President of FRY (from 1993). Took instructions from Milošević.

LJAJIĆ, RASIM. Leader of the Sandžak Democratic Party. Since 2000 a minister in the Serbian government.

LLOYD, TONY. British junior Foreign Office minister dealing with Balkans (1997–99).

MAJOR, JOHN. Prime minister of the United Kingdom (1992–97).

MARKOVIĆ, ANTE. Last federal prime minister (1989–91). Introduced market and, to a lesser extent, political reforms.

MARKOVIĆ, MIHAILO. Serbian philosopher and ideologue of Milošević's Serbian Socialist Party (SPS). Coauthor of infamous memorandum that listed Serb grievances within the SFRY and was widely regarded as a blueprint for a Greater Serbia.

MARKOVIĆ, MIRJANA. Slobodan Milošević's wife. Powerful and influential figure. Belgrade university professor. Founding member of the Yugoslav United Left (JUL).

MARTIĆ, MILAN. President of breakaway Serb state in Croatia (RSK). Former Knin police chief. Fled Croatian offensive in August 1995. Indicted for war crimes by War Crimes Tribunal in The Hague.

MATIĆ, VERAN. Cofounder with Saša Mirković of B92, the leading independent (and opposition) radio station during the Milošević years.

MESIĆ, STIPE. Croatia's representative on the federal Presidency, HDZ leader, and, until a rift in 1994, one of Tudjman's most trusted advisers.

MILES, DICK. U.S. chargé d'affaires, Belgrade (1996–99).

MILOŠEVIĆ, SLOBODAN. President of the Socialist Party of Serbia. President of Serbia until he was elected president of Yugoslavia (FRY) in July 1997. Regarded as most responsible for Yugoslavia's violent disintegration. Although partially rehabilitated for efforts toward peace culminating in the Dayton Agreement, indicted for war crimes during Kosovo crisis. Died in prison before the end of his trial in The Hague.

MILUTINOVIĆ, MILAN. Foreign minister of Yugoslavia from October 1995; became president of Serbia in 1998. Milošević protégé.

MIRKOVIĆ, SAŠA. Cofounder with Veran Matić of Radio B92, the leading independent broadcaster in Serbia.

MLADIĆ, RATKO. General of the pre-breakup Yugoslav army (JNA) and supreme commander of the Army of the "Republika Srpska" (VRS). Indicted for war crimes.

NEVILLE-JONES, DAME PAULINE. Political director of the Foreign and Commonwealth Office in London until the end of 1995. UK representative at the Dayton conference.

ORIĆ, NASER. Leader of Muslim forces defending Srebrenica (1992–95). Former bodyguard of Milošević. Indicted for war crimes.

OWEN, LORD DAVID. European Union cochairman of the International Conference on Former Yugoslavia (ICFY) until early June 1995.

PAGLIA, DON VINCENZO. Spiritual leader of the Catholic lay community of Sant'Egidio, which has mediated in international peace negotiations. Instrumental in bringing about education agreement between FRY and Kosovar Albanians in 1996.

PANIĆ, MILAN. Belgrade-born, California millionaire FRY prime minister (1992–93). Unsuccessful in running against Milošević in Serbian presidential elections of 1992.

PELLNAS, BO. Swedish general. ICFY Mission coordinator on sanctions enforcement on the FRY–Bosnia border.

PERIŠIĆ, MOMČILO. Chief of the General Staff of the Yugoslav (FRY) army (1993–98). Indicted by the International Criminal Tribunal for the former Yugoslavia (ICTY) for war crimes and sentenced in 2011 to twenty-seven years of imprisonment. In 2013, the Appeal Chamber at The Hague acquitted him of all charges.

PEŠIĆ, VESNA. Opposition politician. Strong promoter of democracy and civil society.

PLAVŠIĆ, BILJANA. Bosnian Serb leader. Member of the prewar Presidency of Bosnia. "Vice president of Republika Srpska" during the war and president of Republika Srpska from September 1996. Broke with the hardline Pale leadership and created the Serbian People's Alliance Party in summer 1997. Indicted and sentenced for war crimes. Served two-thirds of her eleven-year sentence. Previously lecturer in biology at the University of Sarajevo.

RIFKIND, MALCOLM. Foreign secretary of the United Kingdom (1995–97).

ROSE, SIR MICHAEL. British lieutenant-general. Commander of UN troops in Bosnia (January 1994–January 1995).

RUGOVA, IBRAHIM. Leader of Kosovo ethnic Albanians (from 1989).

SACIRBEY, MUHAMED. Bosnian Muslim politician. Ambassador to the United Nations since 1992. Bosnian foreign minister (June–December 1995).

ŠEŠELJ, VOJISLAV. Ultranationalist MP who commanded paramilitary unit during war. Intermittently allied with Milošević. Leader of Radical Party. Indicted for war crimes.

SILAJDŽIĆ, HARIS. Bosnian politician. Prime minister (October 1993–January 1996). Split from the SDA in 1996 and formed "ZA Bosna" party.

SMITH, LEIGHTON. U.S. admiral. CINSOUTH, viz. commander of NATO AFSOUTH (Allied Forces Southern European Region). Commander of IFOR (December 1995–July 1996).

SMITH, SIR RUPERT. Lieutenant general, commander of UN forces in Bosnia (January–November 1995).

STAMBOLIĆ, IVAN. Communist party official. Early mentor of Milošević who deposed him from the Presidency of Serbia in 1987. Assassinated in 2000 on the orders, it is widely assumed, of Milošević.

STANIŠIĆ, JOVICA. Head of State Security Service under Milošević. Indicted for war crimes but acquitted in 2013. Secret agent of the CIA.

STOLTENBERG, THORVALD. Norwegian politician. UN-appointed cochair of the International Conference on Former Yugoslavia (ICFY).

SURROI, VETON. Kosovo Albanian journalist, later politician. Founder (1997) and editor of highly influential *Koha Ditore* newspaper in Kosovo.

THAÇI, HASHIM. Leader of the Kosovo Liberation Army (KLA). Elected prime minister after Kosovo declaration of independence in 2008.

TREVISAN, DESSA. Journalist. Veteran *Times* correspondent in Eastern Europe. Fearless critic of Milošević and Tudjman. Accreditation in Serbia withdrawn in 1993 by Milošević.

TUDJMAN, FRANJO. Founding leader of the Croatian Democratic Union (HDZ) and first president of independent Croatia. Widely considered one of the gravediggers of the former Yugoslavia.

UGLJANIN, SULEJMAN. President of (Muslim) Party of Democratic Action of Sandžak. In exile in Turkey from 1993 to 1996.

VANCE, CYRUS. UN special envoy and then cochair of ICFY (1991–93). Former U.S. secretary of state.

VAN DEN BROEK, HANS. EU commissioner responsible for external affairs. Former Dutch foreign minister.

VAN WALSUM, PETER. Dutch diplomat. Political director (1989–93).

VLLASI, AZEM. Ethnic Albanian Kosovo Party leader. Chief of Kosovo Communist Party. Jailed in 1989 by Milošević. Released in April 1990.

VUKMANOVIĆ-TEMPO, SVETOZAR. Montenegrin Partisan. Later high official in the League of Communists of Yugoslavia (LCY).

YELTSIN, BORIS. President of the Russian Federation (1991–99).

ZAMETICA, JOVAN. Personal political adviser to Radovan Karadžić.

ZIMMERMANN, WARREN. Last U.S. ambassador to Yugoslavia (1989–92).

CHRONOLOGY

1980

- President for Life of Yugoslavia, Josip Broz Tito, dies. The Socialist Federal Republic of Yugoslavia (SFRY) is now governed by a Presidency revolving among the six constituent republics.

1987

- Slobodan Milošević as Serbian Communist Party chief visits Kosovo and in an inflammatory speech tells the Serbs in the province that "nobody will ever dare to beat you again."
- Antibureaucratic revolutions orchestrated by Milošević supporters begin, which oust incumbent leaders in Kosovo, Montenegro, and Vojvodina.

1988

- Milošević unseats his mentor, Ivan Stambolić, and replaces him as president of Serbia.

1989

- On the six hundredth anniversary of the Battle of Kosovo, Milošević makes a major nationalist speech at the site of the battle.

1990

- Last Congress of the League of Communists of Yugoslavia held in Belgrade. Alarmed at Serbia's nationalistically driven attempt to dominate the SFRY and humiliated by the rejection of all their proposals for liberal constitutional reforms, Slovenes and Croats walk out.

1991

- Slovenia and Croatia declare independence in June, Macedonia in September. The ten-day war between local forces and Yugoslav People's Army

(JNA) results in JNA retreat. Serb-Croat war begins. Serb areas in Croatia declare independence.
- Major Croatian towns shelled including Vukovar and Dubrovnik.
- Under German pressure, EU agrees to recognize Croatia and Slovenia in January 1992.

1992

- Cutileiro Plan to prevent descent into war in Bosnia signed by Muslim, Serb, and Croat leaders. But after meeting with U.S. ambassador Warren Zimmerman, Bosnian Muslim (Bosniak) leader Izetbegović withdraws his signature.
- Vance Plan creates four UN-protected zones for Serbs in Croatia (UNPAs). Large-scale fighting in Croatia comes to an end.
- Referendum in Bosnia leads to massive vote for independence. Boycotted by Serbs, who had already voted to remain in Yugoslavia. Bosnian declaration of independence followed immediately by beginning of Bosnian war. Bosnian Serb army (VRS) moves to create a separate Serb state, Republika Srpska (RS), over much of Bosnian territory with the intention that it would become part of a new Yugoslav federation.
- Federal Republic of Yugoslavia (FRY) proclaimed, consisting of Serbia and Montenegro, the two remaining republics.
- United Nations imposes sanctions against FR Yugoslavia and accepts Slovenia, Croatia, and Bosnia as members.
- The Yugoslav People's Army (JNA) notionally retreats from Bosnia but leaves Bosnian-born officers and soldiers and all its weaponry to the army of Republika Srpska (VRS). Siege of Sarajevo begins.
- Muslim-Croat War ("war within a war") begins in Bosnia.

1993

- Vance-Owen Peace Plan (VOPP) for division of Bosnia into cantons is accepted by Bosnian Muslims and Croats and by Milošević, but rejected by the Bosnian Serb Assembly despite a personal plea by Milošević. Sanctions against FRY further tightened, leading to hyperinflation exceeding that of the Weimar Republic in the 1920s.
- HMS Invincible Plan of a Union of Three Republics rejected by Izetbegović.
- The Old Bridge in Mostar, commissioned in the sixteenth century by the Turkish sultan, Suleiman the Magnificent, is shelled and destroyed by Croats. It is rebuilt in 2003.

1994

- Peace treaty between Bosnian Muslims and Croats negotiated by the United States and signed in Washington. Muslim-Croat Federation of Bosnia-Hercegovina formed.
- Following Bosnian Serb rejection of the latest peace plan, the Contact Group map, FR Yugoslavia closes border with Republika Srpska to punish RS intransigence and is rewarded with a partial lifting of sanctions.

1995

- In retaliation for NATO air strikes, Bosnian Serbs take some four hundred UN soldiers hostage.
- At Srebrenica, Bosnian Serbs massacre some eight thousand Bosniak males, a war crime subsequently ruled to be genocide by the UN ICTY.
- Croatia launches Operations Flash and Storm, reclaiming all UNPA zones except Eastern Slavonia and resulting in the mass exodus of more than 170,000 Serbs from Croatia.
- "Patriarch" meeting in Belgrade at which all Bosnian Serb, Serb, and Montenegrin leaders agree on a joint Bosnian Serb-FRY delegation to an international peace conference led by Milošević, who is to have the final word if the delegations' views differ. The Serbian Orthodox patriarch witnesses their signature.
- As a result of a mortar shell fired from Serb positions striking the market place in Sarajevo and killing sixty-nine people, NATO launches a series of air strikes on Bosnian Serb military targets and the command and control center. This allows Croatian and Bosnian Muslim armies to launch an offensive against the Bosnian Serbs and the recovery of considerable areas of Bosnian land previously lost to Republika Srpska. Ceasefire agreed to in September 1995.
- At Dayton, Ohio, Richard Holbrooke takes the lead in brokering an agreement subsequently signed in Paris, thereby bringing the war in Bosnia and Herzegovina to an end. Some one hundred thousand killed and missing and two million people internally displaced or refugees.

1996

- FR Yugoslavia recognizes Croatia and Bosnia and Herzegovina.
- Sanctions against FRY are lifted.
- Fighting breaks out between Serbian security forces and ethnic Albanians (Kosovo Liberation Army) in Kosovo.

- Education agreement brokered by Monsignor Paglia of the Sant'Egidio community is signed by Milošević and Ibrahim Rugova, the Kosovo Albanian leader. It is never properly implemented.
- Following electoral fraud in several major Serb towns in local elections, thousands of Serb students and the opposition *Zajedno* (Together) movement demonstrate in Belgrade against the Milošević regime from November to March 1997.

1997

- To bring the demonstrations to an end, the Milošević regime passes a *lex specialis* recognizing the opposition victory. Belgrade and other major cities have opposition mayors.
- Kosovo problem starts to become more acute as KLA kill members of Serb security forces and Albanians in Kosovo perceived as collaborators with the Serb regime.
- Milošević elected president of FRY. Montenegrin leadership changes from Momir Bulatović to Milo Djukanović, who increasingly distances Montenegro from Serbia.

1998

- Eastern Slavonia reintegrated into Croatia, following a three-year period under a UN transitional authority and a peacekeeping force.
- Fighting in Kosovo gradually escalates between Albanians demanding an independent Kosovo and ethnic Serbs and their paramilitary forces.

1999

- Following a massacre of forty-five civilians in Račak in Kosovo by Serb forces, a peace conference is convened at Rambouillet. Serb side refuses to sign the peace agreement, whereupon NATO starts a bombing campaign in Kosovo and FRY. After seventy-eight days of bombing, Milošević signs an agreement ceding control of Kosovo to a UN administration (UNMIK) and a NATO military force (KFOR), but the province still remains a part of the Yugoslav federation.

2000

- Milošević calls early presidential elections but loses to an opposition leader, Vojislav Koštunica, who, after protests and demonstrations at the Milošević regime's renewed attempts to rig the elections, becomes the new president of Yugoslavia. With a new democratic government in place, all sanctions lifted and FRY retakes its place in international organizations.

2001

- Milošević transferred on June 29 to the International Criminal Tribunal for the Former Yugoslavia (ICTY) at The Hague, where he dies on March 11, 2006. The proceedings are terminated three days later without result.

2006

- Montenegro votes to leave State Union of Serbia and Montenegro (successor to the FRY since 2003) and becomes independent.

2008

- Kosovo declares independence.

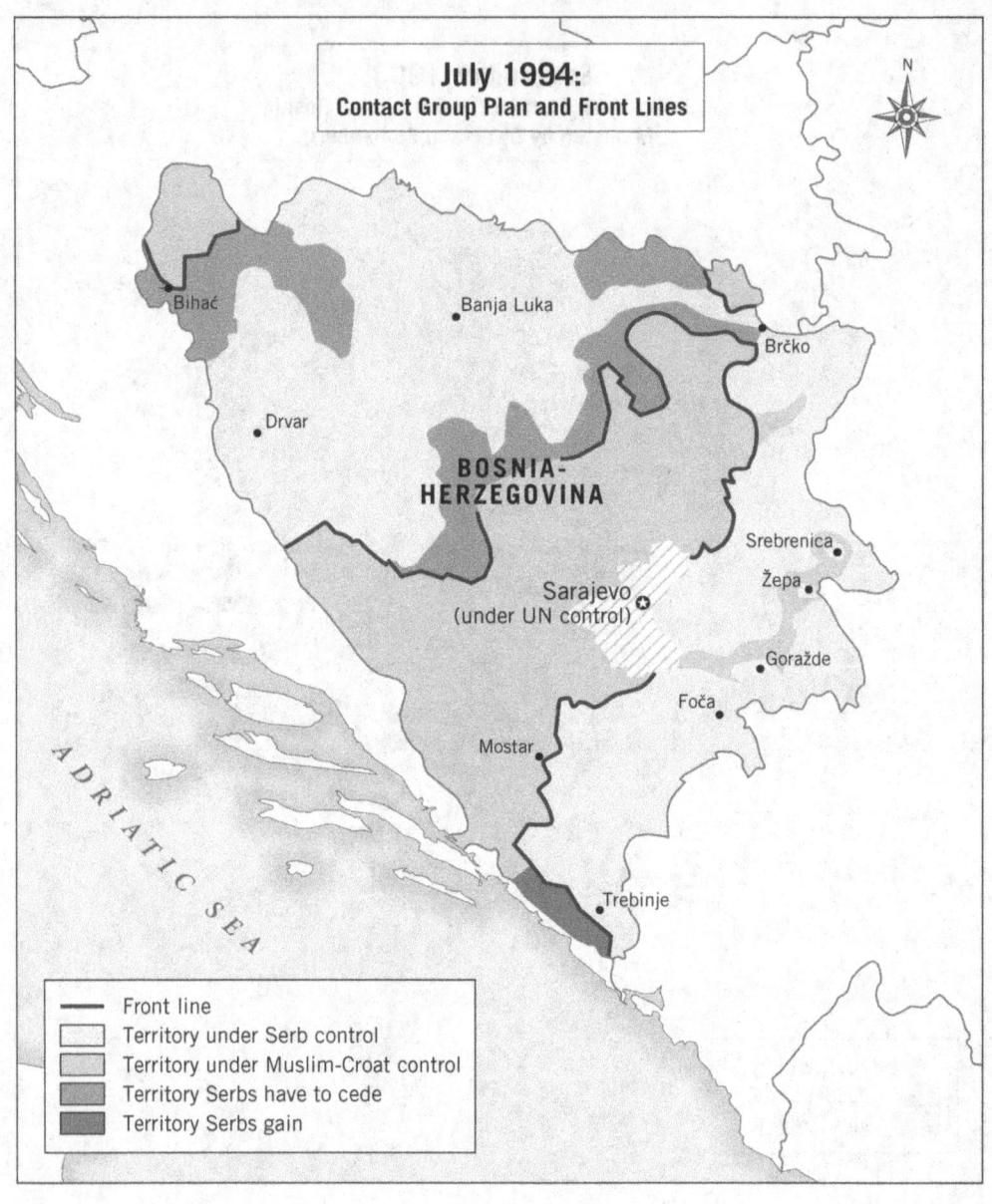

CONVERSATIONS WITH MILOŠEVIĆ

INTRODUCTION

Looking back on the twentieth century, Sir Isaiah Berlin, that great historian of ideas, observed that two factors above all others had shaped human history in that period. First, the development of technology and natural science; the other, the great ideological storms that have altered the lives of virtually all mankind: the Bolshevik revolution and its aftermath—totalitarian tyrannies of both right and left and the explosions of nationalism, racism, and, in places, religious bigotry.[1]

Yugoslavia has been uniquely disadvantaged, exposed as it was to nearly all the ideological storms Berlin mentioned. As early as the 1930s, Rebecca West was lamenting the state of Yugoslavia and fearing it would either fall prey to communism or be overrun by the Nazis. As we know, Yugoslavia was visited by both in reverse order. Several other countries bore the same burdens, but none of them experienced the other ideological storms of nationalism, racism, and religious bigotry in the same mix as Yugoslavia. Nor did any of our analysts (and I include myself in this category as a junior diplomat dealing with the Balkans forty years ago) ever believe that Yugoslavia would collapse in quite such a shocking way. Had we accurately predicted it, we might have taken more precautions to ensure that its dissolution was amortized. As it was, many of the decisions taken by the international community in the early stages of the Yugoslav crisis made an awful situation even worse.

When it looked as though the twin ideological storms of Nazism and communism had burned themselves out, leaving what Sir Michael Howard refers to as "a blasted heath," Yugoslavia filled this void with a new generation of leaders: some were ideologically driven, such as Franjo Tudjman by nationalism and Alija Izetbegović by religion. But the strongest figure to emerge and the one who inspired enormous spontaneous support among the Serbs and Montenegrins proved to be a figure who had no ideological motivation at all, somebody who was content to ride the tiger of nationalism while many suspected that he remained essentially a Communist. The real tiger that consumed him, however, was the pursuit of the unchallenged exercise of power.

Slobodan Milošević was the effectively unrivaled autocratic leader of Serbia and then of the new shrunken Yugoslavia for more than ten years. Although he presided over the most catastrophic decade in Serbian history since the fourteenth century, he managed to maintain power while frequently and aggressively defying the concerted will of the international community. This book does not attempt to provide a definitive answer to how this was possible, but it aims to set the events in their historical context.

The Yugoslav crisis posed serious difficulties of interpretation. Was it a civil war or a war of Serbian aggression? Was it inevitable given the intermittent history of ethnic and religious hatred? Was it a reaction to a unique moment in time—the ending of the Cold War and the consequent dramatic change in Yugoslavia's importance and international stature? Did the international community have the right or obligation to intervene in the internal affairs of a country that was "in the process of dissolution," as the Arbitration Committee led by Robert Badinter put it?[2] The international community had to respond to these hideously difficult questions at a time when its own cohesion was severely strained despite attempts among the Europeans to forge a common foreign and security policy.

Among those who have attempted to interpret the collapse of Yugoslavia, the largest group tend to be advocates of the argument that Milošević and Tudjman, particularly the former, were the gravediggers of the old Socialist Federal Republic of Yugoslavia (SFRY). According to this thesis, neatly sketched by Susan L. Woodward, "a domestic power struggle in the waning days of Communist rule becomes an expansionary project of one nation against the others, in part through politicians' calculated revival of memories about national antagonisms and threats to the survival of their nation in the past from other nations within their common state . . . and in part through their policies to stifle the emergence of pluralist democratic trends (said to be bursting forth in the republics of Slovenia and Croatia) by strengthening the central state and the socialist order. In these analyses there is a strong element of intention and planning, in accordance with the conspiratorial thinking that flourishes in regions and times where uncertainty is particularly pronounced."[3] The most popular camp received reinforcement from Richard Holbrooke, who claimed that "Yugoslavia's tragedy was not foreordained. It was the product of bad, even criminal, political leaders who encouraged ethnic confrontation for personal, political and financial gain."[4]

There are shades here of the unending debate encapsulated in Carlyle's dictum that "history is the biography of great men"—what E. H. Carr called the Bad King John theory of history, for which he had little time, believing instead that the great person "is always representative either of existing forces, or of forces which [he or she] helps to create by way of challenge to existing authority."[5] Few would take issue, however, with the argument that, with respect to a handful of people, the history of the world would have been decisively altered if they had never been born. A. J. P. Taylor argued that "the history of modern Europe can be written in terms of three titans: Napoleon, Bismarck, and Lenin."[6] One curious omission is surely Hitler, repaired by Ian Kershaw, who identified him as "one of the few individuals of whom it can be said with absolute certainty that without him the course of history would have been different."[7] But can one say as much of Milošević? I would not like to be so absolute as Kershaw is over Hitler. The interaction of the nationalist leaders of the former Yugoslav republics made a violent breakup inevitable, and among them Milošević played a dominant role, but was it a uniquely preeminent role? Holbrooke is in no doubt, nor was the last U.S. ambassador to Yugoslavia, Warren Zimmermann, who claimed that Milošević was the gravedigger of the state. Before rushing to judgment, it may be more valuable to examine the course of the breakup of Yugoslavia before Milošević added his own perverse, catalytic contribution.

One of the problems we immediately encounter is the complexity of the issues. As Stevan Pavlowitch remarked, "It cannot be simplified ... without being distorted out of all recognition."[8] A detailed analysis is required to answer not just why it fell apart but the how—and especially the why of the extreme violence. I detect four threads needing to be unraveled: internal structures, international factors, ancient and not-so-ancient hatreds, and the personalities of the leaders. Indeed, without an understanding of the interplay between the constitutional, historical, and economic factors and the baleful role played by international actors and institutions in the critical period leading up to the dissolution of the SFRY, we are left with a two-dimensional approach, an arena inhabited by stage villains and other characters as unreal as those found in a morality play. A close analysis of the causes of the breakup of Yugoslavia suggest that the picture is not quite so Manichaean, and that while the policies of leaders such as Milošević and Tudjman undoubtedly accentuated the bitterness and were directly and indirectly responsible for the extreme violence with which Yugoslavia collapsed, there were objective elements contributing to an inevitable breakup: the policies followed by President Josip Broz Tito from the early 1970s onward, the activities of nationalists in all the republics in the 1970s and 1980s, and the witting and unwitting interventions of the international community. This is not to downplay or underestimate the responsibility of the political leaders in Serbia, Bosnia, and Croatia (and of Milošević and Tudjman in particular) but to point up the fact that had their policies been constructively directed, the inevitable breakup could perhaps have been achieved without recourse to four years of war, even if falling somewhat short of the velvet divorce that occurred in the case of the other last survivor of the Versailles Treaty, Czechoslovakia, in 1993.

It took about a hundred years to create Yugoslavia from the first stirrings of pan–Southern Slav nationalism to the Treaty of Versailles. Yugoslavia existed in two incarnations for some seventy years and then dissolved in the space of a couple of years between 1989 and 1991. The Marxist "withering away of the state" had come about at the federal Yugoslav level just as new states emerged from the empty shell. There was in Yugoslavia no democratic political culture; instead, there was an absence of civic society and representative political institutions. This was a legacy of the unaccountable and manipulative Communist Party politics in which citizens were kept at a distance from decision-making processes, which provided the worst possible basis for democratic transition.

The Kingdom of Serbs, Croats, and Slovenes that emerged at the end of the First World War as a result of the collapse and final demise of the Austro-Hungarian and Ottoman empires stemmed from the efforts of several Slav idealists and Romantics to create a united state to ward off powerful neighbors and to fulfill early nineteenth-century Romantic dreams of a South Slav state. The Slovenes and Croats were thought to have improved their lot, having previously been vassals of the Habsburgs, while the Serbs were all brought together for the first time in modern history in one state. (In practice, the new disposition was almost immediately unbalanced as a result of the Serbs' domination: their king, their capital, very largely their constitution.) As Susan Woodward comments, "The new Yugoslavia created a regional compromise . . . between the principle of national self-determination used to legitimise the dismantling of the Eastern Empires and the principle of the balance of Power, under which the creation of a multinational state in the Balkans would act as a buffer against the emergence of large potentially hostile powers."[9] But even in the early days the tensions were apparent. In 1933 Arnold J. Zurcher wrote, "Yugoslavia inherited people from different jurisdictions. . . . With the exception of ½ million Germans and an equal number of Magyars most of the people . . . may be considered South Slavs; but Croat, Slovene and Serbia are even further apart than Russian, Austrian and Prussian Poles. Cultural traditions, economic standards, religion, political temper and even language separate them. . . . If they are ever to be reconciled it will take more political imagination than Yugoslavia's present rulers appear to possess."[10] A perceptive and prescient comment, flawed only by the bizarre omission of any mention of the Albanians, who were also probably around half a million at that time. In effect, he was saying that Yugoslavia was an artificial creation bringing together people who had never lived together previously and who were separated by more than what united them. The twenty-three-year life of the first Yugoslavia (1918–1941) under the Serb Karadjordjević dynasty had a miserable history peppered with assassinations and failed attempts at parliamentary monarchy. A Croat deputy was murdered in Parliament in 1929 after which King Aleksandar abandoned attempts at a parliamentary monarchy, suspended the constitution, and arrogated to the monarchy dictatorial powers. His own assassination in Marseilles in 1934, orchestrated by Croatian nationalists, led to further Serb/Croat tension. In 1939 a *sporazum*, or agreement, conceded autonomy to Croatia, but it came too late; the first Yugoslavia effectively disappeared from the map of

Europe after the Nazi attack on Belgrade on April 6, 1941, carved up between Germany and Italy and a quisling fascist state in Croatia encompassing Bosnia that was responsible for the murder of many thousands of Serbs, Jews, and Roma. The figures are, inevitably in the Balkans, disputed: the Serbs say seven hundred thousand; the Croatian president Franjo Tudjman claimed that there were "only" thirty thousand; most Western historians tend toward a figure of more than three hundred thousand. What is not in dispute is that the war of liberation against the Germans and Italians and the three-sided civil war between Tito's Partisans, Draža Mihailović's Chetniks, and the quisling Ustasha claimed over one million lives. Tito's Communists emerged the victors. His victory was not Yugoslavia's first glimpse of communism. It had taken root in the first elections in Yugoslavia in 1919 when the Communist Party had finished a respectable fourth with 12 percent of the vote. In 1929 however, when the constitution was annulled by the king, the Communist Party was forced underground.

By contrast, when Tito came to power in 1944, Yugocommunism's prestige was at its zenith. This allowed Tito to carry through his policies, ruthlessly eliminating opposition through brutal purges as necessary. Initially fervent acolytes of Stalinism, Tito and most of his close political allies soon became disenchanted with the Soviet Union's attempts to reduce them to the status of a satellite state. Unlike others in Eastern Europe who had been liberated entirely through the efforts of the Red Army, Yugoslavia's experience had been different. Tito believed he deserved better from Stalin. His treatment was worse. In 1948 Stalin arranged for the expulsion of Yugoslavia from the Cominform as heretics. This at least left Yugoslavia free to embark on its own socialist experiments, often the brainchild of Edvard Kardelj, the party ideologue, one of Tito's most trusted lieutenants, and a former Slovene schoolmaster. (The inherent weaknesses of communism are helpfully illustrated by the manner in which both the Soviet Union and the SFRY dissolved virtually simultaneously, despite their very different routes to the socialist Nirvana.) Nevertheless, the split with Moscow was traumatic for the leadership of the League of Communists of Yugoslavia. Not all accepted it: those who did not were swiftly purged. But it proved domestically and internationally popular. Its more liberal socialist economic model and other civic liberties (passports, foreign travel) allowed a rise in economic prosperity fueled in part by the first *Gastarbeiter* (guest worker) remittances and in part by the West's financial injections to bolster Yugoslavia's important buffer role. This liberalism drew a line, however, at any threat to the party's dominant role. Milovan Djilas, the "father" of Communist dissidents, spent many years in prison for attacking the behavior of the party and its leadership in the 1950s and 1960s. For the average apolitical Yugoslav, however, these were years of contentment and compared particularly favorably to the lot of average citizens in Warsaw Pact countries.

And there was real, not just imported, economic growth. Tito encouraged a work ethic that initially at least bore fruit.

To bolster the 1960s and early 1970s aura of self-confidence, the regime was fond of trumpeting the slogan, which would be ironic if it were not so tragic, that Yugoslavia was "a haven of peace in Europe," comparing itself favorably to the situation in other parts of Europe racked at that time by the activities of the Irish Republican Army (IRA), the Basque ETA, and Baader-Meinhof and the Red Brigades. But even then one did not need to be a practicing political meteorologist to detect storm clouds.

Whatever the country's level of self-confidence, it was not immune to the international wave of protests and demands for political reform of the late 1960s. These led Tito and particularly Kardelj to pursue their final and most disastrous experiments in social and constitutional engineering: the 1974 constitution that followed on their three previous attempts in 1946, 1953, and 1964. (As he told Malcolm Rifkind, the British Foreign Secretary at the time, Milošević believed that the 1974 constitution was Tito's biggest mistake—although he partly exonerated him on the grounds of his great age at the time of its promulgation—and the solvent that broke up Yugoslavia.) Kardelj now decided to devolve administrative, economic, social, and even some political power while reserving foreign affairs, defense, and key foreign trade matters to the center. The extent of devolution down to the republics and autonomous regions created a de facto confederation. Indeed, the new constitution defined the six republics as "States based on popular sovereignty." This was an unprecedented and unparalleled devolution and empowerment of federal units that now had their own presidents, collective presidencies, parliaments, and ministries, including some ministries for foreign affairs. Until the development of the Spanish post-Franco constitutional arrangements, the Yugoslav model was the most advanced (i.e., the most devolved) federal structure in Europe.

Serbia's position was anomalous: it had two autonomous provinces (Kosovo and Vojvodina) with voting rights in most federal institutions (such as the federal Presidency) on a par with the republics, and Serbia's right to change the Serbian constitution depended on the assent of the assemblies of the two autonomous provinces, thereby giving them an effective veto. By contrast, the autonomous provinces could change their own constitutions without the consent of the Republic of Serbia. This was a source of resentment that was to be fully exploited later.

In Yugoslavia as a whole, meanwhile, the de facto, almost de jure, confederation inevitably diminished the power of the federal government and left the republics and autonomous provinces holding the real levers of power. None of this mattered much while Tito was alive. His autocratic style of government left him as the key decision maker, the "only effectively functioning institution,"[11] the defender of the unity of the country and guardian of the national interest. The confederal structures that his heirs inherited post-1980, however, not only were unsuited to prolonging the life of a unified state but also had themselves created a centrifugal dynamic. Yugoslavia was in effect reduced to being what the compound parts by consensus allowed it to be.

Kardelj's 1974 constitution was a heady brew of socialist theory and practice. Its immediate source was the writings of the philosopher and, ironically, future nationalist academician, Mihailo Marković. But it reached back to P. J. Proudhom's federalism, the experience of the Paris commune of 1871, and its more Marxist interpretation. The resulting mix was, Kardelj says, "a system of delegation" and the pluralism of "self-managed interests." But, as Ivan Vejvoda clarifies in his excellent analysis of the deleterious effect of the constitution, which I paraphrase, self-management was ultimately fraudulent; "the real decision making was going on at the highest levels of Communist power."[12] Fatally, however, this governmental power was at the republican or provincial level, not at the federal level.

The empowered (republics' and autonomous provinces') nomenklaturas reinforced the tendency toward the creation of their own states, thereby weakening an already withered federal government. The republics' leaders became increasingly uncompromising and assertive. Federal institutions were reduced to the status of talking shops. Vejvoda highlights education, transportation, and media as areas where centrifugal forces grew ever stronger. There were disputes over a common core curriculum in literature and history. Interrepublican highways were not completed. Each republic and autonomous province had its own television and radio stations, with no national TV or radio stations. When matters came to a head, it was easy to exploit and aggravate these divisions.

Leaving Tito, the president for life, to one side for a moment, the only other effective central institution became the Yugoslav People's Army, the JNA. It was, also, the most reactionary and secretive institution, but until the outbreak of hostilities, it was the last hope for keeping Yugoslavia together. Often referred to as Tito's Praetorian Guard and fervent believers in the Titoist slogan of "Brotherhood and Unity," the JNA held a privileged position and operated effectively as a seventh republic, having its own representative at Presidency meetings. In the republics, however, the army had also been organized into territorial defense units as a reaction to the 1968 invasion of Czechoslovakia by the Warsaw Pact. This led to both a federal and a republic-based command and control system, the latter in 1990-91 proving the ideal breeding ground for the development of the armies of Slovenia and Croatia.

Two other factors hastened the demise of the SFRY. The six constituent nations defined in the 1974 constitution of Yugoslavia—Slovenes, Croats, Serbs, ethnic Muslims, Montenegrins, and Macedonians—were majority nations in all republics except Bosnia and Herzegovina, whose multiethnic character was a microcosm of Yugoslavia. In Bosnia, the particular ethnic split between Muslims, Serbs, and Croats was 43:31:17. A strict parity or rotation basis obtained. The constitution's conferral of statehood on the republics increased the tendency toward nation building around the core nations of each republic, with the other nationalities relegated to minority status—even if they were constituent nations of Yugoslavia. (Albanians, Hungarians, and so on could not be constituent nations. They could only be nationalities, as they had "parent" independent states beyond the Yugoslav border.)

This centrifugal tendency was reinforced by another anomaly of the 1974 constitution, the consensus rule that thwarted the holding of federal elections, which would have allowed the convening of a constituent Assembly (one person, one vote) and an upper chamber representing the rights of the national majorities and minorities. Every proposal to this effect by federal prime minister Ante Marković was systematically obstructed by Slovenia, Serbia, and often Croatia. The republics then proceeded to reinforce their own legitimacy by holding republican elections (as discussed, under the 1974 constitution each republic was a state based on popular sovereignty).

This gadarene rush toward full-blown nation statehood on the basis of the republics became the single most significant element in the dissolution of the SFRY. As economic circumstances worsened—by 1985 the federal government was undergoing a fiscal crisis that led to a bout of hyperinflation, and the decentralized nature of the economy offered endless scope for bureaucratic holdups and financial indiscipline—there was a natural tendency, encouraged by the republican leaderships, toward nationalism and to lay the blame for hardships at the door of the neighboring republics. Mutual recriminations over exploitation and hardship were reinforced by nationalist intellectuals who recited their own historical agenda of the suffering of their people. The 1986 draft Memorandum of the Serbian Academy of Sciences and Arts (SANU) was the most egregious example of the documenting of such grievances, real or imagined. It was often quoted as the point of departure of the renewal of Serb nationalism (but see chapter 15 below).

The speedy disintegration of Yugoslavia is not just explicable in terms of domestic political struggles and constitutional disputes. Not only were the constitutional reforms part of the stricter conditionality imposed by the international financial institutions, but the domestic actors were making their choices in terms of foreign developments. The mixed messages from outside the country reinforced the conflicts within.

Tito's importance to the West lay in his country's strategic importance as a bulwark against Soviet expansionism. But a bulwark needs to be strengthened, and Tito apportioned substantial amounts of Yugoslavia's scarce resources into defense. To make such a distortion of the domestic economy palatable to those who were called on to support his independent brand of communism required a substantial financial injection from his outside supporters. This external support created a dependency culture that was ultimately highly corrosive, however much it contributed in the short term to ever-increasing living standards and consequent political and social stability.

His Third Way, a response to exclusion from the Eastern and Western alliances, that is, his cofounding role in the Non-Aligned Movement, often led to prickly moments in relations with the West and a good deal of gratuitous anti-Western rhetoric that grated in Washington, London, and elsewhere. Yet Tito's position and postures were essentially a Western asset—for which the West paid dearly.

By the end of Tito's life, however, the economic situation had deteriorated dramatically. Yugoslav debt at about twenty billion dollars and adverse terms of trade for Yugoslav exports all contributed. The macroeconomic stabilization program inspired by the International Monetary Fund (IMF) was introduced in 1982, which brought in familiar austerity measures, high unemployment, and declining living standards. The program accentuated social and republican divides by a North-South policy that differentiated between the investment programs for each. Thus the North (Croatia and Slovenia) became more advanced and export orientated, while the South remained labor intensive and with a low wage economy (not dissimilar to the division in Italy between the North and the Mezzogiorno).

The 1974 constitution's decentralization measures were a key element in preventing adequate reform of the central economy. With foreign borrowing, exchange, and debt obligations removed to the republics, the federal government's capacities to address the proposed transition to a market economy could hardly begin to function.

Although the debt crisis was partially eased in the middle of the decade by a huge debt-refinancing program, the continuing tension in East-West relations left little scope for reducing federal defense expenditure. However unjustified and perverse it now seems, this was a period when the perceived threat led to increased defense spending in new high-technology weaponry.

The League of Communists at the time proposed dealing with its problems by a political reform program that would change the balance in center-republican relations back toward the center. Slovenia, however, which along with Croatia had begun to benefit from increased foreign investment flows, took a consistently negative attitude to any proposals to water down the republics' achievements since the 1974 constitution at the expense of the central government. In 1985 Slovenia put forward a proposal for a confederation of sovereign republics (a similar proposal was advanced by international negotiators to try to deal with the Yugoslav crisis five years later). One of Tito's old guard, Stane Dolanc, although a Slovene himself, said that such an outcome, a "free, united Slovenia, joined in a central European Catholic federation, means the destruction of Yugoslavia."[13]

At the same time, a combination of an economic policy aimed at improving the flow of exports to the West and declining domestic investment in transport, construction and mining, timber, and industry were leading to the impoverishment of industrialized areas of Croatia and of Bosnia and Herzegovina, areas that were ethnically mixed. Attempts were made to encourage foreign investment through a program of privatization and suppression of self-management, which led internally to the first massive layoffs due to bankruptcy in forty years. The largest enterprises in Serbia, Croatia, and Bosnia were all threatened with bankruptcy, and as the banking system attempted to avert the consequent debt crisis, a banking crisis began to hit most firms in all republics. This in turn led to republican parliaments refusing to allow taxes due to the federal government to be transferred. They were, moreover, increasingly hostile to IMF conditionality attached to further loans (a phenomenon we have seen recently in Greece).

By 1988, as Susan Woodward points out, "the country was experiencing a social upheaval of revolutionary proportions as a result of the economic hardships occasioned by the debt repayment stabilisation programme," not to mention the stagnation in upward mobility and higher competition for jobs in the public sector.[14] This fed into resentment of those people and those areas considered inefficient and hence of the whole system of republican balance.

Other countries in the East, particularly Hungary, by the end of the 1980s were reforming themselves, whatever the short-term social cost. But with the rapidly evolving situation in East-West relations in the Gorbachev era, the success in arms control talks, and finally the collapse of the Berlin Wall and the end of the Cold War and Warsaw Pact, Yugoslavia's special relationship with the West was at an end. And it was forced to see itself as a competitor on equal but not privileged terms with other Central European countries for Western attention and in particular economic attention.

In 1989, the incoming U.S. ambassador, Warren Zimmerman, crystallized this uncompromising and chilly new message. Yugoslavia no longer enjoyed the geopolitical importance that the United States had given it during the Cold War. Yugoslavia had now been surpassed by both Poland and Hungary in economic and political openness. In addition, human rights had become a major element of U.S. policy. If Yugoslavia wanted to continue its close relations with the United States, it would have to curb human rights abuses in Kosovo. The United States supported Yugoslavia's unity, independence, and territorial integrity. But it could only support unity in the context of democracy. It would strongly oppose unity imposed or preserved by force.

The pivotal neighboring or near neighboring countries, Italy, Austria, and Germany, all had historical and indeed cultural and religious reasons for favoring the Roman Catholic countries of Hungary, Czechoslovakia, and Poland over the Orthodox Eastern areas. For Croatia and Slovenia this was a defining moment. They could see the need to jump ship if they were, to stretch the metaphor, not to miss the boat. The Austrians, the Germans, and the Vatican openly supported Croatian and Slovenian pretensions to disengage from the Federal Republic (and the respective presidents of Croatia and Slovenia warmly reciprocated the Vatican's attentions), and both republics made secret arms purchases in Hungary, Austria, Germany, and Czechoslovakia to prepare their nascent independent national armies.

This intense republican activity and interplay with foreign governments took place against a background of seeming insouciance on the international community's part to the problems of the federal government. Federal prime minister Ante Marković had his calls for economic help rebuffed or held up. His appeals to the United States and the European Community fell on deaf ears. Not until spring 1991 did Marković receive a response from the EC to his request for assistance. The EC's willingness to talk, by contrast, to the Slovenes and Croats left the federal government's hope for international support looking increasingly forlorn. Deprived of the right to relegitimize through federal elections, Marković had nowhere to go and no country to govern either, as was shown in the republics' multiparty elections, which gave the Slovenes and Croats the spur to go for independence while at the same time swinging the Serb majority behind the Milošević approach to the Serbian national question. It was depressing to see prospects of the emergence of a civil society evaporate as voters, far from rejecting nationalism and religion, respectively, embraced them.

Moreover, the federal Presidency's attempts to reduce armed conflict in Croatia between the government and the Krajina Serbs at the beginning of 1991 by securing the border and disarming all paramilitaries and militia groups led to a repeat of Zimmermann's warning by the U.S. government that it would not accept the use of force to hold Yugoslavia together. NATO and the Conference on Security and Cooperation in Europe (CSCE) were at the same time refusing to take any preventive action to reverse the moves toward violent breakup. Given the contradictions, it was not surprising that the pro-Yugoslav lobby lost confidence in foreign support for the federal government's position, however much the rhetoric may have suggested otherwise.

After the declaration of independence on June 25, 1991, by Slovenia and Croatia, the European Community sent its troika of foreign ministers to Yugoslavia, followed shortly after by the CSCE Committee of Senior Officials. This was to be the first test of recently established crisis management mechanisms. The United States was content to play second fiddle. The EC and the CSCE could take the strain. George Bush's secretary of state, James Baker, had declared that the United States "had no dog in this fight," an oblique echo of Woodrow Wilson's adage, "If you want to put out a fire in Utah you do not send to Oklahoma for the fire engine. If you want to put out a fire in the Balkans . . . You do not send to the United States for troops."[15] European activists such as Jacques Delors, president of the European Commission (who famously said in 1991 of the Yugoslav crisis, "We do not interfere in American affairs. We hope they will have enough respect not to interfere in ours"), and the pan-Europeans of the CSCE, such as Austria and Hungary, were keen that Europe should take a more proactive role than had been possible up to the end of the Cold War. Jacques Poos, Luxembourg's foreign minister, raised expectations that Europe could handle it by declaring fatuously, "The hour of Europe has dawned."[16]

And yet, it was at this time that international thinking was at its most muddled. The guidelines were clear. They had been adopted at the Helsinki Conference in 1975: they emphasized the unacceptability of border changes other than by consent, territorial integrity, human rights, and self-determination. Unfortunately, the guidelines were themselves conflictive. As Woodward points out, "instead of choosing between the principles of territorial integrity and national self-determination, the Europeans chose to adapt their norms to their preferences and apply both principles to the federal republics, as if they already were States and the bearers of national sovereignty, and as if international law did not oblige them to apply the principles of territorial integrity and self-determination to the Yugoslav state, its entire population and its external borders. . . . By limiting their role to neutral mediation, they were forced to define the dispute between Slovenia and the federal government as a border dispute between two equal parties. And by defining the conflict as an issue of borders and sovereignty, they foreclosed the option of a domestic solution, . . . and legitimated the view that this was an international conflict."[17]

Muddled thinking was, however, no barrier to or brake on feverish diplomatic activity. It is something of a mystery that the West's response to the onset of the crisis is so frequently described as one of neglect or passivity. Unfortunately all sides saw the international community's activities in a negative light unless their role could be harnessed to suit their purposes. For the Serbs, the international community's attentions were unwelcome unless and until arrangements were in place that allowed for the formation of Serb statelets in those countries that were determined to secede. At the same time, Milošević was unwilling to countenance similar autonomous arrangements for the Albanian community in Kosovo. For the Slovenes and the Croats, the international community's sole value in this negotiation was to allow them independence as soon as possible with as few strings attached as could be negotiated. Once independence had been achieved, they had no interest in a negotiated settlement with the rest of Yugoslavia, nor did they care very much if Bosnia (which, as a mini-Yugoslavia, was bound to be intimately and dramatically affected by the breakup of the SFRY) were to be dismembered. Indeed, from what we know of Milošević and Tudjman's secret discussions at a meeting in Tito's former hunting lodge at Karadjordjevo in 1991, the Croatian leader was as determined to see a Croatian statelet formed there as Milošević was to set up a Bosnian Serb entity.

Within a few months, multiparty elections in both Slovenia and Croatia had brought leaders to power committed to the right of the Slovene and Croat nations to their own state. Decisive referenda in favor of independence in December 1990 and May 1991, respectively, were followed by formal declarations of independence by Slovenia and Croatia on June 25, 1991.

The JNA was sent into Slovenia to crush the secession on the orders of the federal government headed by Prime Minister Ante Marković. The half-hearted nature of the JNA's intervention has been the subject of differing interpretations ever since. Certainly it was far from being a full-blooded crackdown, nor did it enjoy strong support from the Serb authorities. Indeed, there is some evidence to suggest that Milošević was actively urging the Slovenes to secede. Slovene president Milan Kučan claimed that he and Milošević reached agreement on Slovenia's secession as early as January 1991. Milošević, while recognizing the right of the Slovenes to their own state, believed that Serbia should enjoy the same right—that is, of unifying all Serbs in Yugoslavia in one state. Slovenia, not having any significant number of Serbs, was unimportant in this context, but Croatia, with its large Serb minority, and Bosnia, with the Serbs comprising one-third of the population, were different matters. It might have been more acceptable to examine the case for all nations to be unified in their own state if Milošević had ever been prepared to consider that this right extended to the Albanians in Kosovo, the Hungarians in Vojvodina, or the Sandžak Muslims. The European Community's priority at this stage was to hold the federation together. They accordingly dispatched a troika of foreign ministers to neutralize the dangerous course of events created by the unilateral declaration of independence and the deployment by the Federal Presidency of the JNA. But as in so many cases, it is war, however limited, that makes a state. The confrontation between the Slovenian territorial forces and the JNA made any U-turn by Slovenia out of the question. There was no turning back. Within a few months, a real war broke out in Croatia as the Croats, fearing they would be left behind, built up their own territorial forces. In sharp contrast to his attitude to Slovenia, Milošević made it clear that he was only prepared for Croatia to leave Yugoslavia if it were prepared to leave the Serbs and their territories in Croatia behind.

The bitterly contested war, effectively between the Croats on the one hand and the Serbs and Montenegrins (rather than the JNA) on the other, left the Serbs in control of about a third of Croatia's territory. But the propaganda war was won decisively by the Croats as pictures of the Serb and Montenegrin bombardment and shelling of Vukovar and Dubrovnik filled television screens and brought to the attention of Western public opinion the reality of a major war on European soil for the first time since the end of the Second World War.

The television images helped Germany propel the European Union into premature recognition of Slovene and Croatian independence in December 1991, a time when Lord Carrington was at a critical stage in attempting to negotiate a peace settlement. With independence in their pockets, Croatia and Slovenia had little incentive to negotiate constructively. Nevertheless, the UN negotiator, Cyrus Vance, brokered a truce in late 1991 that created four UN-protected areas within Croatia occupied by Serbs, although Croatian sovereignty was recognized over these territories.

It took some time for all members of the international community to peel off the facade. For many, the penny dropped agonizingly slowly. This was not to be a traditional negotiation with any decent compromise at the end. It was for this reason that people such as Lord Carrington needed maximum leverage, which, if force was not going to be used to keep the warring parties apart and to maintain the integrity of Yugoslavia, meant withholding recognition from those parties that wanted it and threatening effective sanctions against those parties that were interested in hegemony rather than preserving a multiethnic state. But the precipitate action in recognizing Croatia and Slovenia at the December 1991 Foreign Ministers Meeting of the EC, against the advice of the European Union's own negotiator Lord Carrington, in the teeth of the opposition of the UN secretary-general, of the U.S. government, and, most significantly of all, of President Izetbegović of Bosnia, removed any incentive for the Croats and Slovenes to negotiate seriously about a comprehensive settlement. They had already got what they wanted—and relatively cost-free in political terms. Further negotiation would only, as they saw it, claw back some of the gains they had won. If recognition was meant to stop the Serbo-Croat war, this had been achieved by Cyrus Vance the previous month. If it was meant to punish the Serbs for what had already taken place, then the main penalties fell on Bosnia.

The decision still stands as a monument to the shortcomings of European foreign policy. Lord Owen summed it up accurately as "a sombre warning of how a dangerous decision, with predicted consequences, can be made in an atmosphere where maintaining unity among the member states becomes an end in itself."[18] It was, in other words, deemed to be more important to keep in step than to be heading in the right direction, despite the dire warnings by those closest to the conflict. Lord Carrington wrote to the chairman of the EC foreign ministers on December 2, 1991, "An early recognition of Croatia would undoubtedly be the break-up of the conference.... This might well be the spark that sets Bosnia-Herzegovina alight." The European Community even overruled its own decisions. Five weeks before the recognition of Croatia and Slovenia, the EC's declaration in Rome on November 8, 1991, stated, "the prospect of recognition of the independence of those republics which seek it, can only be envisaged in the framework of an overall settlement."[19]

Before considering a request for recognition from Bosnia, the European Community required a referendum on independence, a poll that was predictably boycotted by the Bosnian Serbs who had held their own referendum previously on remaining with Yugoslavia. Again, thanks to the confusions inherent in the Badinter Commission's opinions, the European Community acted inconsistently. Yugoslavia was deemed to be a dead letter. Self-determination and territorial integrity were principles applied only to the republics but not within the republics, nor to the Federal Republic. A referendum in Yugoslavia as a whole would certainly have resulted in a large majority in favor of keeping the SFRY together.

Having opposed the premature recognition of the independence of Croatia and Slovenia, the president of the Bosnian Presidency, Alija Izetbegović, was now faced with an impossible dilemma. He saw very clearly the bleakness of a future Yugoslavia from which Croatia would have withdrawn. His choices were stark: to announce Bosnian withdrawal from Yugoslavia, thereby inevitably provoking the Bosnian Serbs to fight to remain within it, or to acquiesce in a Serb-dominated truncated Yugoslavia. After opting for independence, Izetbegović believed that he would be quickly recognized and that the West would help him defend his borders. He was half right.

The international community's disarray was complete when it recognized Bosnia in April 1992. To compound its previous error by moving swiftly to recognize Bosnia without the prior presence of a UN prevention force was, as Lord Owen said, "foolhardy in the extreme."[20] Efforts to bring about a negotiated settlement were set aside as the Serbs precipitated a full-scale war. Some would argue that the war would have taken place anyway. We can never be confident. But the attempt to prevent it was torpedoed as the EC compounded its previous error in prematurely recognizing Croatia and Slovenia by its premature recognition of Bosnia. By this time, however, the Europeans were not isolated. The U.S. position had shifted by 180 degrees. It had now become a fervent advocate of recognition.

The fault lines of the history school that sees the ancient ethnic hatreds and conflicts as inevitably born out of the history and character of the Balkan people has fewer adherents. But the case is not to be discarded out of hand, not least because it helps explain why the breakdown was so violent. Some have argued that the collapse of the federal state left a vacuum that led to a legal void. The republics, feeling themselves unaccountable and thus free of responsibility, were in no position to constrain violence. The argument continues that national politics stemming from the centrifugal evolution of the party and state (nationalism from above) had by the late 1980s and early 1990s joined up with nationalism from below, which had been kept in a deep freeze under Tito and now emerged with the thaw of the collapse of communism. This double intensification of nationalism proved to be a challenge the political leadership could not meet peacefully. The long period of Communist structures, the lack of accountability, the inability of society to react and take a grip on politics, the festering national grievances, real or invented, and the complexities of intra-Yugoslav relations all created a chemistry of breakdown likely to generate large-scale violence.

This in a nutshell is the argument put forth by, among others, Ivan Vejvoda. It is persuasive, but it takes inadequate account of the impact that the violence of the Second World War and immediate postwar years had on what had been—except in the largest towns—until the 1970s and 1980s a basically agrarian society—that is, one where even the city dwellers were only one or two generations away from the village.

The atrocities by all sides in the war of liberation against the Axis powers and the concurrent internecine wars of 1941–45, glimpsed brilliantly in Milovan Djilas's *Wartime*, illuminate the quite literal "take no prisoners" approach to warfare, adopted when it became clear that the Germans were killing all captured Partisans.[21] Only the Jews suffered so directly and on a greater scale than the Yugoslavs in terms of seeing members of their families killed and mutilated before their eyes. It was the Serbs who felt these grievances most acutely, yet under Tito Croatian Ustasha atrocities were underplayed. Mention of Partisan atrocities was even less tolerated. If these memories were publicly suppressed, they were not forgotten. And when the opportune moment came, the press was mobilized to exploit these tribal emotions to the benefit of the power policies of the Federal Republic's leaders. Noel Malcolm vividly conveys the way the state media became a propaganda tool in Bosnia and Serbia: "It was as if all television in the USA had been taken over by the Ku Klux Klan."[22]

While we are right to reject historical determinism with its implication that the Balkans are hopeless and will always be a source of indiscipline and fractiousness, we should not ignore the effect such a view has had on the Balkan people themselves, particularly those who lived under Ottoman rule. To a depressing extent the "Wild East" stereotype of the Balkans we retain has become a reality because the inhabitants of the region know they are expected by westerners to behave badly. Put another way, the people of the Balkans had become so inured to being regarded as the cat's-paw of the Great Powers that had to intervene to pick up the pieces in 1878, 1913, 1944, and from 1991 onward that there was an element of living down to their reputation.

But if we reinforce our stereotypes of the Balkans as a disaster area, as Samuel P. Huntington chose to do in his controversial *Clash of Civilizations and the Remaking of World Order*, excluding the Orthodox nations from European civilization, the prospect of bringing the benefits of the Enlightenment to those parts of the Balkans where the Ottomans shielded the local population from it is postponed.[23] There is no reason to suppose that an underlay of poverty, ignorance, and foreign oppression in a largely rural society is a perpetual barrier to progress.

The fault line of history was in place long before there were Croats and Serbs to straddle it. It was to be a century or more after the division of the Roman Empire in AD 395 that the Serbs settled south and east of the dividing line, the Croats north and west. Early tensions between Western and Eastern Empires were compounded by the creation in 1578 of a Military Frontier (or *Krajina*) to prevent further Turkish incursions. The zone, barren after repeated wars between the Holy Roman Empire and the Turks, was to be repopulated with dispossessed colonists from Serbia who were to be given land, autonomy, and religious freedom. Their relative independence and military spirit also created a tension with the Croats, fostered by the Catholic Church (which since the mutual excommunications of 1054 had regarded the Serbs as schismatics), which was to persist down the centuries. The poverty of the Krajina Serbs, as Jasminka Udovićki notes, "played a distinct role in forming the perception of Serbs as a backward and inferior race. For Catholic Croats prideful of their efficiency, law and order, considering themselves ... to be more culturally developed, the Serbs were primitive semi-Orientals."[24] For the Serbs of that region the state of ignorance and backwardness was a function of foreign oppression: be it Habsburg or Ottoman. Thus a Krajina Serb poet in 1842, Ognjeslav Utjesenović Ostrozinski, wrote self-pityingly, "The whole world sees morning but in the Balkans daylight never comes."[25]

Paradoxically, therefore, it was at that time and in Croatia that the first stirrings of a movement toward the unification of the South Slavs could be detected. The Illyrian movement that started in the 1830s and 1840s was revived in the 1860s under the name of Yugoslavism. One of its leading lights was a remarkable Croatian Catholic bishop, Josip Strossmeyer, who gave of his own wealth to promote the cause of unification and founded the University of Zagreb and the Yugoslav Academy.

A contemporaneous movement in Croatia was, however, heading in a very different direction. The Stranka Prava, founded by Ante Starčević and Eugen Kvaternik, demanded a specifically Croat state, regarding other South Slavs as inferior. The Slovenes were "mountain Croats" and the Serbs an "unclean, servile race" with Asian standards of hygiene and without culture.[26] The resentment and contempt felt by the Croats strengthened the Krajina Serbs' sense of military toughness and imbued in them also a desire to be reunited ultimately in one state with Serbia. As Udovićki points out, "Had the Krajina never been used as a human shield keeping Europe out of reach of the Ottomans the history of Croatia-Serbia relations could have turned out rather differently."[27]

Inter-ethnic relations were at least as fraught in Bosnia. The Ottoman conquest of 1463 ushered in a powerful Muslim political and landowning hierarchy bearing down on the Croatian and Serb communities. The conversions to Islam by the indigenous Slavs were probably less on religious grounds from those anxious to distance themselves from both Catholic and Orthodox Churches than economic or social. Conversion had an attraction to anyone aspiring to public or military service. Moreover, Islam was open to all.

As the Ottoman Empire declined, however, the Turkish governors and landlords penalized through taxation the overwhelmingly Serb serfs to such an extent as to provoke six uprisings between 1834 and 1862, each ruthlessly suppressed.[28] The major uprising in Herzegovina in 1875 led to full-scale war against the Ottoman Empire the following year and within two years to the Treaties of San Stefano and Berlin, which have done so much to shape the present borders and to sow the seeds for future resentment and rivalry.

It is hard to overcome the cultural distortions that have accrued over hundreds of years and that have led to historical baggage few leading politicians even today seem willing to abandon. The Ottoman yoke, worn lightly in some ways, nevertheless kept the influence and effects of the Enlightenment at bay. Therefore, the civic values the Enlightenment held dear—human rights, the right of the individual, free expression, and assembly—never had a chance to get a real foothold. The media is a case in point. There is an unhealthy inclination to equate political power with control over the media. "The others had control for long enough; now it's our turn" is a depressingly typical reaction born of the Communist/Balkan legacy, where power sharing and checks and balances are exiguous and every game has to be won 5–nil, not 3–2.

The catalog of ethnic conflict thereafter can be as brief as it was bloody. The first Balkan War in 1912 was the occasion for the Serb reconquest (or occupation, as the Albanians would say) of Kosovo. The First World War found the Serbs and Croats fighting in opposing armies, although there were exceptions. Many Croatian Krajina Serbs, for instance, fought for their Habsburg masters against the Serb army. After the war, the overweening and proprietorial Serb attitude provoked tensions particularly among the Croats, who felt not without cause that it was largely the force of Serb arms that had played the decisive role in the creation of the new state, and ensured that the first Yugoslavia (as it became known officially in 1929) got off to a bad start and never recovered. Finally, the internecine war among the South Slavs, carried on with equal ferocity to the war of liberation against the Axis powers, left, as Udovički remarks, "deep scars in the collective memory of the Serbs and served as a stock for the engineering of Serbian nationalism in the late 1980s."[29]

The scars are even slower to heal as a result of what Freud describes as "the narcissism of minor difference." In a 1917 essay, Freud observed that "it is precisely the minor differences in people who are otherwise alike that form the basis of feelings of strangeness and hostility between them."[30] For those like Aleksa Djilas, who see the wars in Croatia and Bosnia as essentially replays of the 1941–45 civil war largely on the same territory, Freud's analysis must strike a chord. Serbs, Croats, and Muslims are all South Slavs, speaking the same language but differentiated by religion and custom. Michael Ignatieff in writing about Freud's observation points out how Freud focuses our attention on the paradoxical relation between narcissism and aggression. "It is precisely because differences between groups are minor that they must be expressed aggressively. The less substantial the differences between two groups, the more they both struggle to portray those differences as absolute."[31] In transposing the argument to the wars of the 1990s, the read-across is clear.

The Axis forces had no time for the concept of Yugoslavia after their invasion in 1941. Goebbels described the then Kingdom of Yugoslavia as "a questionable patchwork of states" that could be undone if the Germans would "do something with the Croats"; some of the Italian fascists in turn also planned to detach Croatia from Yugoslavia and, in Count Ciano's words, to organize the Kosovar Albanians "into a dagger pointed at the side of Belgrade."[32]

Following the struggle against the Italians and the Germans, a conflict overshadowed by the internecine war between the Partisans, Chetniks, and Ustasha, the second Yugoslavia, the Socialist Federal Republic of Yugoslavia, got off to an even worse start as Tito's settling of scores added hundreds of thousands more to the death toll already incurred in the fighting and in the Croats' concentration camps. Tito's collision with Stalin in 1948 was a near-run thing. Stalin's failure to invade is as puzzling as Hitler's reluctance to invade Britain in 1940. But Tito's authoritarian rule survived that test, and the West was happy to pour money into Yugoslavia while it could provide a convenient strategic breakwater against the Communist world. With the triple blow of the death of Tito, the collapse of the Soviet Union and consequent withdrawal of Western aid, and the breakdown of the original post-1945 one-party centralization into polycentric federalism and eventually rampant nationalism, the second Yugoslavia's fate was sealed.

Milošević, as the chief engineer of its demise, was pursuing policies that, while amplifying the unmistakable sounds of Serbian nationalism, acted as the unwitting recruiting sergeant for Slovene and Croatian nationalism (and indeed subsequently for the Kosovo Liberation Army). Moreover, Milošević's brand of Serbian nationalism and hegemony gave the Slovenes and Croats a far more internationally respectable rallying cry than selfish economic self-interest. Whether the breakup would have occurred without Milošević may be a matter of conjecture for some. I am convinced that it would have happened in any event, given the disastrous conjuncture in which Yugoslavia found itself at the end of the 1980s. Although comparisons in subjective areas such as nationalism are not always helpful, Czechoslovakia's problems seemed far less daunting than Yugoslavia's, yet that federation too dissolved.

The Serbs have always been central actors in this drama. They have a national slogan, "only harmony can save the Serbs." It is a slogan they are fond of quoting, and it is now represented on the national flag. But it remains just that, a totem, a symbol that is never acted on. In the last century, the Serbs even managed to have two dynasties running in parallel, until the Obrenovićs were finally deposed in the most ghastly manner by regicide in 1903. And while the Serbs in Serbia proper may pay lip service to the cause of Serbian unity, they largely regard their Bosnian Serb brothers across the Drina as crude country bumpkins. And the retention of power by Milošević was greatly facilitated by the inability of the opposition parties ever to agree for very long about anything among themselves. This created no sense of shame or embarrassment. Each group claimed they had been betrayed by the other. How can you remain a Serb and tolerate betrayal?

The reality is that although Serbia is part of the European continent, more than a whiff of its Ottoman past persists. As Wayne Vucinich argues in his book on the Ottoman Empire, "Centuries of feudal bondage contributed to . . . a state of lethargy, indifference, indecision, and a tendency towards submissiveness which grew out of the necessity for survival. . . . Coupled with subservience is cleverness, expressed in attempts to get around obstacles, including those erected by authority by using none too ethical . . . or even illegal means."[33] The notion persists that it is perfectly permissible to cheat and steal from the government. The apparent acceptance of war profiteers' behavior, the incomprehension at our attempts to stamp out corruption, at least in the administration of aid to Bosnia, the ambivalent attitude to war crimes generally, and the pervasive Balkan love of smuggling can all be traced back to this root. And the Communist period reinforced the suspicion of government, distrust of neighbors, and the need to look after number one and to work the network of influence for personal gain.

If we regard it as inevitable that with the death of Tito, the Serbs would have looked for a strongman to redress what they saw as their legitimate grievances and reestablish the hegemony they enjoyed in the first Yugoslavia, Milošević's rise and the death of Yugoslavia can be seen less in terms of his unique personality than in the opportunities offered in the late 1980s to a chance taker willing to harness himself to the convenient instrument of choice, nationalism, and capable of using the utmost brutality and ruthlessness to snuff out opposition and to muzzle the press.

Nor should we look at Milošević in isolation from the other republican leaders. While Milošević dreamed of becoming the new Tito, the leader who came closest to aping Tito's style was Croatian president Franjo Tudjman, with his white field marshal's suit and his holiday hideaway on Brioni. Tudjman, the youngest Partisan general, had been prosecuted for his nationalist views under communism. He either kept them under wraps while a Partisan or subsequently developed them. If any of the republic leaders can be considered to have been a twenty-four-carat nationalist, it was Tudjman. In several aspects of national life, he reawakened old memories of the fascist "Independent State of Croatia" of 1941–44. Tudjman had a well-founded reputation for speaking his mind to foreign visitors, treating them to his unflattering views of the Muslims and his revisionist view of geography, namely that Croatia is not part of the Balkans. In 1995, he famously drew on a menu card (at a banquet in London marking the end of the Second World War) his proposed map of Bosnia carved up between Serbia and Croatia. Paddy Ashdown, the Liberal Democrats party leader who was the pupil at this history lesson, was aghast. With the expulsion of some 170,000 Serbs from Croatia, Croatia is almost as mono-ethnic as Slovenia. Without attracting any of the opprobrium attached to Ante Pavelić, the wartime leader of the Croatian state, or indeed to Milošević over his treatment of the Kosovo Albanians, Tudjman successfully cleansed the Krajina of Serbs much as Pavelić would have wished.

The Slovenian leader Milan Kučan owed his position to a career inside the Communist Party hierarchy, but he was clear sighted enough to see that communism's time was rapidly running out, and he sensibly transmogrified himself into an Eastern European liberal, portraying himself as battling against an old-style Communist regime in Belgrade. While Kučan achieved remarkable things for Slovenia, it was done in the most dry-eyed way. Kučan believed that Slovenia would actually be held back by the rest of Yugoslavia, with the possible exception of Croatia, and he was presented with the best of opportunities, the militant nationalism Milošević deployed to extend his power beyond the borders of Serbia. Nevertheless, to see Kučan as a Balkan version of Czechoslovakia's Václav Havel is going too far. He was motivated by his own element of nationalism, which put Slovene interests far ahead of those for preserving Yugoslavia.

And then there was Alija Izetbegović, the only one of the six presidents to emerge from the first multiparty elections in Yugoslavia who had no Communist Party credentials. Indeed, he had been the object of repeated persecution under the Communists for his involvement in religious and nationalist groups, neither of which was tolerated under Titoism. He served three years in prison shortly after the Second World War for his involvement in the nationalist group *Mladi Muslimani* (young Muslims). In the 1980s, Izetbegović was again imprisoned after a political show trial that alleged he was planning to overthrow the Communist regime and to replace it with a Muslim state. After his release from prison in 1988 he became president of the SDA (Muslim nationalist party), the first of the separate community political parties founded in Bosnia in the run-up to the 1990 multiparty elections. His religious writings were often quoted against him by Croat and Serb opponents. As a man of strong academic and religious convictions, he was unused to the deals and compromises that are the small change of politics. As a result, all international negotiators found him a strain to deal with, often preferring his more Western-oriented lieutenants Mohammed Sacirbey or Haris Silajdžić. He was often portrayed in the Western media as the personification of his people's victim status, and there was indeed pathos about his person. He was in chronic ill-health and at one stage was not expected to survive for long beyond the Dayton Agreement. Nevertheless his mind was as sharp and twisting as any of his Balkan colleagues (Milošević called him the Grand Vizier), and he was not of a conciliatory or forgiving nature. His unwillingness to offer public reassurance to the Serbs of Sarajevo after the Dayton peace accords played into the hands of Radovan Karadžić and Momčilo Krajišnik, who were urging all Sarajevo Serbs to abandon the city and their traditional suburbs.

The other republican presidents, Kiro Gligorov in Macedonia and Momir Bulatović in Montenegro, were largely peripheral figures. Macedonia's exit from Yugoslavia was the smoothest and the least problematic—perhaps just as well given the domestic problems it faces together with its troubled relations with neighboring Greece. Bulatović had come to power on the back of the Milošević-inspired "antibureaucratic" revolution in Montenegro and was widely regarded as little more than a Milošević stooge. His only rebellion—to disagree publicly with Milošević over the acceptability of Lord Carrington's plan presented at the Hague conference in autumn 1991 for a loose alliance of independent states with special status and guarantees for minorities—was quickly snuffed out. He was summoned to Belgrade and browbeaten into submission. It was his last independent act.

The conclusion I draw is that these four interwoven strands cannot properly be considered independently. Without the post-1974 centrifugal internal structures and the disastrous interplay with international factors—notably the dramatic downgrading in Yugoslavia's strategic credit rating with the collapse of communism—Yugoslavia still had a chance. With these twin albatrosses, Yugoslavia's dissolution was guaranteed. The lifting of "the lid on the cauldron of ancient ethnic hatreds," to use Warren Christopher's phrase,[34] by cynical, manipulative, and ruthless politicians—notably Milošević and Tudjman—working to an atavistic nationalist agenda, even if it was not one with which they personally identified, ensured that the breakup would be violent, brutal, and bloody.

CHAPTER 1
The Pyromaniac Fireman

Slobodan Milošević was born in 1941 in Požarevac, a small agricultural center relatively close to the Danube about an hour's drive east of Belgrade. While born in Serbia—and he described himself as Serbian—he was of Montenegrin descent (indeed his brother, at some stage Yugoslav ambassador to Russia, always described himself as Montenegrin). In public, he did not talk much about the links or differences between Serbs and Montenegrins, although, on one occasion, he spoke of them as "two eyes in the same head." His father studied for the Orthodox priesthood (Milošević himself was happy to use Serbian Orthodoxy to further his nationalist agenda) and taught theology and languages. His mother was also a teacher, which no doubt explains the good account Milošević gave of himself at school. It was there that he met his future wife, Mirjana (Mira) Marković, who came from a Communist background and never wavered in her faith. Both his parents committed suicide; his father while Slobodan was at college in the early 1960s: his mother in the early 1970s. Psychiatrists will no doubt discuss at great length how much his wife filled the void left in his family life by his parents' suicides.

While at college studying law, Milošević became friends with a man to whose career he would link his own for the next fifteen years. Ivan Stambolić, having converted to academic studies from the labor force, was five years older than Milošević and immediately focused his attention on building a political career.

It was through his personal connections with this future president of Serbia, rather than through a lengthy climb up the Communist Party hierarchy, that Milošević made his mark. Although he was a minor party official in his undergraduate days, when he was known, no doubt affectionately, as "little Lenin" at the University of Belgrade, his early career thereafter suggested that, unlike Stambolić, politics were not his prime interest. After a short spell as an adviser in the City Council of Belgrade, he moved on to become deputy to Stambolić, who was running the state-controlled conglomerate Tehnogas. Stambolić's political flair ensured his recognition as one of the Young Turks who had made their reputation exclusively in the postwar period, owing nothing to Partisan credentials. He worked his way up from being general manager of Tehnogas to the presidency of the Belgrade Chamber of Commerce, president of the League of Communists of Serbia, and finally Serbian president.

Stambolić was not only Milošević's political mentor; he was also a close personal friend who felt no reserve at sharing with Milošević his political experience and tradecraft. Initially, however, Milošević's career, while linked to Stambolić, followed its own trajectory. After taking over the running of Tehnogas, he became the head of a major Belgrade bank—often traveling to the United States—and it was only when Stambolić became president of the League of Serbian Communists—ten years after leaving Tehnogas—that Milošević took on a party position. Even that was undertaken on a part-time basis while he continued to run Beogradska Banka. Thereafter their paths converged. Milošević followed closely in Stambolić's track, always one step behind: head of the Belgrade party, then general secretary of the Serbian Communist Party, and finally, with the overthrow of Stambolić, president of Serbia.

If Milošević was unusual in being parachuted into senior political positions without the traditional apprenticeship, he, in turn, brought to politics his own talents honed as a manager with often extensive contacts with the outside world, particularly the United States. Milošević's approach to decision making and power politics was not for faint-hearted apparatchiks. He was direct, determined, and an excellent learner. He listened well, made up his mind, and defended his decisions, often with great stubbornness. And having arrived in politics at the top table, he found himself immediately among those who made policy, rather than those who merely executed it and accepted the received wisdom. It is the experience he acquired at this time that singled him out from traditional party hacks, who were consistently cautious in expressing their own opinions unless they coincided with those of their masters.

Milošević's ultimate betrayal of his friend and patron is well documented. Having been sent by Stambolić to Kosovo in April 1987 to represent the Communist Party and to listen to the complaints from both sides about the worsening situation in the province, Milošević seized center stage with his famous call to the Serbs of Kosovo (of whom over two hundred thousand had left by the mid-1980s, convinced that they had no future in the province) to stay in Kosovo "for the sake of your ancestors and descendants" and his promise that "nobody should ever dare beat you again."

Although Milošević was to some extent the victim of unforeseen (by him) circumstance in Kosovo that day, he quickly turned the nationalist movement of Kosovo Serbs to his advantage. As Aleksa Djilas perceptively noted in his profile of the Serbian president, Milošević succeeded "because he understood the power of fear and knew how to use it for his own purposes ... discovering ... that the best way to escape the wrath of the masses was to lead them. It was an act of political cannibalism. The opponent, Serbian nationalism, was devoured, and its spirit permeated the eater. Milošević reinvigorated the [Communist] party by forcing it to embrace nationalism. . . . Milošević had learnt the secret of demagoguery in post Communist Europe. Far from transcending nationalism, as communism had taught, he embraced it eagerly. Once seen as a functionary of a discredited regime, he was now the voice of Serbian nationalism."[1] Within a year of his first public appearance in Kosovo, he was the most popular figure in Serbian living memory.

Watching the television pictures of Milošević more than twenty years on, it is not easy for a Western observer to appreciate the power of his limited oratory. Unlike other Communist Party chiefs, however, he did not read lengthy speeches larded with Marxist jargon to his audience. He did not use notes and spoke in simple short sentences. That itself was a sensation at the time. What he actually said was regarded as anti-Yugoslav and brought him a rebuke when he returned from Kosovo. Undaunted, he plotted and planned his ascent to the top of the Serbian Communist Party.

At the celebrated, indeed televised, Eighth Session of the Central Committee of the Serbian League of Communists in September 1987, Milošević's supporters mobilized their forces and isolated Stambolić. The Serbian president's traditional political wiles appear to have deserted him as though he did not believe that his closest friend could wield the knife. He recalled later, "When somebody looks at your back for 25 years, it is understandable that he gets the desire to put a knife in it at some point. Many people warned me, but I didn't acknowledge it."[2] Although the vote at the Eighth Session was in theory about the expulsion of the Belgrade party boss, Dragiša Pavlović, a Stambolić supporter, it was clear to all who the real target was. Pavlović was expelled from the Presidency during the Eighth Session, and Stambolić was officially dismissed in mid-December 1987.

While many leaders outside Serbia welcomed Stambolić's replacement by Milošević, feeling that Milošević was, unlike the feared Stambolić, someone they could control, Milošević nursed an innate belief that he could become the new strong man to take over control not just of Serbia but of Yugoslavia. The next stage of his campaign was therefore to ensure that he controlled the federal Presidency. To that end he needed to have his own placemen from at least half the republics and autonomous provinces (Kosovo and Vojvodina had full voting rights on the federal Presidency). Removing the incumbents in those autonomous provinces and promoting an "antibureaucratic" revolution in Montenegro allowed Milošević to control four votes on the Presidency. The tactics were always the same: a traveling road show of Serb nationalists from Kosovo would organize rallies and provoke confrontation with the authorities, who, physically intimidated by the crowds and denied help from the army, eventually would opt for resignation. By this time, the smaller republics were becoming thoroughly alarmed. Realizing belatedly that they had far more to fear from Milošević than they ever had from Stambolić, they were determined to avoid being picked off in the same way as the autonomous provinces and Montenegro.

Milošević's image as the Balkan butcher was, of course, clearly lodged with me by the time I reached Belgrade. But behind the inevitably oversimplified picture emerged a more complex and often paradoxical figure. He was, for instance, uncomfortable in crowds—surprising given the way he rose to prominence—and was almost never seen out in public. Equally he had little interest in the pomp and circumstance of office, although in my last few weeks in Belgrade a presidential guard appeared outside his residence dressed in full ceremonial guard not seen since Tito's days. He was basically uninterested in the trappings of power—just the real thing.

He had very few real close friends. He discarded colleagues and friends when they had served their purpose but removed them in a way that usually prevented their being able to damage him. His only real friend was his wife. Mira Marković was a philosophy professor at the University of Belgrade and founded a Marxist successor party to the League of Communists in 1990, which she later developed into a broader-based movement known as JUL, the Yugoslav United Left. Lord Owen pointed out the paradox of pro-Yugoslav antinationalist Mira Marković cohabiting with a man "widely believed to have been the chief instigator of [Yugoslavia's] break-up." She told David Owen and his wife that she understood that Milošević had failed to convince them that he was not a nationalist. "I will tell you why he is not. I would never have married or stayed married to him if he was a nationalist."[3] Milošević's attention to her views increasingly led to the exclusion from Milošević's circle of anyone of a liberal Western bent. Mira Marković's own placemen were invariably ideologically sound from her point of view and frequently intensely loyal to her rather than to her husband. She constantly sought to promote them into positions of influence, claiming that, unlike most of his party lieutenants, her men were true believers. Her power and baleful influence on her husband made her widely feared.

The joke went the rounds in Belgrade of an occasion when Milošević and his wife were in the car when it ran out of petrol. Although as a result of sanctions there was an acute shortage of petrol, Mira persuaded a petrol pump attendant to fill up their car. When he asked her who the attendant was, she replied, "my first love." "So," retorted Milošević, "if you had married him, you would have been a petrol pump attendant's wife." "No," said Mira, "if I'd married him, he would have been President of Serbia."[4]

Milošević's favored operating style was conspiratorial. He was accurately described as a "chamber politician" by the philosopher Ljubomir Tadić in 1993; in other words, as a man who likes to work with small groups of people busily promoting and removing members from his circle of trusted advisers. It created the atmosphere of fear and uncertainty (on which he thrived) among those with whom he worked. Those who stood up to him quickly earned not respect but enmity. Thus the Bosnian Serb leaders Karadžić and Krajišnik, formerly Milošević's creatures, became, as he saw them, too puffed up, capable of defying his wishes for prolonged periods. Like other autocrats, including Tito, he preferred to avoid being seen to wield the axe himself. Others were usually appointed to fulfill that role. Nonetheless, there was never any doubt over who took the final decisions on the removal of people from their positions. It was purely because Milošević had decided that they had outlived their usefulness or their loyalty was suspect. And sometimes, he was perfectly prepared to demonstrate his power personally. At a party meeting, for example, which removed several top officials, including his former closest colleague, Borislav (Bora) Jović, and the nationalist ideologue professor Mihailo Marković, he merely read out the names of those being politically liquidated without a word of explanation. With the sole exception of his wife Mira, nobody else's views were solicited or relevant.

The "cold narcissus," as the psychologist Žarko Trebjesanin described him, and the man of ice whose lack of emotion chilled some, such as former U.S. ambassador Warren Zimmermann, was nonetheless capable of great personal charm, as many international visitors and negotiators found. He was remarkable in recalling the most minute details of the private lives of some individuals. My young colleague David Austin, the talented embassy press attaché and a terrier-like negotiator, was regularly asked about the progress of his baby daughter, Grace, when he was working for David Owen's successor, Carl Bildt. Yet Milošević never expressed any regret or sadness over the fate of thousands who had died, whether they were Serbs, Albanians, Muslims, or Croats. It was as though their fate was merely a question of bureaucratic statistics, not personal suffering and tragedy.

The historian Milorad Ekmečić described him as "a genius of petty manoeuvring."[5] In other words, a man with no strategy and little sense of anticipation. He reacted incredibly quickly to events when they happened, but without any long-term vision, it was not surprising that his overall track record was disastrous. He tended to lurch from one extreme to another. Pushing his luck too far and then recoiling too far in the opposite direction, making unnecessary concessions when his bluff was called. His biographer, Slavoljub Djukić, described him as "at one and the same time a pyromaniac and a fireman, the Ubu Roi of the Balkans."[6]

* * *

Bora Jović, the Serbian Presidency representative and a close Milošević ally and collaborator at the time, paints a vivid picture of the less than fraternal infighting of the Federal Presidency in his diary of the period.[7] He describes in meticulous detail the dramatic political clashes particularly between Slovenes and

Serbs over the handling of the crisis in Kosovo and the former's attempts to force through constitutional amendments to facilitate secession from Yugoslavia. The bitterness of the invective led to a progressive decline in interrepublic relations and undermined every attempt by the federal government to find a compromise.

Despite their amendments being declared unconstitutional by the Federal Presidency, the Slovenes insisted on them. Serbia responded by announcing the visit of Milošević's traveling circus of nationalists, "the meeting of truth." When the Slovenes banned the rally, the Serbs canceled the meeting but instigated instead a boycott of Slovene goods in Serbia. At the last Congress of the League of Communists of Yugoslavia in January 1990, the Slovenes walked out after all their suggested amendments to the resolution on the future development of the Communist Party were humiliatingly defeated. They were followed out of the meeting by the Croats. The Congress was abandoned after a fifteen-minute recess called by the Montenegrin president and Congress chairman Momir Bulatović, a recess that, as he later put it, "lasted throughout history."[8]

Within a few months, multiparty elections in both Slovenia and Croatia had brought leaders to power committed to the right of the Slovene and Croat nations to their own state. Decisive referenda in favor of independence in December 1990 and May 1991, respectively, were followed by formal declarations of independence by Slovenia and Croatia on June 25, 1991.

One of the strongest opponents of the premature recognition of the independence of Croatia and Slovenia had been the president of the Bosnian Presidency, Alija Izetbegović, who saw very clearly the bleakness of a future Yugoslavia from which Slovenia and Croatia would have withdrawn. His choices were stark: to announce Bosnian withdrawal from Yugoslavia, thereby inevitably provoking the Bosnian Serbs to fight to remain within it, or to acquiesce in a Serb-dominated truncated Yugoslavia. After a referendum boycotted by the Bosnian Serbs, who had already voted to stay in Yugoslavia, Izetbegović declared Bosnia independent, an independence that was quickly recognized by the United States and the EC.

The well-armed and well-prepared Bosnian Serb army (drawn largely from the ranks of the JNA serving in Bosnia) quickly overran much of the country, occupying, by the time the battle lines were consolidated, around 70 percent of Bosnia. For nearly three years the front lines remained largely unchanged, although major cities were the subject of ferocious bombardment mainly from the Serbs but also in case of Mostar from the Croats. The international community reacted by imposing draconian sanctions against Serbia and Montenegro, the rump Yugoslavia that had also by this stage lost the republic of Macedonia, and by declaring a no-fly zone over Bosnia.

There then followed an unhappy period of transatlantic tension as the incoming Clinton administration maintained President George H. W. Bush's determination not to commit ground troops to stop the fighting. (As mentioned, Bush's secretary of state, James Baker, had declared that the United States "had no dog in this fight.") Clinton, however, advocated a policy of lifting the arms embargo and bombing the Serbs into withdrawing from conquests made, "that traditional U.S. long-distance and low-risk instrument, bombing."[9] The Europeans were more focused on promoting diplomatic solutions and dealing with the humanitarian crisis as well as containing the fighting to ensure no spillover into the rest of the region. Moreover, as it was the Europeans who had the troops on the ground who would be most at risk of attack or of being taken hostage in the event of air strikes, they failed to see why a military solution should be dictated by those who were not prepared to put their troops in harm's way.

At a meeting in London in 1992 called by the British prime minister John Major, agreement had been reached to establish a permanent International Conference on Former Yugoslavia (ICFY) to negotiate on all aspects of the crisis. The cochairmen were Lord Owen (who had succeeded Lord Carrington as the European negotiator) and Cyrus Vance, who represented the UN secretary-general. The parties had drawn up a proposal for a tricanton division of Bosnia at Lisbon in March 1992 before the war had begun in Bosnia. But President Izetbegović of Bosnia had withdrawn his support for the proposal, some say under pressure from the U.S. ambassador to Yugoslavia, Warren Zimmermann (a claim that Zimmermann himself contested). Vance and Owen replaced the Cutileiro plan, as it was known, with their own in January 1993. The Vance-Owen peace plan (known by the acronym VOPP) divided Bosnia into ten cantons in an attempt to preserve a multinational and multiethnic Bosnia. Despite winning the backing of President Milošević and, initially, Radovan Karadžić, the Bosnian Serb leader, the plan was rejected by the Pale Assembly of Bosnian Serbs largely as a result of the interventions of General Ratko Mladić and the Bosnian Serb vice president, Biljana Plavšić (who at one stage in the late 1990s was seen as the best hope for a pro-Western Bosnian Serb Republic but who was later imprisoned for war crimes).

Owen and Vance's successor, the former Norwegian foreign and defense minister, Thorvald Stoltenberg, drew up a new peace plan in August 1993 known as the Invincible plan as revisions to it were negotiated on board HMS *Invincible*. This again partitioned Bosnia, on a 51 (Muslims and Croats) to 49 (Serbs) percent basis and allowed for the possibility of the Bosnian Serbs opting out of the new state after a period of five years. This again foundered on Muslim opposition—specifically Izetbegović's. To add to the Muslims' plight, they became engaged on a second front in 1993 with the Bosnian Croats, a war that was every bit as cruel and vicious as the fight with the Serbs.

The end of the year therefore saw the battle lines virtually frozen and diplomacy benighted. The United States had not abandoned its preference for lift and strike and had damned the Vance-Owen plan with the faintest of praise. Owen and Stoltenberg were treated with increasing suspicion by the Clinton administration. The Bosnian Muslims had little interest in negotiating a peace agreement while they enjoyed numerical superiority and could hope to exercise pressure through Congress on the administration to lift the arms embargo, if necessary covertly. Early 1994 saw renewed U.S. diplomatic activity culminating in the Washington Agreement of March 1994, which brought to an end the bitter fighting between Bosnian Muslims and Croats and united them under the flag of convenience of the Muslim-Croat Federation. With the formation of the Federation, the Muslims and Croats turned the corner militarily and were able to rely on substantial support from the United States and Germany.

It was at this time, with the situation on the ground virtually static and the various peace plans shelved, that I set off for Yugoslavia. David Owen, frustrated at the lack of progress, had suggested the formation of a Contact Group of the five key international players involved in the Bosnian crisis: the United States, Britain, France, Germany, and Russia.

My first official encounter with Yugoslavia had come in the 1970s when I was appointed to the junior desk of a two-man Balkans section in the Foreign Office's Eastern European and Soviet Department. My main focus tended to be on Romania, Bulgaria, and Albania, but these were not always full-time jobs in those halcyon days. Romania was a maverick within the Warsaw Pact and had close relations with Yugoslavia. Despite the trouble Romania caused the Soviet Union, we had some difficulty stomaching the repressive domestic regime of Nicolae Ceaușescu. His family's outrageous behavior whenever they traveled abroad made them an object of ridicule among diplomats. His son in particular used to behave toward female fellow guests at state banquets like a latter-day Tom Jones with a serving wench. These approaches were not universally welcomed. Having read what other heads of state and their guests had had to endure, our permanent under-secretary minuted on one graphic account, "This man and his family must not be allowed near Her Majesty." I had moved on by the time this recommendation had been overturned and never found out how badly the junior Ceaușescus behaved during their state visit to Britain in 1977.

Albania, by contrast, was no problem at all. I only had two files on Albania: one was called the Corfu Channel incident, the other Albanian gold. As the two issues were inextricably linked—we were not prepared to release Albanian gold we held in the Bank of England (having recovered it from the Italians of the end of the Second World War) until they paid us compensation for sinking two of our battleships in the international waters of the Corfu Channel in 1946. I could at a pinch have incorporated the two files into one.

As it was, the main activity on the files tended to be a parliamentary question every six to nine months asking what progress if any had been made toward solving these matters. We had no diplomatic relations with Albania precisely because they refused to negotiate on our compensation claim, which had been adjudicated by the International Court of Justice. This meant that there never was any progress to report.

At the time that I was serving on the Balkan desk, Yugoslavia had been given its last and most disastrous constitution by Tito in 1974. Although much effort was spent in analyzing the constitution, none of us appreciated how corrosive it was ultimately to prove. While Tito was still regarded very much by the West as an invaluable asset in the Cold War, a cloud was cast over our bilateral relations at the time by the arrest and imprisonment of a couple of plane spotters from Richmond-on-Thames who had visited ten military airfields without detection and who, when they were finally picked up by Tito's security people, found themselves accused of espionage. Although the charge was preposterous, I suspect that the Yugoslavs thought that only professional spies could have visited so many military establishments without detection. It was easy to picture the security police advancing this line with their political masters to cover their embarrassment and incompetence. Eventually a bilateral ministerial visit unlocked the prison cells, but the Yugoslavs were stubborn, unreasonable, and abrasive in any discussion of the matter. It was to be nearly twenty years before I dealt with them again. But it was a useful if small-scale dress rehearsal for the confrontations to come with Milošević and the Bosnian Serbs.

CHAPTER 2

Early Belgrade Days

The invitation to head the mission in Belgrade came from the Foreign Office personnel department in time-honored fashion. It was spring 1993, and the war in Bosnia had been raging for nearly a year. The code word "challenging," meaning a job nobody else was keen to undertake, cropped up once or twice. But I was not too worried. None of the other options seemed particularly attractive; I had maintained a keen interest in Balkan affairs, and I thought my involvement in Yugoslav affairs in the Foreign Office twenty years previously would stand me in good stead.

My wife, Elizabeth, an ex-Australian diplomat, and I had some six months to go before we left our previous post in Madrid. During that period, it seemed on more than one occasion improbable that there would be a mission in Belgrade left to head. The German government in particular was adamant that all European Union missions should be closed down completely. The discussions on lifting the arms embargo and carrying out air strikes against the Bosnian Serbs continued intermittently throughout 1993, with those who had no troops on the ground (the United States and Germany) arguing most vehemently, while those who did (UK, France, and Spain) opposed just as resolutely.

Finally in February 1994, shortly after General Michael Rose (whom I knew from my days in charge of counterterrorism in the Foreign Office) had taken over as commander of UN ground forces in Bosnia, a shell on the marketplace in Sarajevo, which killed sixty-nine people, prompted a real possibility of an imminent air strike. This was averted by a negotiated settlement brokered by the Russian deputy foreign minister Vitaly Churkin, who bludgeoned the Bosnian Serb leaders in their headquarters in Pale into agreeing to withdraw their heavy weapons from a twenty-mile exclusion zone around Sarajevo, while the Russians agreed to send in their own troops under UN colors to supervise the agreement.

Foreign Secretary Douglas Hurd and I watched the announcement of Churkin's deal with the Bosnian Serbs on television together in his office. I was receiving my last briefings before departure. Hurd echoed the advice I had been given previously by the European Union's negotiator, Lord Owen, who strongly believed that the key to the resolution of the crisis in Bosnia lay with Milošević. This may seem obvious with the benefit of hindsight, but at the time most of the negotiations were carried out with the Bosnian parties themselves—with scant results. Hurd and Owen believed that without Milošević's engagement the long haul to peace would stretch still further. The difficulty was how to engage Milošević and at the same time detach him from covert support for the Bosnian Serbs. Milošević at the time was sulking in his tent after his failure (and, as he saw it, consequent humiliation), despite a personal intervention and appearance at the Bosnian Serb Assembly in Pale, to persuade the Bosnian Serbs to accept the Vance-Owen Peace Plan (VOPP) the previous spring. Efforts to persuade him to use his undoubted influence had been met with the mantra "lift sanctions and I may be able to help you." The international community wished to see something up front from the Serb side before contemplating any relaxation of the sanctions. Douglas Hurd and David Owen's message to me was that, while the front-line diplomacy would be continued by the international negotiators, anything I could do to help them understand Milošević's thinking—to get inside his head—would be invaluable.

With those orders, Elizabeth and I set off a few days later for Belgrade via Zagreb, where we spent a few educationally testing weeks. While we were studying in Zagreb, a partial evacuation of the Belgrade embassy took place under the threat of NATO air strikes in the event of Bosnian Serb noncompliance with the agreement with Churkin to withdraw their heavy weaponry from around Sarajevo. We took the opportunity to improve our language skills by staying with two elderly widows who spent a very high percentage of their time watching TV in preference to talking to their guests. The language school where we learned the local variant of Serbo-Croatian (*ijekavski*) feigned incredulity when they heard that we were studying in Croatia prior to going to live in Serbia. "Of course the languages are similar," they would say, "but they are quite different" (shades of Herder's contention that language equals nation). Although our language teacher knew we were going to live in Belgrade, she systematically corrected our Serbian pronunciation learned from the BBC Serbian service to the, for her, acceptable Croatian variant. All of this slowed down our, or at least my, already leaden progress toward adequacy in Serbo-Croatian. Elizabeth had taken an early lead in the language sweepstakes, which she never relinquished. Our teacher also gave us a useful introductory lesson into the use of nationalism in language; she studiously avoided using the word "Serb" and used instead the term "Chetnik." We were soon to see the reverse side of the coin when less sophisticated Serbs would refer to all Croats as "Ustasha."

The previous month had seen Serbia hit rock bottom. Hyperinflation had peaked at 352 trillion percent. But when we finally arrived in Belgrade, the very worst seemed to be over. Admittedly the airport was closed to international flights, and the streets were virtually empty with the exception of the omnipresent street vendors of petrol dispensed in plastic bottles by the liter. But the currency had stabilized thanks to a new economic reform program put in place by the central bank governor, Dragoslav Avramović. The farmers had started to bring their produce back to the market, and the fields of the Pannonian plain were well on the way to providing a fine harvest, the surplus of which was later to be sold off overseas by Serbian government ministers for substantial personal profit. Our staff at the embassy were politely amused to see that we had arrived in Belgrade with our car groaning with foodstuffs bought in Hungary as we had failed to update ourselves on whether markets were operating normally.

Sanctions throughout our time worked only fitfully. A short while after our arrival, my wife and her parents came across a major smuggling operation at the Iron Gates, a gorge on the Danube between Serbia and Romania, while they were indulging in a rare touristic outing. They observed a flotilla of small boats crossing the Danube in both directions and unwisely decided to photograph this picturesque scene. The owners of the small boats, having seen themselves being photographed, took it very much amiss as a result of which Elizabeth and her parents had to beat a hasty retreat.

We had expected to find Milošević as omnipresent in Belgrade as Tudjman had been in Zagreb, where scarcely a day went by without a press conference or public appearance by the "Father of the Nation." But the heady days of mass rallies were over. Not only were there no pictures of Milošević in public places, but the man was inaudible—no press conferences and only a tiny handful of speeches (perhaps four in my first couple of years) and to be seen only on the front pages of *Politika* and in Trappist mode on state television, meeting the odd small delegation or visitor.

Largely invisible he may have been, but his brooding presence permeated every quarter of Belgrade. A one-man show, "l'état c'est moi," might have been coined by him. It was impossible to hold any political discussion without his name cropping up almost immediately. As biographer Slavoljub Djukić said, "All the normal institutions exist, but only one functions: Slobodan Milošević."[1] It was as though he was the only three-dimensional figure in Serbian politics while the others were cardboard cutouts.

One of the characters on the political scene who was distinctly non-two-dimensional was the charismatic former nationalist, now peacenik, Vuk Drašković. On one of our first evenings in Belgrade, Elizabeth and I had dinner with Vuk and his wife, Danica. Vuk looked as though he should have played the lead in Franco Zeffirelli's *Jesus of Nazareth*. He was an unashamed apologist for the Chetnik leader Draža Mihailović (who was executed by the Partisans after the war, despite having formerly been supported by the Allies in the fight against the Nazis), a former journalist and a writer, some of whose books (*The Knife*, for instance) were chillingly nationalistic. He had, however, converted to the cause of peace and in the course of a demonstration against the government the previous year been locked up and beaten by the security police. His brutal treatment at the hands of Milošević had nonetheless not prevented him from meeting the Serbian president a few weeks previously in the wake of the December 1993 Serbian parliamentary elections, when Milošević's Socialists had failed to gain an outright victory. Drašković gave us a colorful account of the meeting.

In response to Drašković's rhetorical "How are you? *Kako ste?*" Milošević had responded with great vigor that he was "very, very well indeed." Drašković could not refrain from commenting that, if true, this placed Milošević in a tiny minority in Serbia given the desperate straits in which the divided Serb society found itself after two years of sanctions and a war on its doorstep. Milošević had breezed on to discuss with Drašković the possibility of his entering the government. Drašković had on close inspection declined the poisoned chalice. If his party could have held the Interior Ministry, he would accept. If not, no. Milošević had refused to discuss the Interior Ministry, having too much communism in his makeup even to consider surrendering the levers of police power to a nonbeliever such as Drašković. But he tried to tempt him with up to ten cabinet seats for his party. Drašković was not having any. Milošević accordingly made other arrangements to secure a parliamentary majority, seducing a small moderate businessmen's party, New Democracy, out of their loose coalition with Drašković and into his camp. Drašković preferred to remain in opposition—where he languished, after a period as deputy prime minister under Milošević and a post-Milošević period as foreign minister.

Danica, his wife, whose features are as striking as her remarks tend to be dramatic, volunteered the startling prophecy that she expected the streets of Belgrade to be running in blood by June—we were in March. The prospect of a civil war was one she appeared almost to welcome. Fortunately for the rest of the population, her Cassandra-like prophecy failed to materialize. It provided, nevertheless, a vivid reminder, if one were ever needed, of how extreme statements and even actions in the Balkans often passed as normal or at least as unremarkable in those days.

By way of contrast to this pro-monarchy, pro-Chetnik couple, I decided to call on one of the heroes of the Partisan struggle, the veteran dissident Milovan Djilas. Tito's former comrade-in-arms turned his bitterest internal critic was a man I had long admired from afar. The veteran dissident—indeed, the man who coined the concept before the word was current—was now in his eighties, but he retained all the sharpness and acumen so evident in his political writing. "Welcome to the home of dissidence," he said, showing me in. Although I had many questions to put to him, I did not want to tire him out as he was clearly physically frail.

I was particularly interested in hearing his views on the significance of the so-called AVNOJ borders,[2] the administrative borders between and within the republics, drawn up by Djilas and two other senior Partisans, Aleksandar Ranković and Edvard Kardelj, under Tito's direction, in 1943 at the height of the war at Jajce in Bosnia. It was the status of these borders that a group of international jurists, headed by former French justice minister Robert Badinter, were charged by the European Community in 1991 with examining.[3] Djilas said that he and Tito always considered them administrative units of convenience, first and foremost. Republican and nationalist sentiment would in any case be blurred in the new socialist paradise, which he and Tito were set on creating. The idea that they could ever be considered international borders had simply never occurred to Tito or himself. It puzzled him and astonished me that the members of the Badinter Commission never troubled themselves to sound him out as the only surviving draughtsman of what was to become a highly contentious border delineation. He spoke a little of the difficulties he had experienced in writing some of his books in prison and of getting them smuggled out and eventually published. He then complained that although everybody spoke of his political and historical works, he was never given any credit as a novelist. I replied, "Mr. Djilas, with the greatest of respect, you have been a Partisan general, the first figure in the struggle to destroy communism from within, and your political writings are still regarded as classic texts. Don't you think it's a bit much to expect also to be acclaimed as a great novelist?" Djilas, amused, conceded the point.

I later reread his description of the discussions on the inter- and intrarepublican borders at the Communist Party's Central Committee meetings in Jajce in November 1943.[4] Moša Pijade, a leader of the Partisan uprising in Montenegro, had put forward a proposal for the territorial autonomy of the Serbs in Croatia. He produced maps that had his proposed borders marked. Djilas continues, "The idea was a new one and the Serbs in Croatia had served valiantly in the uprising.... I think I saw dejection even on Tito's face: perhaps, as a Croat, he found it awkward to oppose." Djilas records that he was the first to oppose Pijade's ideas, claiming that they would provide the fuel for Croatian nationalism. His co-draftsmen Kardelj and Ranković agreed with him. "Tito calmly accepted our stand, while injecting the class motivation: 'with us this will be more of an administrative division, instead of fixed borders, as with the bourgeoisie.'"

Djilas goes on to mention casually that the original intention of the Communist hierarchy was to make the whole of Bosnia-Herzegovina an autonomous region as part of Serbia. However, in the light of the fighting that had occurred in Bosnia and as a result of an appeal by the local Communists, the central committee agreed to reexamine the question, and Bosnia's republican status was finally confirmed the following year.[5]

Our heavy baggage from London arrived two weeks after our arrival, but we had barely time to unpack when the embassy was yet again partially evacuated to Hungary after the renewed threats of air strikes against the Bosnian Serbs. These came to virtually nothing and resulted principally in the shooting down of a British Harrier jump jet, which had been flying too low and too often over Bosnian Serb positions. Nevertheless, dependents and nonessential staff crawled wearily yet again up the inadequate highway to Budapest, returning after the danger was deemed to be over some five days later. The anti-Western fury artificially created in the state media was quite unpleasant for a time and resulted in a flurry of death threats to the embassy and its staff, an occasional feature of our time in Belgrade.

CHAPTER 3

Close Encounter with the Bosnian Serbs

The Three Ks

With the return of the evacuees from their enforced midweek break in Budapest came a message from the Foreign Office that the new under-secretary for Yugoslavia, Roger Bone, would arrive shortly to familiarize himself with the region and to make contact with the Bosnian Serb leadership. Roger arrived from Sofia (there were no flights to Belgrade as a result of sanctions), where I'd sent a driver to pick him up. He arrived about two hours before I expected owing to a misunderstanding with my driver. Roger had asked how long the car journey from Sofia to Belgrade would take and added as a guess the thought that it might be a couple of hours. My driver had taken it as a challenge to accomplish the journey in that time (it normally took about four hours), hence Roger arrived after a white-knuckle ride severely shaken if not stirred.

As soon as Roger had recovered, the Bosnian Serb vice president, Nikola Koljević, was duly fielded and received a vigorous protest about his army's behavior at Goražde. Koljević was far from the stereotypical picture I had formed of the Bosnian Serbs. He was defensive but not defiant, mild mannered, and preached no history lessons. After our protest, he telephoned Karadžić from my residence to ask him what was going on in Goražde.

Karadžić spun him some line about provocations and exaggerated foreign press reactions. I had, however, been briefed only hours before by the United Nations High Commissioner for Refugees (UNHCR) spokesperson in Belgrade, Lyndall Sachs, who gave me a graphic account of the situation on the ground as seen by UNHCR representatives. (She also volunteered her views on the shortcomings of the safe areas policy, claiming that in the long term, it would lead to the loss of more lives than it would ever save—prophetic in the light of what happened in Srebrenica fewer than eighteen months later.) Lyndall's briefing meant that we were able to rebut the Karadžić line forcefully. Koljević looked uncomfortable and apologetic and fell silent. He was to be a frequent actor on my small stage in future months.

Less than a month later, the Foreign Office minister of state in charge of Yugoslavia, Douglas Hogg, arrived for an intensive visit to Belgrade and Kosovo.

He was the first European Union minister to pay a visit to the troubled province since the Yugoslav crisis began.

His first contacts, however, were with the Serb leadership. This gave me my first opportunity to meet Milošević. Diplomats did not normally meet Milošević. He was affronted by the withdrawal of ambassadors by all Western countries in May 1992 and declined to receive the chargés d'affaires who were left behind or appointed to head those embassies. The odd exception was made for delivery of high-level messages from presidents or prime ministers. Acting on David Owen's advice, I had asked for a call through his chef de cabinet, Goran Milinović, but was not in the least surprised that I had not at that stage been received. I was therefore particularly curious to meet the person described by the *Guardian* as "the most dangerous man in Europe."[1] One of the Foreign Office under-secretaries in London had told me before I left that at a meeting in Brussels with European foreign ministers in December 1993, Milošević had "oozed power." There was, however, little sense of either danger or power at that first encounter.

The Serbian presidential building is in the old center of Belgrade. A late nineteenth-century creation, it is depressingly grimy on the outside and, at that time, gloomy and unwelcoming inside. It was also almost totally deserted. None of the bustle you would find in a Western ministry. In the course of perhaps forty visits, excepting bodyguards and security men, I never met more than two or three people in the building besides Milošević. The pattern was always the same. If the meeting was as part of a delegation, as on this occasion, it took place in an ornate drawing room on the ground floor with heavy nineteenth-century furniture and modern paintings on the wall. Milošević would invariably stride in purposefully, fix his visitor with an intense blue-eyed stare, and then warmly shake his hand with a good deal of cordiality as though the visitor were the most important person Milošević had ever met. These simple tricks of the trade were, I imagine, learned in his banking days when he was a commuter to New York. Certainly it was in marked contrast to the more buttoned up, diffident Eastern European style.

At this first encounter, I found the experience of meeting "the most dangerous man in Europe" underwhelming. He was leaden rather than dominating; he allowed the conversation to drift for lengthy periods without attempting to steer it. He continued to be subdued and listless but rallied fairly strongly toward the end. The conversation was, however, circular and unproductive. Milošević insisted that sanctions must be removed before he would actively engage in support of the peace process; Douglas Hogg warned him that failure to take positive measures to bring the Bosnian Serbs to heel would lead inevitably to further sanctions against Serbia and Montenegro. While there had been some talk of a carrot for Milošević a few weeks earlier, the Bosnian Serb operation at

Goražde had so alienated Western opinion that sanctions relief was nowhere on the agenda. Milošević repeated his line; we rehearsed ours. No progress. As we left the meeting, Douglas Hogg remarked, "He has a certain rough charm. I need to keep reminding myself of all the terrible things he's done."

Later that day we met the three key Bosnian Serb leaders known as the three *K*s: Karadžić, Krajišnik, and Koljević. To have the leaders of the Bosnian Serbs assembled on a terrace for afternoon tea with Douglas Hogg was, as my wife commented, an odd way to mark our twentieth wedding anniversary. Karadžić did all the talking for his side. To reverse Clemenceau's description of the Socialist leader Jaurès, all Karadžić's verbs were in the past tense.[2] Much of the negotiation concerned the principle of the territorial division: 51 percent to the Muslims and Croats and 49 percent to the Serbs, a principle that had been agreed to onboard HMS *Invincible*. Karadžić countered by claiming that the concession was only in the context of the agreement hammered out at the HMS *Invincible* talks. It was not to be quoted against the Bosnian Serbs out of that context now that those talks had failed. Douglas Hogg insisted that the principle of 51/49 percent division had been agreed to. There was no going back. No, replied Karadžić like a carpet salesman, it was a one-day special offer. As he left, Karadžić stopped by our piano to look at a photo of our three children. The way he then asked after them made me distinctly uneasy.

The consequences of European and U.S. insistence on this *acquis* were not to become clear for some months to come, but they were later to provide a fig leaf for Karadžić's intransigence at a time when, in retrospect, he had his best hand to play. As the group left, the Bosnian Serb vice president, Koljević, a Shakespearean scholar, took me aside to say that he would like to continue our conversation and would be in touch. We met several times over the next few months as the Contact Group refined the map they were preparing to give to the parties on a "take it or leave it" basis.

At one stage in June 1994, Karadžić himself came to my house to show me a map that he said he could not put forward himself. He would be killed if he did so; he would, however, be prepared to have it "imposed" on the Bosnian Serbs. When I asked him to leave the map behind, he said it was his only copy. But he would be prepared to trace it for me. He was for once as good as his word. Some adhesive tape and a fresh copy of a map of Bosnia were provided, and using my dining room window as a drawing board, he traced a copy. It was an intriguing document, but I could see immediately that it would be wholly unacceptable in its present shape as it came nowhere near the 51/49 percent division of territory. Karadžić admitted that it was still some way from those percentages. Nor could he give any explanation of how those percentages would be reached. Nonetheless I sent the map back urgently to London for evaluation by the Contact Group and to see what they could learn from it of the Bosnian Serbs' bottom line.

I was actively engaged at that period not only with the Bosnian Serb leadership but also with those who might be supposed to have some positive influence on them. Included under this rubric were the former Federal Republic of Yugoslavia (FRY) president Dobrica Ćosić (dismissed from office by Milošević's maneuverings though ostensibly at the behest of Vojislav Šešelj's ultranationalist Radical Party, which exercised a certain malign influence on the body politic), his close adviser Svetozar Stojanović, and the ideologue of Milošević's Socialists and high priest of nationalism, Professor Mihailo Marković.

These contacts yielded meager pickings. Ćosić, who was a very near neighbor in the residential quarter known as Dedinje, came over as particularly intransigent and unlikely to play a positive or constructive role in influencing the Bosnian Serbs. He once asked me in all seriousness why it was objectionable to aim for a Greater Serbia when we had our own Great Britain. Attempts to persuade him that Great Britain was no more than a distinction between us and Brittany were met with incredulity.

As the summer wore on, it looked increasingly likely that it would be only through direct contacts with the Bosnian Serbs that any progress could be registered. Koljević was a regular visitor in that period, constantly looking for ammunition to try to persuade his harder-line colleagues in Pale that they should accept whatever the Contact Group proposed, provided it was from a Bosnian Serb perspective reasonable.

Given the secretive workings of the Contact Group and their decision to withhold even from their own embassies details of the mapmaking, this made negotiations with Koljević particularly complicated. Nevertheless I was clear from my contacts with him that some at least of the Bosnian Serb desiderata had to be satisfied if there was to be any chance of their accepting the map. These desiderata, which were not always consistently maintained, included compact and defensible territory; access to the sea, however minimal; the Posavina corridor linking the eastern and western parts of Bosnian Serb territory; the absorption of the three enclaves in eastern Bosnia into the Republika Srpska; and a resolution to the problem of Sarajevo.

When the Contact Group map was finally presented to the parties in July 1994, the Bosnian Serbs immediately believed that it had been designed to be rejected by them as it met none of their basic demands. Most damaging of all in their eyes was the way it fragmented Bosnian Serbian territory in a way that made it virtually indefensible. I had warned the Contact Group through the Foreign Office of the Bosnian Serb bottom line, but the history of the Group's mapmaking as revealed in David Owen's book *Balkan Odyssey* makes it clear that the U.S. representative Charles Redmond was the chief draftsman and that the British and French felt that it was largely the Russians' responsibility to argue the Bosnian Serb case. That they failed to do so has never been satisfactorily explained. My own impression is that Vitaly Churkin, who was in charge of Yugoslav affairs under foreign minister Kozyrev in the Russian Foreign Ministry, was so disenchanted with the Bosnian Serbs (particularly after Goražde) that he felt no urge to defend their corner and so instructed his representative on the Contact Group.

After the usual Bosnian Serb consultative processes, they delivered their response to the map with typical histrionic flourish in a sealed pink envelope. The anticipated rejection led swiftly to action by Contact Group ministers to ratchet up sanctions both on the Bosnian Serbs and on Belgrade.

In this climate it was felt worthwhile to have one last go at persuading the Bosnian Serbs. Accordingly the Contact Group's UK representative, David Manning, and I traveled to the Bosnian Serb capital, Pale, a ski resort near Sarajevo, to attempt to persuade Karadžić to accept the map. Karadžić was in a defiant mood. He was suffering from a heavy cold and distinctly unenthusiastic about the meeting with us. This did not, however, constrain him from the delivery of a lengthy historical analysis of the reason why the Serbs were once more the Guardians at the Gate keeping the Muslims at bay on behalf of Christian Europe. (The reality was, of course, that far from Bosnian Serbs being guardians of Christian Europe, their behavior served as a recruiting sergeant for homegrown Islamic extremism in Europe.) We got nowhere and left in a depressed and subdued mood, holding some stamps of the Bosnian Serb entity, the Republika Srpska, which in a last-minute gesture he had given us as if embarrassed at having been such a disobliging interlocutor.

When we called on Milošević, on our return to Belgrade, his reaction was robust: he was, he said, determined to put a real squeeze on the Bosnian Serbs. He was transformed from the man at our first encounter. He was seriously engaged and animated. He told us that he would be meeting the Bosnian Serb leadership later that day and would let us know how the meeting had gone. We pressed him on what he would do if they continued to reject the map. He would go no further than to say that the leadership would feel the consequences, but he left us with the impression that frustrated as he was, he was not prepared yet to isolate the Bosnian Serbs as a whole for the impertinence of their leadership in defying him.

He called us to his office the next afternoon to report failure. It was a brief encounter. He had been up all night (it showed) to try to persuade the Bosnian Serb leadership. He was clearly very tired and reticent about his next move. It was obvious to us both, however, that he had another card to play.

David Manning departed, but in Belgrade we did not have to wait long to see Milošević's reaction. The Writers' Club in Belgrade, even in those days of sanctions and power cuts, was a popular venue for politicians, journalists, academics, diplomats, and the occasional paramilitary leader, such as the notorious Serbian warlord Željko Ražnatović, alias Arkan. I was dining at the club three days after our encounter with Milošević on the last night before it closed for the summer break. Dragan Hadži Antić, the editor-in-chief of *Politika*, the state-controlled (i.e., Milošević) daily, was also dining there that night but left, I noticed, rather abruptly and uncharacteristically early. The reason was to be found in next morning's edition of his paper, which splashed with an interview with Milošević (a rarity in itself) that was little more than a prepared statement by Milošević couched in very tough language about the damage that the Bosnian Serbs were doing to the overall Serb cause despite the enormous sacrifices the Serbs had already made on behalf of their cousins across the Drina. This unprecedented attack on the Bosnian Serbs caused a sensation among the Belgrade political and diplomatic classes.

Four days later the Serbian government issued an even tougher statement that announced the closure of the border between Bosnia and Serbia for everything except food, clothing and medicine, cut off all relations with the Bosnian Serb republic, and denied the leadership access to the FRY. The statement concluded with a blunt warning to the Bosnian Serbs not to resort to the device of a referendum to reject the Contact Group map, a warning that Karadžić characteristically ignored.

The stage was now set for a major showdown between Milošević and Karadžić. David Owen, who had been working for many months to split off the Serbs from the Bosnian Serbs, was quick to capitalize on the opportunity presented by the blockade on the Serb/Bosnian border imposed by Milošević. Most commentators in Belgrade including myself were skeptical about the chances of Milošević accepting international observers of his blockade. This would amount to a diminution of national sovereignty, which Milošević had never been prepared to accept previously. He had once before closed the border with Bosnia after the Vance-Owen Peace Plan (VOPP) had been rejected by the Bosnian Serb Assembly. But this had lasted only a matter of days. With international supervision Milošević would have to be serious about enforcing the blockade. Owen and Stoltenberg, however, moved with great speed to convince Milošević of the advantages to be obtained from international supervision, and within six weeks of the Serbian government's announcement of the blockade, the first international observers began to arrive, an operation placed in the experienced and skilled hands of Swedish general Bo Pellnas, who had worked in a variety of capacities for the UN throughout the Yugoslav crisis and who became a firm friend and ally in the months ahead.

Milošević duly gained his reward when the Security Council voted in October 1994 to suspend sanctions on sporting links, cultural relations, and international air services. In terms of restoring the shattered Yugoslav economy, these measures had no significance at all. Psychologically, however, they were an important fillip to the long-suffering Yugoslav public for whom deprivation of their participation in international sporting events was particularly keenly felt and deeply humiliating. Sporting events were, it might be said, in those days paradigms of Serbian life in a war zone (at least off the field). There was one memorable football (soccer) game between the two leading Belgrade clubs, Red Star and Partizan, which degenerated into a series of fights with smoke bombs being thrown and the pitch reduced to zero visibility. As the smoke swirled around us in the stands, I noticed one man carrying a child out of the stadium, which I regarded as a good deed. As he came closer, I saw that he had a beltful of hand grenades strapped to his midriff. The mind boggled at what might have happened if one had accidentally been knocked off his belt in the general melee.

CHAPTER 4

A First Private Meeting with Milošević

I continued to see a good deal of Koljević, who initially was allowed to travel from Bosnia back to Belgrade, where his family lived. Of the three Bosnian Serb Ks, the professor (as Nikola Koljević liked to be called) was the least well known. He was often trotted out as the semirespectable face of the Pale leadership—his excellent English, his academic background, and his knowledge of Shakespeare were regarded as assets—but he was not memorable. He has often been dismissed as part alcoholic, part Milošević stooge (hence having no clout in Pale), and part nationalist ogre responsible for targeting the priceless library in Sarajevo. All of this gave a somewhat distorted picture.

By the time I met him in April 1994, the worst excesses of nationalism seemed to have been burned out of him. He never made disparaging or racist remarks about Muslims or Croats in my hearing, and I find it hard to think that a combination of his grasp of military targeting and his extreme myopia would have been a great asset to the Bosnian Serb artillery. In fact, he rarely, if ever, before the Dayton Agreement evinced much interest in Sarajevo. Banja Luka was his town, and in the endless discussions of the map, the prospect of a unified Sarajevo under Muslim control did not bother him.

Much later, after Dayton in the winter of 1995/96, he worked tirelessly but ultimately futilely against his Pale colleagues in trying to persuade the Serbs to stay in their suburbs even if under Muslim-Croat Federation control. He would beg me repeatedly to get the international community to offer guarantees and to muzzle Izetbegović, whose anti-Serb remarks at the time worked very much with the grain of Krajišnik's and Karadžić's rhetoric. They appeared to have a demonic desire to leave the Serb suburbs of Sarajevo as deserted smoking ruins, a final act of criminal petulance, more redolent of a spoiled child in the nursery than would-be leaders of their community, against a city that both professed to hold dear and that had been the second largest Serb city in the former Yugoslavia.

For Koljević this was one more disappointment and disillusionment to add to many others. His estrangement from the Pale clique had by then become complete, although he still felt enormous difficulty in cutting himself off from Radovan Karadžić, his friend of over thirty years. I doubt that Karadžić felt the same compunction. I had seen him humiliate Koljević, talking over the latter's pronouncements on policy with some fatuous remarks about the merits of a bottle of wine as though Koljević's views were of no possible importance or relevance.

But all this was some way in the future. From our first meeting, when Koljević was given a verbal mauling about the terrible shelling of Goražde and its civilian population, he gave the impression that he wanted desperately to be seen to be doing the right thing as far as the West was concerned. He also demonstrated a genuine, I believe, ignorance of a good deal of what was happening on the ground in Bosnia.

In our attempts to drive wedges between Belgrade and Pale and to gauge the weak links in the Bosnian Serb leadership, Koljević was a willing if sometimes unconscious partner. He was the weak link. He was also close to Milošević, making him doubly useful. In the inevitable trade-off, he wanted to know how serious the international community was about the threat of further sanctions. He claimed to have become a believer in the need to end the war, to reach what he would describe as an honorable settlement, giving up about 20 percent of the territory held by the Bosnian Serbs in return for some or (ideally) all of the eastern enclaves. My role was to impress on him how serious we were about further sanctions (even though we were under no illusions that this would offer a quick fix) while persuading him of the advantages of settling then, arguments that he would deploy later with his as yet unconvinced colleagues.

Milošević, of course, was aware through his security people of my contacts with Koljević and the Bosnian Serbs and, given his Communist schooling, was typically suspicious. Was this a Western attempt to sideline him, to marginalize Serbia, and to close a deal directly with Pale? Why, he asked Koljević (who promptly relayed the question to me), was I seeing so much of the former Yugoslav president, arch-nationalist, and father figure of the Bosnian Serbs, academician Dobrica Ćosić? Two reasons, I replied. First, I was bound to see a fair amount of Ćosić: he was my neighbor, and his home was thirty yards from my front door. Second, he had undoubted influence with the Bosnian Serbs and with Karadžić particularly. If he could be persuaded to influence them in favor of the Contact Group's proposals, he was now worth cultivating. Moreover, I added to Koljević, if Milošević was so interested in what I was doing, he could ask me directly. After a further few weeks' reflection, he decided to do so.

We had now reached a critical point in the peace process. Pale remained unrepentant and unmoved by the Drina blockade; the head of the Bosnian Serb army, Ratko Mladić, was attacking one of the UN-protected safe areas, Bihać, and early talk of an end to the war or even a ceasefire seemed wildly optimistic. It was against this background that my first tête-à-tête meeting with Milošević took place.

As I was to discover, all such small-scale meetings took place in Milošević's set of offices on the first floor: a suite of three interconnecting rooms, a waiting room on the right, his personal secretary's office in the middle, and his own office on the left, leading off from which were further rooms that could be used for meals. His office was large and traditional. No televisions, no gizmos. A huge desk with relatively little paperwork on it—Serbia was clearly not a paper-driven autocracy—and a large photograph of his wife on the wall to the left of his desk. Milošević invited me to sit down on one of four or five armchairs surrounding a circular glass table on which was placed a large clock. Despite the obvious indicator, he rarely gave the impression of being particularly hurried. Formalities were invariably preserved. Mr. President: Mr. Roberts. The usual Serbian offerings would be made: coffee, fruit juice, and rakija, or the Serb national drink slivovica, plum brandy. It always seemed wise to stick to the coffee and juice.

At our last meeting, shortly after Milošević had failed to persuade the Bosnian Serbs to accept the Contact Group plan, he had looked tired and dispirited. On this occasion he was in confident and optimistic form. He gave no impression of being under pressure or of being wracked by much self-doubt. Much of the meeting focused on Bosnia, although we also discussed at length the crisis in Croatia and Serbo-Croat relations. Milošević told me that he had recently received twenty members of the Bosnian Serb Assembly, who were increasingly dissatisfied with Karadžić and his determination to prosecute the war.

Milošević said that the group had told him that up to fifty members of the Assembly now wanted to accept the Contact Group plan. Milošević did not believe that they yet had the numbers, but he was sure that a majority (forty-three) would emerge within the next few months, which could then bypass Karadžić. Milošević claimed to be working hard to bring more and more members of the Assembly on side. (If he was, he would have been deploying the usual mixture of threats and bribery.)

Milošević was increasingly critical of the Bosnian Serb leadership. He claimed not to understand how Karadžić could fail to accept the Contact Group plan, which allowed the Serbs half of the cake while the other two communities in Bosnia had to share the other half. The deal was not perfect, but it was fair. Moreover land swaps were inevitable.

When I asked him about Mladić, Milošević said that there was very strong conflict between Karadžić and Mladić. When he had last seen the latter, Milošević had told him that he was on the way to becoming the last Nazi general of the twentieth century, supporting a fascist regime. Paradoxically, Milošević went on to claim that Mladić and the Bosnian Serb army had never been guilty of atrocities. These had been conducted by "political" paramilitaries organized and abetted by primitive elements in Karadžić's political party, the SDS, or Serbian Democratic Party. (As I noted at the time in my report, which was, of course, prior to the Srebrenica genocide, "some re-writing of history here." It was a frequent line from the Serb leadership to claim that all war crimes and atrocities had been carried out by irregulars, far removed from the formal army structures.) Milošević continued that while the international community had committed many mistakes over events in the former Yugoslavia, it was now committing its biggest mistake in not offering him any support. To suspend or lift sanctions on significant trade relations would be the most powerful signal to the Bosnian Serbs that the game was up.

I told Milošević that I would have to disabuse him: it was wholly unrealistic to expect further concessions from the international community without further movement from Belgrade. The Contact Group was working on a twin track approach involving mutual recognition of the former Yugoslav republics. If Milošević bought in to this approach and honored his commitments on the border closure, significant sanction relief was possible. Milošević insisted that the focus should be entirely on bringing Karadžić to accept the Contact Group plan.

He then raised the question of the supporters of Fikret Abdić, who had been displaced by the fighting in Bihać. Abdić, a prominent Bosnian Muslim businessman, had won more votes than Izetbegović in the 1990 elections for the Bosnian Presidency, but for complicated reasons Izetbegović was elected by the seven-man Presidency instead.[1] The whole future course of Bosnia was altered by this decision. Later Abdić led his core supporters around and in Bihać in northwest Bosnia against Izetbegović's Sarajevo-led government, declaring his region independent from the rest of Bosnia. Milošević, not surprisingly, found Abdić an admirable Muslim whose supporters were not being helped by UNHCR for fear of antagonizing Izetbegović. Milošević maintained that after the war businessmen like Abdić would return to dispossess the nationalists. Even Izetbegović, claimed Milošević, recognized this. On HMS *Invincible*, while sitting in Milošević's cabin, Izetbegović had said to Karadžić, "After the war, both of us will be finished." Not a sentiment with which Milošević rushed to identify.

Concluding our discussion on Bosnia, I said that I wanted to be absolutely clear. Milošević was saying that there was no future in pursuing a multitrack approach. He agreed that we should stick to the Contact Group plan, however long it took to work. I asked him how long he thought it would take—three, six months? He said he hoped less time. I said that I hoped so too, as within six months pressure to lift the arms embargo would resurface in a way that might make it unavoidable. If this were the case, we and others would withdraw our contingents from the United Nations Protection Force (UNPROFOR). That, said Milošević, would lead to a great deal more bloodshed. The first to suffer from a lifting of the arms embargo would be the Croats. Izetbegović had only agreed to the Federation as a marriage of convenience. The hatred between Muslims and Croats in central Bosnia-Herzegovina, claimed Milošević, was undiminished.

His mention of the Croats led me to refer to the threat then current of a Croatian attack on the Krajina Serbs. I told him that the UK and the United States were trying to prevent this major and dangerous escalation. Milošević said that the Croats would be making a major mistake if they tried to attack the Krajina. Not only would it set back the prospect of a peaceful settlement, but the Croats would have no chance of a military success. The Krajina Serbs were very able fighters and were highly motivated to defend their territory. I asked whether, in the event of a Croatian attack on the Krajinas, the Yugoslav army (VJ) would intervene. Milošević said that they would not. But the Krajinas, he repeated, could defend themselves.

In retrospect, it is curious that Milošević retained such an exaggerated respect for the ability of the Krajina Serbs to look after themselves. Within nine months they would have lost nearly all the territory they had occupied and over 170,000 of them would have been driven from Croatia, from territories there that they and their families had occupied for hundreds of years. It was also odd that we were working with the United States to prevent a Croat attack. As Richard Holbrooke helpfully clarifies in his account, *To End a War*, only a few months later he (Holbrooke) was urging the Croats not only to take under their control all Serb-held territory in Croatia but also to occupy as much land in Bosnia as possible.[2]

At the end of our meeting, I raised as a personal request, the position of Dessa Trevisan, the veteran *Times* correspondent whose press accreditation had been withdrawn a year previously. Milošević said that he used to enjoy good relations with her but that she had fallen under bad influence and had come out with many antagonistic remarks against the regime. I said that was no reason to refuse her accreditation. What did he expect her to do? Echo the uncritical and sycophantic reporting of the state media? Her career had been long and distinguished, and her credibility was very high in the UK. Milošević said after a pause, "She can come and live here. There is no problem. Her links are with Belgrade." (Nevertheless, every time I tried to cash in that chip in the next three years I found obstacles placed in my path. Yes, she could come back but, no, she was not going to have her accreditation returned. In retrospect, I should have written to Milošević immediately to clarify exactly what he and I meant by her being able to return and on what terms.)

The meeting concluded on what I thought was a positive note, however. I felt that it might be possible to establish a working relationship with Milošević, which I hoped to turn to the British government's advantage, knowing, of course, that Milošević would do his best to exploit the relationship, experienced as he was in using and manipulating both international and domestic actors. I was under no illusions; it was a risky business, but the Foreign Office was more than prepared to take the risk in the interests of advancing the peace process.

Ten days later, I was back in Milošević's office carrying out a démarche on Foreign Office instructions about the now critical situation in Bihać, one of the six UN-designated safe areas. I asked Milošević to use all his influence on Pale to prevent an attack on the Bihać safe area and in particular on the town. Its fall would provoke a humanitarian disaster on a major scale. Milošević, invoking Balkan confidentiality, "for your ears only," said that he had heard from his intelligence network in Bosnia that Karadžić had issued written orders for the Bosnian Serb army to take Bihać. As soon as he had learned this, Milošević had been in touch with General Mladić to urge him not to proceed. Mladić had promised Milošević that he would disobey Karadžić's orders and would not enter the city.

Milošević said that he would not put his hand in the fire to say that Mladić would do as he had said, but he believed that Mladić would stick to his promise, and the Bosnian Serb army was deeply loyal to him. Mladić was in strong personal conflict with Karadžić at present. As a result of Mladić's increasing popularity, Karadžić was looking for the opportunity to remove him, while at the same time blaming him for any atrocities committed. In comparison with Karadžić, Milošević thought Mladić was an honest man (a change of tune from his earlier description of Mladić as on the way to being the last Nazi general of the twentieth century). He was meeting Mladić secretly in Belgrade that night, a fact of which Karadžić must remain unaware, when Milošević would do his best to ensure that Mladić stuck to his promise.

Milošević added that while we were talking, a group of deputies from the Pale Assembly were waiting to speak to him. He had been in discussion with them and had broken off to receive my representations. He would continue to talk to them after I had left. He believed in his pincer strategy, undermining Karadžić through Mladić on the one hand and through the dissident Assembly members on the other. He then went through his ritual about the need to lift sanctions against the FRY to speed up the whole process. I reminded him of my instructions; I noted that he could clearly exercise influence on Pale. Milošević said that he had no influence there. Karadžić had sent him many messages asking to be received. He had constantly turned him down. I said that he was splitting hairs; Pale was for us shorthand for the Bosnian Serbs. If Milošević could influence and restrain the behavior of the Bosnian Serb army through Mladić, rather than through Karadžić, we would be content.

Although Milošević was clearly relishing the maneuvering, wheeler-dealing, and manipulating, I concentrated more on what lay behind his remarks. Clearly he wanted to impress on me his ability to control events through Mladić. On the other hand, he was obviously nervous at being placed in the position of taking responsibility for all acts carried out by the Bosnian Serbs. Part of his game plan was to discredit Karadžić at the expense of Mladić and, by extension, of himself. To shore up his position among the Serbs, he had to be seen as the sole effective political interlocutor for the international community.

CHAPTER 5
Meeting General Mladić

Milošević's refusal to accept that a twin track approach had any merit and the corollary, his preferred solution, to pursue acceptance of the Contact Group's map (however long it took, and however little the Contact Group did to support his efforts), were to become leitmotifs over the next few weeks. Milošević was determined to keep the international community working through him and pressuring Karadžić and the Bosnian Serb leadership. He did not wish to be distracted from this aim by what came to be known as Plan B, namely, mutual recognition between the FRY, Bosnia, and ultimately Croatia.

Nevertheless, the expectation that Pale would succumb quickly to the twin pressures of the international community and Milošević faded as the autumn of 1994 gave way to winter. The blockade of the Drina River seemed reasonably tight and was so certified by Lord Owen and Thorvald Stoltenberg, the cochairmen of the International Conference on the Former Yugoslavia (ICFY) on the advice of General Bo Pellnas, the head of the ICFY monitoring mission, in their report to the Security Council. Suspension of sanctions on cultural and sporting links and air services was renewed for a further one hundred days. There was always going to be some seepage, but the word had clearly gone down from Milošević to his crony and customs chief, Mihail Kertes, that all cooperation was to be extended to Pellnas. But the economy of Republika Srpska had been at subsistence level for a very long time. Trade flows were relatively unimportant. Belt tightening could go another notch or two.

The attempt to break the logjam came from an unexpected quarter. Karadžić had always had good links into certain elements in the United States. He talked regularly to U.S. Serbs, some of whom had power and influence with the Democratic Party and, it appeared, at former president Jimmy Carter's eponymous center. It was never clear to me to what extent the U.S. administration was involved in the Carter initiative. It is fair to assume that while State Department officials were not the prime movers, they thought it worthwhile and gave the proposed initiative a fair wind. It had some obvious attractions from their point of view. If it worked, they would have achieved a breakthrough that owed nothing to Milošević. And indebtedness to Milošević was something they would, if given the option, always prefer to avoid for obvious and understandable domestic reasons.

The Contact Group visited Belgrade in December 1994 and made clear that they did not welcome Carter's initiative, which they thought was an undesirable distraction from the prime aim of overthrowing Karadžić through the votes of dissident Assembly members. I handed over a message two days before Christmas from Douglas Hurd to Milošević urging that he should continue to work on the Pale Assembly. Milošević said that he was surprised at the negative attitude of the Contact Group to the Carter mission. The fact that it had taken place had to be accepted. He believed that it was important to try to bridge the efforts made by Carter and those of the Contact Group. He and the Group had discussed a text on future constitutional arrangements in Bosnia that when issued should make Milošević's task in winning over wavering members of the Assembly easier. (It had no noticeable effect.)

Carter visited Pale shortly before Christmas 1994. He was unable to persuade Karadžić to accept the Contact Group plan even as a basis for negotiation, but he forced through agreement on a four-month cease-fire that on the face of it was a positive development. It was, however, far from being a cessation of hostilities. Karadžić viewed it as a welcome respite for his overextended forces, who had a long front line to defend. The Croats and Muslims saw it as a valuable opportunity for further rearmament and training. The regular Croat army was in particular receiving training from an ostensibly private American firm of recently retired U.S. generals. The Muslims too were receiving arms from a variety of sources; even some NATO forces were involved in delivering arms to them according to eyewitness accounts from Dutch soldiers in the eastern enclaves. And the Bosnian Serb army was receiving some limited support, probably in terms of crucial spare parts delivered by the Yugoslav army (VJ).

It was about this time that I called on General Momčilo Perišić, the VJ's chief of defense staff, to test his determination to maintain the border closure. He was remarkably frank. Yes, of course, he implemented the politicians' decision. No, he did not agree with this political split between Serb leaders. The Serbian people were united even if their leaders were temporarily at odds. The people's sentiments would prevail in the long term. As for his relations with General Mladić, they had been brother officers in the old Yugoslav army, the JNA. By implication their bonds of friendship were far more important than any temporary division between politicians. Perišić pronounced the Serbo-Croat word for "politicians" with particular contempt.

Carter's continuing attempt to get the Bosnian Serbs to accept the Contact Group plan made no headway. He seemed at one point to come agonizingly close, and the Contact Group helped by making it clear that the map need be accepted only "as a starting point," with the clear indication that swaps of territory were possible (indeed, they had always been regarded as inevitable and even desirable). There was also renewed emphasis on the constitutional proposals prepared by the ICFY's legal expert, Paul Szasz, and leaked to both parties by the United States and the Russians. They were a far cry from what was eventually agreed to at Dayton, providing as they did for only the lightest of umbrellas over the two entities. In particular, the provision for special parallel relationships (a euphemism for "confederation" echoing the references in the Washington Agreement setting up the Muslim Croat Federation to the possibility of confederation between Croatia and the Federation) offered a huge incentive for Karadžić to sign up. Karadžić, however, had other ideas.

I decided to ask Milošević what he thought Karadžić was up to. He said that it was quite simple. Karadžić wanted to destroy the Contact Group and cut a separate deal with the United States. He failed to understand that the Americans would not allow themselves to be picked off in this way. In which case, I asked, why had Karadžić turned down the approach from Carter? Milošević said that Carter had to push the official Contact Group line for the moment. Karadžić counted on Carter being brought back into play once the present round of Contact Group activity had run its course. Milošević had heard, and he was sure Karadžić had also learned, that Carter was preparing new maps. If true, that was news to me. The Americans in Belgrade strongly denied knowledge of such mapmaking, which would, of course, have fatally undermined the position of the Contact Group. Milošević was clearly concerned at the possibility of being marginalized. But he need not have worried. Carter backed off when Karadžić remained adamant about refusing the Contact Group map even under more flexible conditions.

If Carter could not move him, neither could the Contact Group. They also went to Pale that winter to pressure the Bosnian Serbs, despite the evident unhappiness of the Bosnian government at both the Carter initiative and the unexpected flexibility in the Contact Group's position, particularly after the apparently adamantine position adopted only six months earlier. They returned empty-handed.

With the prospects of progress so bleak, I asked the Foreign Office whether they would like me to have one last go to see if there was anything to be rescued from the ruins of the negotiation. I had not been to Bosnia since the fruitless visit with David Manning the previous summer, and I had no illusions that this visit would be any more successful. But it seemed to me worth trying, as the alternative was clearly going to be a progressive breakdown of the ceasefire as spring approached (Haris Silajdžić, the Bosnian prime minister, was already saying as much), and another fighting season began. The Foreign Office agreed.

I duly met Krajišnik and Koljević in late January 1995 at the Bosnian border town of Zvornik. The hotel where we met was freezing; there was virtually no heating oil for nongovernmental use in Bosnia. We kept our overcoats on during the seven-hour meeting while Krajišnik and Koljević played their traditional hard cop/soft cop roles. In Pale, Krajišnik was known as Brezhnev. His inflexible mindset, his peasant cunning, and above all his infinite capacity for prevarication and his patience in persevering with his chosen line all combined to make him a formidable and wearying interlocutor. Koljević told me months later that Krajišnik thrived on these lengthy meetings with political opponents. He enjoyed wearing down, exhausting, and frustrating them. Successive High Representatives in Bosnia had to suffer far more frequent punishment at Krajišnik's hands.

My line was straightforward. This was a historic opportunity to settle. The map was to be considered as a starting point. Territorial swaps were in both sides' interests. And parallel special relationships would allow the Bosnian Serbs a confederal relationship with Serbia, just as the Washington Agreement allowed the Muslim Croat Federation to confederate with Croatia. Such a configuration would interestingly echo discussions held as far back as 1991 on a new post-SFRY confederation.

Krajišnik, reflecting Karadžić's views, clearly believed that time was on the Serbs' side. The Contact Group had softened their approach; they might soften it further. I tried to demonstrate why this was not the case. The balance of forces was moving decisively against the Bosnian Serbs. The blockade of the Drina and sanctions were progressively weakening the Republika Srpska (RS).

Krajišnik then revealed the nodal point of his argument (although I heard later that in this he was merely the spokesman for Karadžić, for whom this had become a mantra). The international community talked about accepting the Contact Group map as a starting point, said Krajišnik. But this meant that the map was an *acquis*. In other words, the Contact Group map was already a bottom line as far as advantage to the Serbs was concerned. Any subsequent negotiations could only make matters worse for them.

When I pointed out how perverse this interpretation was, Krajišnik replied that this had been their experience during the talks on the HMS *Invincible*. Karadžić had accepted the idea of a 49/51 percent split of territory as part of a package that included crucially the possibility of a referendum to allow the Bosnian Serbs to secede from Bosnia-Herzegovina after five years. The international community had simply pocketed the "concession" of 49/51 percent and withdrawn the referendum that had been an integral part of the package and without which Karadžić would never have accepted the territorial division. It had, said Krajišnik, echoing Karadžić's line to Douglas Hogg nearly a year earlier, been a one-day special offer.

Despite seven hours of talks, I was unable to disabuse Krajišnik of his belief that a starting point meant what it said. It should not be regarded as a high-water mark for the Bosnian Serbs. It would mark instead the beginning of the negotiating process that would improve the maps from both sides' point of view while maintaining the territorial division of 49/51 percent.

I returned to Belgrade exhausted and deeply depressed. Not only did my trip have no positive results, but it led to yet another wholly unnecessary transatlantic spat. As I had made no progress, it was thought in London unnecessary to brief other members of the Contact Group. But the U.S. government got wind of the talks and was clearly suspicious of our motives. Holbrooke complained bitterly about my visit to our Washington Embassy, which compounded U.S. suspicions by denying that such a visit had taken place. While there was no justification for Holbrooke's hostility, it illustrated graphically the misgivings that the United States held for British and French motives and the peculiar inconsistencies and double standards that it was fond of applying to the crisis. The United States had sent its own Contact Group representative, Charlie Thomas, on a solo trip to Pale barely a few days previously without consultation and without warning. U.S. policy seemed to be that it was entitled to do what it wished without consultation, but its allies could behave similarly only at their peril.

When I next saw Milošević (whom I had warned of my impending visit to Zvornik, as he would inevitably have found out about it through his border authorities and secret police), he was predictably smug. His message summed up was "Ignore and isolate Pale; deal only through me. It may be slow while you continue to keep me shackled under sanctions, but I will get there."

Indeed, the Contact Group turned back wearily and unenthusiastically to Belgrade and to Plan B, mutual recognition between Bosnia and the FRY. In doing so they had to contend with a credibility problem as a result of what was referred to as the Russian natural gas episode. Early in the winter, Charlie Thomas (the U.S. representative) had promised Milošević in the presence of the rest of the Contact Group that the United States would allow the UN Sanctions Committee to agree to the import by Serbia of Russian natural gas on humanitarian grounds for heating throughout the winter months. Despite Thomas's promise, every time the question was raised in the UN Sanctions Committee, the U.S. representative there blocked its adoption. Milošević took this badly and told me and everybody else he met at the time that the Contact Group had thereby lost its credibility and demonstrated a "total absence of style." For once he had a point. For months afterward, whenever the Contact Group or the international community tried to strike a deal with Milošević, he would be entitled to ask how he could trust us when we had failed to keep our word over the Russian natural gas. Pretty rich coming from Milošević. But we had handed him a strong stick with which to beat us.

Shortly afterward, in early 1995, Milošević arranged for me to meet General Mladić in Belgrade. My aim was to reinforce the message we had been trying to convey to the Bosnian Serbs through Milošević that the Contact Group plan should be accepted, that attacks on the safe areas should cease, and that delivery of humanitarian supplies should be allowed unhindered. I also wanted to gauge his mood and assess his obviously complex and warped personality. The meeting took place in a Serbian government villa about three hundred yards from my residence in Belgrade. Mladić looked comfortably at home as I was ushered in accompanied by George Busby, a first secretary in my Chancery, an excellent analyst of the Serb scene, and the best Serbo-Croatian speaker in the British Foreign Service. The usher was a fellow general of Mladić's, General Gvero, who behaved more like a ward nurse taking visitors to a mentally unstable patient. Mladić was out of uniform, wearing an undersize black shirt, and was cocky, boastful, and swaggering in his manner. He was entirely devoid of charm but clearly had a high regard for himself. He read us the standard Bosnian Serb text of the Serbs as the Guardians of the Gate of Europe, keeping the unbelievers at bay. His hatred of Muslim fellow Slavs was unbridled and unconcealed.

The more we argued—and there was no meeting of minds on any topic—the angrier he became. His bull neck bulged; he became almost puce with rage. He recalled how his first silk shirt had been made from British parachutes dropping supplies to the Serbs during the Second World War. Every Bosnian Serb boy, he said, had such a shirt as Britain had dropped so much aid to the Partisan army. Now he announced he would never buy a silk shirt from Britain again. The Royal Air Force now dropped only bombs. Although the conversation continued for three full hours, we found almost nothing worth recording from the point of view of the war in Bosnia. It was wholly unproductive, disappointing, and above all distinctly disagreeable. Showing us out, General Gvero was apologetic, muttering something of the order of "You have to excuse the general, he's not at his best today."

When I next saw Milošević, he was keen to hear what I thought. He was still vigorously promoting the idea of Mladić taking over the governance of the Bosnian Serb entity and deposing Karadžić. I told Milošević how dismal an experience it had been, and what a poor impression Mladić had made. Milošević was clearly disappointed. "He sometimes feels he has to try to impose his personality on first acquaintance," said Milošević. I replied that I was not interested in this kind of verbal arm wrestling. It failed to address the crucial issue: how to bring the war to an early end and in the meantime to minimize civilian suffering. He never suggested that I meet Mladić again. Three months later Mladić was indicted as a war criminal by the International Criminal Tribunal for the Former Yugoslavia (ICTY).

CHAPTER 6

Point Man for the Contact Group

The next few months were largely devoted to the almost theological question of mutual recognition by the FRY and Bosnia as a way of bypassing and ultimately sidelining Pale. A whole series of meetings now took place between the Contact Group and Milošević in various configurations and at varying levels. The British and French political directors Pauline Neville-Jones and Alain Dejammet were very much to the fore, visiting regularly in the period from February to April 1995. Pauline possessed a formidable intellect that many of her colleagues, domestic and international, found intimidating. But I had always got on very well with her. She listened carefully to advice, asked invariably shrewd and penetrating questions, and conducted negotiations with Milošević and others with the utmost vigor. Working to their script, I filled in for the itinerant political directors in the final stages and secured, after a week of four conversations and meetings with Milošević, his agreement to a formula for mutual recognition that would also offer him the prospect of some (unspecified) sanctions relief.

At the first of these meetings I handed over a message from the British Foreign Secretary urging Milošević to put aside the quibbles and wordplay and recognize the state of Bosnia. Milošević was initially very resistant. He would, he said, recognize the union of the Muslim-Croat Federation and the Republika Srpska (the Bosnian Serb entity). Moreover, he would be prepared to come to a summit meeting with Izetbegović in Paris and recognize the two defined entities and announce his willingness to recognize the union of the two as soon as it came into existence.

I replied that what mattered to us was that he should recognize the Bosnian state, which had internationally recognized borders, as a demonstration that he had no territorial claims on it. Milošević countered by claiming that if he recognized the state of Bosnia, who would recognize him and his almost universally unrecognized country, the FRY? Izetbegović was not in a position to do so. Moreover, recognition of Bosnia would act as a disincentive for Izetbegović to negotiate with the Bosnian Serbs. He would claim that he already enjoyed recognition and had no need to agree to constitutional negotiations on a union.

I told him that the situation on the ground was unraveling badly in Bosnia. An agreement on mutual recognition would put pressure on the Bosnian government to agree to extend the cessation of hostilities and send a powerful signal on the political front. Milošević claimed that he had already announced that he had no territorial claims on Bosnia and repeated that he could announce his readiness to recognize the union of the two entities as soon as it would be formed. He then asked what would be available in terms of sanctions relief. I said that there would be no question of his coming to a summit without knowing exactly what was on offer in exchange for a satisfactory formula on recognition.

Milošević said that he would look carefully overnight at the Foreign Secretary's message and the latest Contact Group paper and would see me the next day. Our meeting the following morning turned into what was in effect a joint drafting session in which Milošević advanced alternative paragraphs to the Contact Group text. His suggestions were, I could see, unacceptable. I put some countersuggestions to him, which he clearly didn't like, although he did not specifically reject them.

He broke off from the drafting session to describe two recent meetings with secret envoys from Tudjman and Izetbegović, respectively. It had amused him, he said, that apart from the fact that they were serving different masters, their messages were identical: "To hell with foreigners. We can only solve this problem ourselves." Both envoys had, according to Milošević, urged early meetings between their presidents and Milošević. Indeed, Tudjman had sent a further emissary to underline the urgency of a bilateral meeting. Milošević said that he expected to see Tudjman privately very soon—usually bad news for the Muslims—and was also keen to have an early meeting with Izetbegović. His personal emissary had provided Milošević with some interesting glimpses into Izetbegović's mind and preoccupations. Milošević believed that he could set Izetbegović's "grand vizier" mind at rest very quickly in a bilateral meeting.

I said that the international community would always have preferred to see the parties to the conflict agree to solutions among themselves. It was precisely because they had lamentably failed to do so that we had intervened in the first place. Milošević backtracked at this point. He was not trying to eject the international community. Once bilateral meetings had taken place, it should be possible to bring everyone together in accepting the Contact Group plan. This exchange illustrated the infinite capacity for self-deception with which so many Balkan politicians were infected. It is hard to believe that a bilateral meeting with Milošević would ever have set Izetbegović's mind at rest. Indeed, if he were aware that a parallel bilateral was being contemplated or had taken place between Milošević and Tudjman, Izetbegović would have had every right to be seriously worried.

Milošević then digressed further away from the drafting exercise to events in Pale. Karadžić was, maintained Milošević, pestering him continually with messages. The latest from "that lunatic" had been a plea to Milošević to guarantee that he would not hand Karadžić over to the War Crimes Tribunal and would instead appoint him director of a psychiatric hospital in Belgrade. Milošević had replied that he would look at Karadžić's requests if and only if Karadžić accepted the Contact Group plan. Since then there had been silence.

The next day Milošević telephoned me with his response to my counterproposals. He preferred to stick to his position. After about three weeks of cogitation and redrafting by the Contact Group, I put revised language to him. He asked me to call to discuss his reactions. Essentially we were now arguing about two points: whether in exchange for recognition sanctions would be suspended or lifted—Milošević obviously was working hard for lift—and the vexed question of how to describe the independent Republic of Bosnia, as he wanted to use the word "Union" while we wanted the word "State." After a good deal of haggling I suggested on a personal basis that perhaps the problem could be got round by dropping both words and speaking simply of the FRY recognizing Bosnia and Herzegovina within its internationally recognized borders. After some hesitation, Milošević said he could agree to this.

On sanctions I said that there was bound to be a difference between us. The most that the Contact Group would be able to offer in exchange for recognition of Bosnia would be "meaningful suspension" of sanctions—that is, suspension of sanctions on major trade items though perhaps not on all the strategic goods that he would like. But if the border remained closed, I said, suspension would be indefinite. Milošević promptly complained that suspension left him open to imaginary claims of violation of the border closure between the FRY and the Bosnian Serb entity. I said that he knew as well as I did that we were in a negotiation. He would have to make a judgment whether the deal to be struck was one with which he was prepared to live. I took his silence in response to this as a positive indicator.

The Contact Group sent me back a week later to say that the language to which Milošević and I had agreed at our previous meeting was, if he confirmed it, an important move that would represent a substantial step forward. The Contact Group would meet again shortly at a very high level. This would be a critical meeting that could result in the present downward spiral being reversed, given the right conditions. I hoped he could help us create those conditions and give a powerful impetus to ending the war. The situation on the ground remained very fragile. The Sarajevo government had said publicly that they would extend the ceasefire agreement only if Milošević recognized Bosnia within its internationally recognized borders and kept the FRY/Bosnia border closed.

Milošević had no problem in confirming our previous agreement, but as I expected, he vigorously pursued the question of the lifting of all sanctions. I repeated my line about his lack of realism. A more realistic target might be the suspension of trade sanctions in nonstrategic goods and perhaps the lifting of currently suspended sanctions (sport and cultural contacts and international air flights). Milošević said that suspended sanctions only left him open to blackmail over alleged helicopter flights and the like across the border. He could not expect public backing for recognition if the offer were to suspend sanctions only. I said again that he would have to make a judgment on whether the deal on offer was worth it. Milošević added that he was considering holding a referendum on recognition and sanctions relief to wrong-foot the nationalist opposition within Serbia.

Before I left, Milošević commented that he had recently seen General Mladić and had urged him to declare the current political leadership in Pale irresponsible and to take over the reins of government and negotiation with the Contact Group. Mladić had considered the suggestion and had replied that he would come back to Belgrade in a few days' time, accompanied by his senior military commanders.

Milošević seemed quite fixated at this time with his scheme to push Mladić into taking political power in Pale. I wondered whether he might have found the read-across to Serbia disturbing. It was no secret that his relations with the commander of the Yugoslav army, General Perišić, were no better than correct.[1] If Perišić saw his brother officer taking political power in Pale, it might give him some ideas. The Yugoslav army had traditionally played an institutional role in politics and had been effectively an extra voice on the presidency of the old SFRY.

It is hard now in retrospect to believe that Mladić might have been an improvement on Karadžić. Milošević clearly believed that he would be able to persuade Mladić to do his bidding. Everything I had seen and heard of Mladić, however, suggested that he was very much his own man, who took instructions from anyone only with the greatest reluctance. And it was Mladić who had spoken out against the Vance-Owen plan (VOPP) in Pale in 1993, opposing both Karadžić and Milošević. Perhaps Milošević had a financial pull on him. It was well known that the Bosnian Serb army's pensions were paid by the Yugoslav government. It might alternatively have been the Bosnian Serb army's desperate need for some military spare parts that only the Yugoslav army could supply.

While Karadžić and the Bosnian Serbs were clearly uppermost in Milošević's mind now, he also had time, as he told me, to harass the Krajina Serbs in Croatia. The Krajina Serbs' leader, Milan Martić, was threatening at about that time to go for formal unification with the Bosnian Serbs. Milošević said that he had put that on ice, telling Martić that if he chose to go ahead with unification, the Krajina Serb statelet, the Republika Srpska Krajina (RSK), would suffer the same sanctions that Serbia now imposed against the Bosnian Serbs. This was a serious threat to the Krajina Serbs, who relied on Yugoslavia for a good deal of money and food. He said that Martić, while disliking his rival among the Krajina Serbs, Milan Babić, had felt obliged to invite him to form a government as he was the leader of the largest party. Milošević had suggested to Martić that he should avoid this option by dissolving the Krajina Serb parliament and calling early elections. However, Martić had not felt strong enough within the RSK to do so. Babić had asked to call on Milošević "just for five minutes." Milošević had said no. Babić was not a serious person; like Karadžić, he never got up before noon. Milošević said that he had given instructions that not even the doorman at the Serbian Presidency building should receive Babić! Probably exaggeration, but not entirely to be discounted.

This was my most intense period of working with Milošević. It was entirely on a one-to-one basis, and it was clear that while I was clearing my lines with the Foreign Office and through them with the Contact Group, he consulted nobody—except perhaps his wife. Her influence on him was legendary and never in my experience other than baleful. She had a remarkable hold on him, despite the fact that while he was largely rational, she was totally ideological.

After an exchange of drafts on one occasion, his sharp eye detected a bureaucratic muddle that had escaped my and the Contact Group's attention. Although we disagreed frequently, the atmosphere was always calm and businesslike (no raised voices) while never being particularly cordial. Doing business with Milošević was in many ways far easier than with many other officials of the regime. Of course, he knew what he wanted could never be contradicted by any other individual within the regime, and he had the power to see any of his own decisions executed within Serbia and often beyond. But he was a surprisingly good listener—never interrupted—and got the point first time.

As a negotiator I found him in his own way impressive: clear thinking, determined, and apparently reasonable, particularly when you held a major trump card in the shape of sanctions in your hand. Milošević knew how to aim for the maximum but to settle for second best if he judged that a sufficiently large "critical mass"—a favorite Milošević phrase—of positive elements had been assembled. If he had a fault as a negotiator, it was his tendency at times to overreach himself in going for broke. As a diplomat, I found the experience demanding: to attempt to outmaneuver—or even to keep your footing against—a man who had destabilized not only a country but also a region in a manner not seen in Europe for half a century was an enormous challenge. Modest successes such as those over the recognition formula were naturally satisfying. But over the whole period of my mission such successes were depressingly rare.

While the outcome of the negotiation on recognition was deemed broadly satisfactory by the Contact Group, when it came to a discussion of the sanctions relief that would flow, the United States was very cautious. At the high-level meeting I had mentioned to Milošević, Holbrooke announced to the other Contact Group political directors that the United States would now take over the running of negotiations as that nation would have the most difficulty in conceding anything to Milošević at all. His deputy Robert Frasure would leave for Belgrade shortly to pursue the discussions bilaterally with Milošević. Frasure duly arrived. He was a fine strategic thinker with a well-developed sense of fun and an amusing world-weary cynicism. He duly spent three days in May 1995 locked up with Milošević in Karadjordjevo, an old Tito villa about a hundred kilometers north of Belgrade. After his sojourn with Milošević, Frasure returned to Belgrade on May 18 and reported back. I saw him just after he had spoken to Holbrooke in Washington for two hours.

When he briefed me on the deal he had hammered out, involving the suspension of sanctions on nonstrategic goods and allowing the import of sufficient oil to supply Serbia's nonmilitary needs, I told him that I judged it to be immediately acceptable to Britain, France, and Russia. Indeed, I thought it was surprisingly generous up front to the Serbs. It was the sort of deal that, had the British or French negotiated it, would no doubt have led to carping comments about "being soft on the Serbs." He said Holbrooke had been positive and optimistic about wider U.S. support. Dick Holbrooke's optimism proved for once to be unjustified. When the deal had been fully dissected in Washington, it was thrown out, and Frasure was told to renegotiate it. The impression given was that Madeleine Albright, Vice President Gore, and Warren Christopher, in that order, all had deep reservations.

Various refinements were introduced, but the core question of a sanctions reimposition mechanism proved the breaking point. No method could be found to bridge the gap between the U.S. determination to be able to reimpose sanctions without falling foul of a Russian veto and Russia's determination not to allow the United States unilaterally to decide on the reimposition of sanctions. The United States refused to accept the United Nations secretary-general or Security Council having the decisive say. After Frasure had had another couple of meetings with Milošević, the United States turned the problem over to Carl Bildt, the incoming EU representative and cochairman (with the UN's special representative, Thorvald Stoltenberg) of the International Conference on Former Yugoslavia (ICFY), who had just taken over from Lord Owen.

David Owen's resignation after three thankless years was no surprise, but I very much regretted his departure. Both the timing and the manner seemed to me unfortunate. I could well understand how weary and frustrated he must have been at the endless sniping from the warring parties and allies alike and at his inability to make real progress on Bosnia. But he was the architect of the Contact Group, and the almost casual manner in which his departure was announced did not seem to do justice to the enormous effort he had put in over three years. How different his reputation would have been if the Vance-Owen plan (VOPP) had been accepted and implemented. Although David Owen had gained a very prickly reputation at the Foreign Office in the 1970s,[2] he had very greatly mellowed in the intervening twenty-one years and, while keeping all his energy and intellectual sharpness, was now a pleasure to work with.

I need not have been concerned, however, about his successor, who got to grips very quickly with the minutiae of the dossier. Bildt came to Belgrade for a couple of briefing meetings and proved himself a good listener with a very clear idea of where he was heading. He picked up the baton that Frasure had set down and negotiated several further improvements to the formula. He then went off to Washington to seek U.S. backing for his efforts. The U.S. administration, however, was no more prepared to back him than they had been prepared to support Frasure.[3] The diplomatic channel once again appeared blocked.

CHAPTER 7

The UN Hostage Crisis

All this was taking place against a background of deterioration on the ground. The four-month cease-fire broke down progressively as the Muslims realized that the net effect of the cease-fire was to allow the Bosnian Serb army to regroup and reorganize—they were defending an exceptionally long frontline with a significantly smaller number of troops—while the Muslim-Croat Federation forces were keen to launch offensives using their new equipment and arms drawn from diverse sources. As the Muslims and Croats increased the pressure on the Bosnian Serbs, this in turn led to counterattacks.

These reached a climax in the week after the Milošević/Frasure talks at Karadjordjevo were concluded. After a day in which 2,700 firing incidents were recorded in Bosnia by UNPROFOR, General Rupert Smith issued an ultimatum to the Bosnian Serbs requiring them to return heavy weapons that they had removed from UN storage depots. When the ultimatum expired without their return, air strikes were ordered, which resulted in a furious reaction by the Bosnian Serbs, who took some four hundred UN troops hostage and launched violent attacks throughout Bosnia, especially on Tuzla, where a shell killed seventy-five people.

I went to see Milošević at this critical moment with a prime ministerial message to ask him to use all available means to secure the UN troops' release. Milošević claimed to be affronted by the Bosnian Serbs' actions, which, he opined, were a humiliation for all Serbs. But the real affront, he continued, was undoubtedly caused by the monumental public relations disaster that Karadžić and Mladić were, not for the first time, inflicting on the Serbian nation as a whole. Comparisons with Saddam Hussain's behavior in taking hostages as human shields were frequently invoked at that time. I asked Milošević what he proposed to do in practical terms to secure the release of our troops. When he said darkly but delphically that he would be taking drastic measures, I pressed him further. He replied that he would be sending to Bosnia his feared secret security chief Jovica Stanišić (the man of whom it was said that he knew literally where the bodies were buried), who would be issuing dire threats. "Like what?" I asked. Milošević was disarmingly frank. "Stanišić will tell Karadžić that I will have him killed if he doesn't release the hostages. He knows I can do it." Perhaps unfortunately, it did not come to that.

Encouraging, if that is the right word, as Milošević's reaction was, it was felt in London that our outrage should be conveyed to the Bosnian Serbs directly. I was accordingly instructed to travel to the Bosnian border town of Zvornik to deliver our message, having first received guarantees from the Bosnian Serbs—to the extent that they were worth believing—that I would not be taken hostage myself. I was to convey a formal written warning from the British government that vital British interests were at stake and that Karadžić and his crew would bear all the responsibility if harm came to any of our soldiers. The Bosnian Serbs who met me were the vice president, Nikola Koljević, and Karadžić's spokesman, Jovan Zametica. After they had read the message, they pressed me on the possible implications. I replied that I took the warning to mean that we would launch a military attack on the Bosnian Serbs if our soldiers were ill-treated or worse, and I made sure that the two Bosnian Serbs understood the consequences. Koljević consulted Karadžić regularly by telephone during our meeting, but his instructions to his colleagues and their replies to me indicated that he was being typically evasive and unwilling to give any guarantees for the soldiers' safety and early release. Another disappointing and unsatisfactory visit to Bosnia, indeed my last in wartime. When I next returned, the war was over.

But while I had made no obvious headway, Milošević had not been idle. The feared Stanišić had indeed been dispatched to Pale. Eventually, after several visits by the Serb security chief, and after Milošević agreed in secret to a Bosnian Serb army request for urgent military spare parts, the hostages were released. They came out in dribs and drabs, no doubt coinciding with the delivery of the spare parts. The British contingent arrived in three tranches. The timing and manner of their release in Serbia was shrouded in typical Balkan fog. On the first occasion, Milošević's office claimed not to know where and when they were being released and referred me to the Ministry of the Interior. Even in the best-run democracies, Ministries of the Interior have never developed a wide reputation for *glasnost*; the Serbian interior ministry took a highly restrictive attitude to information sharing, which did not go far beyond confirming that I had indeed called the ministry number.

Frustrated and angry, I dispatched a member of my defense attaché's staff to the Serb/Bosnian border to see whether the troops would be released as soon as they reached Serbian soil. They were not, but it at least allowed us to pick up some vague hints that they might be taken to the capital of the northern Serb autonomous region of Vojvodina, Novi Sad, a medium-sized town about an hour's drive to the north of Belgrade. This made sense to me; given the secrecy with which the Serbs were operating, their aim would clearly be to throw the media off the scent. And Novi Sad was on the right side of Belgrade if the ultimate plan was to have the soldiers flown out the next day to the UN headquarters in Zagreb without going through the capital.

I accordingly drove to Novi Sad through a torrential downpour, arriving in the former Habsburg town at about three o'clock in the morning. It was an eerie and lonely experience. Although the streets were largely deserted, the presence of a traffic policeman incongruously in the middle of the night suggested that I had guessed right. Even better, the policeman helpfully indicated to which hotel the UN troops were being brought. When I arrived at the hotel, the security police were surprised and distinctly hostile. I had got there before the UN troops had even arrived from the border. They eventually turned up about an hour later, and a further hour after that, when they had been examined by a Serb doctor, I was allowed to talk to them, to discover their state of health, and to take their details.

This first batch, largely from the Royal Welch Fusiliers, were not in particularly good shape. Several of them were suffering from fractures incurred when the armored personnel carrier in which they had been traveling, after being taken hostage, had fallen off a mountain road. Fortunately it had not caught fire. We were lucky that a few broken bones were the worst injuries they had suffered. Bob Frasure's death in an automobile accident was to be a vivid reminder of the dangers of mountain travel in Bosnia only weeks later. I telephoned details of the Royal Welch Fusiliers back to my deputy, the wholly admirable Tony Crombie, who, typically, selflessly manned the embassy switchboard single-handedly throughout the night, for retransmission to the Ministry of Defence. Names were inadequate as there was inevitably in a Welsh regiment many more than one fusilier called Jones, and some indeed bore the same Christian names. Army numbers were therefore essential to avoid confusion and uncertainty among waiting relatives. (My concern was not mirrored by the UN. The first UN representative from Belgrade turned up eleven hours after I had arrived there to collect what were, after all, technically their own, not national, troops.)

Around midday the next day I emerged from the camp where they were being treated to travel back to Belgrade while one of my colleagues relieved me. The legendary British journalist John Simpson of the BBC had just arrived in Novi Sad and interviewed me. When the piece went out, he described me as "the usually debonair Ivor Roberts looking dishevelled and unwashed." I wondered how he would have looked if, instead of sleeping in his bed in Belgrade and making a leisurely trip to Novi Sad for lunch and a spot of interviewing, he had been up all night.

A week or so later, I returned to the charge with Milošević when there appeared to be problems about the release of the last batch of UN soldiers. Milošević said that the holdups had been because the soldiers were widely spread out, and to reach them required travel through areas that were under Muslim attack. Moreover, there was always a danger of some irregulars attacking the hostages. (It all sounded specious to me.) He added that the intervention by the

Greek ministers of defense and foreign affairs, who had dashed dramatically to Pale a few days earlier, had actually delayed the release of the second batch of hostages. Karadžić had naturally been hopeful that the Greeks would be bearing gifts when they arrived. The Greeks had explained that the idea of a Greek intervention had arisen at a recent NATO meeting. (Milošević commented ironically that he knew how much attention NATO paid to Greek views.) In any case, Karadžić had already agreed to release the hostages, and the first batch had arrived in Serbia before news broke of the Greek intervention. Milošević said that the Greeks were, of course, friends of the Serbs, but in many ways they were "not a nation but a profession." Milošević's pique at the Greek intervention was to an outsider amusing but understandable. Milošević did not want to see the credit for securing the release of the hostages shared with anyone.

I also raised with Milošević the question of free passage for UN convoys reprovisioning the eastern Bosnian enclaves. Milošević claimed to have spoken to Mladić about it recently, emphasizing that UNPROFOR must be allowed to function normally and carry out its full range of activities. Mladić had agreed but asked that General Smith should get in touch with him discreetly to take the initiative. Mladić was still, said Milošević, in strong conflict with the political leadership in Pale, and it would be easier for him to respond positively if he could be seen to be reacting to an UNPROFOR initiative, rather than acting on his own.

This serpentine logic led me to ask Milošević if he believed that the Bosnian Serbs wanted UNPROFOR to stay. He replied that it was impossible to say with confidence what anybody in Bosnia wanted. He knew that his own view was clear. UNPROFOR's departure would be very bad news, indeed. He hoped that Carl Bildt would use the impetus of his new arrival as a means to persuade both sides to agree to a fresh cessation of hostilities, even if it was only an informal gentleman's agreement (no sense of irony from Milošević), to allow him to get into the stride of his new mission.

Milošević then asked me about Bildt's role. Would he be the sole negotiator for the Contact Group? I said that it was not clear whether that would be the case, but he would certainly be engaging on the Bosnian as opposed to the Croatian question in a way that his predecessor as ICFY cochairman had not done recently. Milošević said that Bildt's fellow cochairman, Thorvald Stoltenberg, had recently been in touch to suggest that he and Bildt come to Belgrade to meet him. Milošević had agreed, but he thought that Lord Owen's departure was a major loss. He wondered whether the departure of the British cochairman suggested a disengagement on our part from the political and diplomatic negotiations. I explained that this was a fundamental misunderstanding of the cochairman's role. Lord Owen had enjoyed a good deal of support from the British government, but he had been a European negotiator who always saw himself as at the disposal of the current president of the European Union Council of Foreign Ministers. Meanwhile Bildt was an excellent successor who would enjoy plenty of support from the British government both in terms of military and diplomatic advisers (I was "donating" a member of my own staff, David Austin, as an expert on minority questions.) Milošević said that Bildt had been fairly anti-Serb in his comments a few years ago. I said that he was not alone in taking that position. Milošević ruefully agreed; he hoped that Bildt would try to make progress from his earliest meetings and would not simply want to make a series of familiarization visits.

I reflected later whether Milošević's attachment to UNPROFOR was sincere. Milošević could see the advantages in UNPROFOR's continuing presence, provided its role was minimalist. While it acted as a guarantee against the lifting of the arms embargo and air strikes, it was clear that UNPROFOR was not going to be a deterrent to the overrunning of the eastern enclaves if that is what Milošević and Mladić were considering. But I had no proof that this was on the agenda. Milošević had often made the point to me that he saw no advantage for the Bosnian Serbs in trading the eastern enclaves for land around Sarajevo as in the long term he believed the Muslims would in any case melt away from the eastern enclaves to the Sarajevo suburbs.

For the Muslims, UNPROFOR's presence was the reverse side of the coin. Provided it was exercising a proactive deterrent role, containing Serbian aggression, and ensuring humanitarian supplies to the safe areas, it was better than nothing. But if it was preventing the lifting of the arms embargo and the possibility of NATO air strikes to redress the military balance, then it was a fine judgment whether the UN presence was worth it. The Sarajevo government continued to agonize over this question.

CHAPTER 8

Srebrenica

No sooner was one crisis over that summer than another began. Carl Bildt was making good progress in his negotiations with Milošević, but again the United States had difficulty in swallowing the deal. Meanwhile the situation on the ground deteriorated further. A major Muslim offensive to break the siege of Sarajevo failed, only to be followed by an upturn in activity around one of the UN safe areas, Srebrenica. For radical Islamists, the massacres at Srebrenica will always be one of the earliest signposts pointing their way toward jihadism. Savage fighting in spring and summer 1992 had left a particularly bitter legacy there. After initial Bosnian Serb attacks on Srebrenica had been repulsed, some one thousand Serb civilians in the villages outside the town had been killed subsequently by raiding parties from the Muslim garrison in Srebrenica, whose commander, Naser Orić, in a previous incarnation (i.e., before the war) had been ironically a bodyguard of Slobodan Milošević. After the leader of the local Serbs was ambushed and killed, there was a mass exodus of Serbs from Srebrenica to Bratunac, a nearby town. "The Muslims had won control of the town [Srebrenica], but the Serbs exacted a terrible price for their defeat: in the Bratunac football stadium they executed scores of male Muslim prisoners."[1] There was therefore a deep sense of foreboding about Srebrenica. In June 1995, attacks from within the protected area on the outlying Serbian villages were met with an increasingly ferocious Serb advance on the enclave itself. Air attacks were called for by the Dutch UN contingent but were not authorized until it was too late. After two bombs were dropped, which led to threats of more hostage taking, the Dutch defense minister asked that air operations be stopped. Meanwhile the 82nd Division of the Bosnian Muslim army gradually melted away in circumstances that have still not been fully or satisfactorily explained.

According to Laura Silber and Alan Little, the Muslim leadership regarded Srebrenica and the other enclaves (Žepa and Goražde) as a burden. They quote General Rasim Delić, the Bosnian government commander: "These were isolated areas, we did not have physical contact with our forces. Each offensive on any territory carried the danger that the Serb aggressor would make a move on Srebrenica and Žepa. Our government made many ceasefires, many political concessions in order to save Srebrenica and Žepa."[2] Naser Orić himself was withdrawn from Srebrenica in April, three months before the enclave came under attack. Silber and Little have argued that it suited the Bosnian and American governments to see Srebrenica fall in order to allow the Bosnian army to push forward elsewhere and avoid the constant threat of retaliation against the exposed eastern enclaves. In the case of the United States, which was preparing a new initiative, the loss of the eastern enclaves would make the final map drawing that much easier. No evidence to support this theory has been produced, but there were many rumors to the effect that Srebrenica had been virtually abandoned militarily. (Orić's withdrawal may have been a clear signal of this and was so interpreted by a demoralized civilian population within the enclave.) Whatever the wider strategic considerations, nobody could have envisaged the horror that was about to engulf Srebrenica.

The Serbs began to shell the enclave seriously on July 9. With the garrison's abandonment of the enclave and the UN being present in insignificant numbers, the town fell within three days. The hapless civilians were left to the mercy of General Mladić. The men were taken away from the women and children and never seen again. As we now believe, eight thousand men and boys (including some not yet teenage) civilians were either executed or killed in fighting and ambushes as they attempted to flee. It was the most appalling single incident in the whole war, and the worst massacre in Europe since the end of the Second World War. As the ICTY judge said in November 1995 in confirming the indictment of Karadžić and Mladić on charges of genocide, crimes against humanity, and violations of the laws or customs of war, "The evidence tendered by the Prosecutor describes scenes of unimaginable savagery: thousands of men executed and buried in mass graves, hundreds of men buried alive, men and women mutilated and slaughtered, children killed before their mothers' eyes.... These are truly scenes from hell, written on the darkest pages of human history."[3]

It is worth noting that the safe areas policy, copied from the First Gulf War, was, in the case of Bosnia, fatally flawed. The United Nations Security Council adopted a measure to create safe areas in Bosnia, which should in principle have eased the humanitarian crisis for civilians caught up in the war. The idea was that the safe areas should be demilitarized and that UN troops should protect the safe areas and help ensure the transport of humanitarian supplies to the civilian populations. This laudable aim was unfortunately undermined by the failure of the international community to provide adequate means in the shape of UN troops (blue helmets) to defend adequately the safe areas. The UN secretary-general estimated, on best military advice, that he needed some thirty-four thousand troops; he received fewer than seven thousand. Moreover, the safe areas were almost never demilitarized and became caught up in a cycle of Muslim attacks out of the areas, leading to brutal Serb retaliation and ultimately, in Srebrenica, to the horrific massacre of eight thousand Muslim men and boys, rightly deemed an act of genocide by the International Court of Justice (ICJ).[4] The failure of the safe areas policy was a classic example of willing the aim but not being prepared to will the means.

The extent of the horrors and the massacre at Srebrenica was completely unknown at the time. It seemed initially like yet another gruesome and bloody episode in the conflict, but nobody was aware of how egregiously awful the events in the enclave were. Having returned from meetings in London with the new Foreign Secretary, Malcolm Rifkind, where I was at the time of the fall of Srebrenica, I called on Milošević on instructions on July 14. Milošević claimed to have been surprised by the events in Srebrenica—a flagrant example of his being economical with the truth, though I couldn't prove it—and unable to contact Mladić directly, although he had sent the general a message that he should guarantee the safety of the civilians and the UN troops. Mladić, according to Milošević's account, had replied to say that he was going to Srebrenica himself to ensure that there would be no reprisals (an uncharacteristically humane Mladić reaction, if it had been true). As we now know, although only rumors were emerging at the time, his intention seems to have been exactly the opposite. Milošević continued that he had pressed Mladić to ignore the orders, which he knew Karadžić had issued, for the next most exposed enclave, Žepa, to be taken. Mladić had returned an ambiguous reply on this point. Milošević said that Žepa was very vulnerable, being little more than a village. He expected to meet Mladić later that day and would press him to release civilians, allow free access for the UNHCR, and permit humanitarian aid convoys to Srebrenica. But he believed that Mladić would only agree to guarantee this and the integrity of Žepa and Goražde if they could all be shown to be demilitarized, as the original UN Security Council Resolution had required.

I said that he should understand how grave the situation had now become. The withdrawal of the UN would have serious and far-reaching consequences, but the Bosnian Serb action against the eastern enclaves heightened the prospect of its taking place. It looked as though the Bosnian Serbs only wanted UNPROFOR to stay provided it did nothing. This was obviously a situation that neither the Sarajevo government nor the international community could be expected to tolerate.

I mentioned the first media reports of atrocities in Srebrenica. Milošević attempted to divert the conversation onto the atrocities committed by the Croats during their successful May offensive against the Krajina Serbs (Operation Flash) to reincorporate western Slavonia into Croatia. I pointed out that the Croats were at least allowing the reestablishment of a UN presence to monitor human rights there. It was essential that the UN should be allowed back in to Srebrenica as soon as possible to ensure that no atrocities were committed. Milošević said that he agreed and would make the point to Mladić that day. What really passed between Milošević and Mladić at their meeting we shall probably never know, although Mladić told Bildt and General Smith at a dinner with Milošević at about the same time to "forget Žepa." The clear message was that he was going to take it.

Mladić seems to have preferred to take what instructions he chose to obey from Belgrade rather than from Pale at this stage of the war. But while Milošević may well have colluded or conspired with him or even suggested the attack on Srebrenica and Žepa—whatever he chose to tell me—there would appear to have been no logic to Milosević's sanctioning or supporting the massacres, as he would have been the first to know how badly they would have played at a time when he was most anxious to play the peacemaker. Mladić, meanwhile, appears to have been on an adrenalin high, determined to humiliate the international community again after the earlier hostage drama had failed to achieve his objectives. And Mladić had a particular animus against the Dutch peacekeepers as he associated the Dutch government with a particularly anti-Serb line in the abortive peace negotiations in the early stages of the war.

Two tailpieces. Some months later I asked Koljević if he knew what had really happened at Srebrenica. Koljević said that he had carried out his own inquiry. According to the story he had been able to piece together, the massacres had been carried out without Mladić's knowledge and against his wishes. The Bosnian Serb troops who had executed the Muslim men and boys had been deserters who had been rounded up and put in the front line. In an attempt to show their zeal and commitment, they had taken it on themselves to carry out the mass executions. I said that it defied belief that nobody in command knew of or could stop executions on this scale. We were not talking about ten or twenty people; we were talking about several thousand. Mladić was there in Srebrenica; we had all seen him on television. It must all have been planned in advance: he must have both known what was going on and planned it. Koljević said that the account he had given me was based on eyewitness accounts. He could add nothing further.

Shortly after the Dayton Agreement had been signed in Paris, I gave a speech in Belgrade on the subject of human rights (before it became part of the Foreign Office syllabus under Robin Cook's stewardship), pointing out that the Dayton Agreement had been signed, almost to the day, on the nine-hundredth anniversary of the launching of the First Crusade by Pope Urban II in November 1095. When the Crusaders finally took Jerusalem more than three years later in 1099, they broke all the promises given when the city surrendered, and they massacred all the Arab inhabitants, daubing themselves in their victims' blood as they entered the Temple and the holy places. I drew the audience's attention to the depressing echoes of the events of the First Crusade in the fighting in Bosnia. The Serbs were fond of claiming the moral high ground after the atrocities suffered by Serbs under the Ustaše and the Nazis (the example most regularly quoted was the murder of, by some accounts, as many as seven thousand men and boys by the Nazis in the Serbian town of Kragujevac on October 20–21, 1941). Where, I asked, was the moral high ground after Srebrenica, where, by a grim coincidence, a similar number had been executed? My remarks were listened to in stony silence.

At the time of the fall of Srebrenica, I was, as described above, in London and attended a midnight crisis meeting with the incoming Foreign and Defense secretaries, Malcolm Rifkind and Michael Portillo, who had been in their jobs only a matter of days after Douglas Hurd's resignation. This resulted in a move to send a substantially strengthened Rapid Reaction Force to Bosnia. At the subsequent London conference, it was decided to send a warning to General Mladić from three air force generals (UK, France, and U.S.) to the effect that any threat of encroachment on any of the remaining safe areas would be met by the extensive use of air power. I was back in Belgrade by this time to set up, through Milošević, the meeting between the Western generals and Mladić. One of my staff who was present as an interpreter told me afterward that Mladić was particularly impressed by the seniority of the officers sent to convey the warning. As a soldier, first and foremost, he attached inordinate importance to hierarchy and rank.

CHAPTER 9

The End of the Krajina Serbs and NATO Bombing

Not all activity was focused on Bosnia. In Croatia, David Owen and Thorvald Stoltenberg had throughout their respective tenures been working on a plan to restore Croatian sovereignty over the UN protected areas there in exchange for a substantial measure of Serb autonomy, the so-called Z-4 plan. They had already negotiated an economic agreement between the Croats and the Krajina Serbs. This, however, disintegrated as a result of the Croatian offensive in western Slavonia in May 1995. In a thirty-hour assault, Operation Flash, which was euphemistically described by the Croats as a police operation aimed at reopening the main Zagreb-Belgrade highway—closed by the Serbs after a stabbing incident at a petrol station on the highway—the Croats regained control of western Slavonia and swept 18,000 Serbs out of the region. Nobody knows exactly how many civilians were killed as the Croatian army sealed off most of the area. Defense Minister Gojko Šušak announced in parliament that 450 people had died, although there was virtually no military opposition to the Croat offensive. Little and Silber describe how "the next day refrigerator trucks were seen going down the newly opened highway and the Croats began a massive clean up campaign, using chemicals to wash down the roads."[1]

With no support forthcoming from Belgrade, the Krajina Serb leader Milan Martić ordered two rocket attacks on Zagreb, which killed seven people and wounded forty. Martić was quickly indicted by the International War Crimes Tribunal for his attack on innocent civilians. By contrast, nobody was immediately indicted for the attacks on the Krajina Serbs in the May operation or indeed the much larger attack three months later in August (Operation Storm). Operation Flash caused shock waves among the Krajina Serbs. Western Slavonia was always the most exposed part of the Krajina, but it somehow never occurred to the Serbs that the Croats would simply be allowed to overrun a UN protected area without any international reaction. It was a lesson that, as we have seen, would have dire consequences in Srebrenica two months later. Belgrade tried to make partial amends for its failure to support its brethren in Croatia by sending one of its own generals, Mile Mrkšić, to reorganize the army and by rounding up Krajina Serb males who had fled from Croatia at the beginning of the fighting in 1991. Large numbers were sent back to the Krajina to become part of Mrkšić's reorganized fighting force. (I had to issue special letters to two Krajina Serb gardeners working for the embassy to prevent their being press-ganged into military service.) Neither the new recruits nor the reorganization of the army proved to be of much use. The Krajina Serb leaders continued to squabble among themselves and with Milošević. Milošević insisted in conversations with international negotiators at the time that the Serbs in Knin were the toughest Serbs of all and would never be militarily defeated. He told me as much the week before their final defeat, and Carl Bildt got the same message the very day that Franjo Tudjman launched Operation Storm.

The Krajina Serbs appeared to realize by the end of July that the Croatian army offensive inside Bosnia was threatening the future of their statelet dramatically and agreed to talks in Geneva on August 3 under the aegis of the UN secretary-general's special representative, Stoltenberg. All talk of the previous Z-4 plan that the Krajina Serbs had so foolishly and recklessly rejected was now dead. The Croats demanded virtual unconditional surrender. The Serbs in Geneva agreed. The American ambassador to Croatia, Peter Galbraith, met Milan Babić, the Krajina Serb leader, in Belgrade to tell him that the game was up and that he had to accept the Croatian terms. I saw Babić later the same day and repeated the stark message. Babić, however, was still playing the fool, claiming that he would issue a statement accepting the Croat terms only when he had received authority from his Assembly to do so.

In retrospect, it is doubtful whether even a complete and absolute surrender by the Krajina Serbs would have prevented Operation Storm, but we shall never know. The operation was launched at dawn on August 4. According to the UN garrison commander in Knin, five hundred people were killed on that day in the Knin area alone. Within two days Knin, the capital of the RSK statelet, had fallen, and the biggest single movement of people in Europe, since the Sudeten Germans' departure from Czechoslovakia at the end of the Second World War, had begun. Some 170,000 Serbs fled their ancestral homes in Croatia for Serbia. Very few ever returned. It was also the moment in which the balance swung decisively against the Serbs for the first time since the Yugoslav wars began in 1991. They were never to regain the initiative. Within days most of the Krajina Serb statelet apart from Eastern Slavonia had disappeared, and within two months the Bosnian Serbs were to lose over 20 percent of the territory of Bosnia that they had occupied since May 1992. Again the War Crimes Tribunal, despite intensive shelling of civilian areas, including the town of Knin, made no immediate move to indict Croat leaders. The EU negotiator Carl Bildt pointed out this anomaly after Operation Storm and was thereafter in effect declared persona non grata by President Tudjman, who felt correctly that Bildt was inviting the tribunal to indict him.

(This never happened in Tudjman's lifetime, but in 2000, a year after Tudjman's death, Graham Blewitt, a senior ICTY prosecutor, announced, "There would have been sufficient evidence to indict president Tudjman had he still been alive." And the tribunal's indictment of Croatian general Ante Gotovina lists Tudjman as a key participant in a "joint criminal enterprise" aimed at the "permanent removal of the Serb population from the 'Krajina' region by killing, force, fear or threat of force, persecution, forced displacement, transfer and deportation.")

As a complement to the dramatic military activity, the United States decided to engage on the diplomatic front decisively. On August 11, President Clinton's national security adviser, Tony Lake, set off around Europe to promote a new U.S. initiative. The seven-point outline plan effectively sidelined the EU and the Contact Group while Richard Holbrooke and Bob Frasure got to work with a deal on triple recognition, the possibility of exchanges of territory, and constitutional principles. It was a radically new line aimed at doing away with what my U.S. colleague described as "the nickel and dime approach" we had all been working on. But disaster struck. While Holbrooke and his party were trying to gain access to Sarajevo, one of the armored vehicles taking them down Mount Igman fell off the road and exploded. Frasure was one of those killed instantly. It looked for a time as though the peace process would once again be at least on hold, but Holbrooke was determined to press ahead. He was not the only person pursuing radical initiatives at that time.

On Friday, August 25, Milošević held a secret meeting with all the key Bosnian Serb leaders—political and military—and every member of the Yugoslav, Serb, and Montenegrin constitutional hierarchy in the presence of Serbian Orthodox Patriarch Pavle. In short, all the church and state institutions throughout Serb lands were united in one place in what became known as the Patriarch's Meeting. Milošević did not require any decisions at that meeting, but he invited attendees to let him have a very early response to his suggestion that he should lead the political negotiations that were clearly now going to be required and that he should have the casting vote in the joint Serb/Bosnian Serb delegation. The same cast met again on Monday, August 28. When I later asked the Bosnian Serbian vice president Koljević what had made Karadžić capitulate, he replied enigmatically, "We had no choice." Whatever that meant, and it sounded ugly, they duly signed the document relinquishing their negotiating rights to Milošević. The use of the patriarch was a master stroke. Pavle later withdrew his assent when some of his hard-line nationalist bishops realized what he had done, but it was too late by then.

Before the Bosnian Serbs had even returned to Pale, however, NATO bombs had started to fall on their headquarters after the shelling of the Markale market in Sarajevo on the previous day, August 28, (killing forty-three people) had been attributed by UNPROFOR to the Serbs. By destroying so much of the Bosnian Serb army (VRS) communications, the course of the war was decisively altered in a way that made the final mapmaking at Dayton much simpler. Koljević tried to persuade me that the bomb could not have come from Serb lines. I said that he was wasting his breath. I had no technical information on the UN investigation into the bomb cratering, but even if, for the sake of argument, the Bosnian Serbs had not launched this particular bomb, what about the innumerable mortar and artillery rounds they had used to shell Sarajevo for three years with the loss of thousands of lives? Koljević gloomily conceded the point. I suggested that he concentrate his efforts instead on persuading Mladić to comply with the UN demands for the withdrawal of heavy weapons.

Koljević took me at my word and promptly launched into a blazing row on my telephone with Mladić, which made as usual no difference to Mladić's course of action. The confusion in Serb ranks reached such a state that a couple of days later Koljević produced a letter signed by himself complying with all the conditions required by General Bernard Janvier to call off the air strikes. Within hours a separate statement by Mladić defiantly rejected the NATO conditions and contradicted Koljević's letter. It was clear to all that only Mladić's agreement to comply had any real meaning. Whether Koljević enjoyed the support of even his political colleagues in Pale must be open to doubt. Mladić's refusal to comply was accompanied by claims that to withdraw Serb heavy weaponry would leave the Serb communities in Sarajevo at the mercy of Izetbegović's army, not a line calculated to evince much sympathy from NATO.

And so the "pissing match," as my U.S. colleague called it, between Mladić and Generals Janvier and Smith continued with a great deal of orchestration by Holbrooke going on behind the scenes. It was eventually Mladić who blinked under enormous pressure from Milošević and rather less pressure from Holbrooke, who was unenthusiastic about calling off the bombing campaign. Holbrooke, who blew very hot and cold about the bombing—initially strongly against—finally concluded that the bombing strengthened his negotiating position with Milošević, an argument that had some force. The difficulty was to be found in calibrating events with sufficient care to ensure that the Bosnian Serb army was not so weakened as to bring about the prospect of the complete collapse of the Republika Srpska. This might in turn have resulted in Milošević being forced to send in troops from Serbia and Montenegro to prevent such a calamity and to stem the awful prospect of nearly a million refugees coming to Serbia. There was a deep irony in the timing of the concession by Mladić in withdrawing his heavy weapons. The NATO planes had run out of justifiable targets and would have had to call a halt to the bombing themselves, knowing that they would not get Security Council endorsement for additional targeting given the Russians' veto.

CHAPTER 10

Dayton from the Sidelines

Richard Holbrooke's shuttle diplomacy in the weeks leading up to the Dayton Agreement was carried out with typical American brio and panache, liberally laced with his own brand of New York chutzpah. Holbrooke played the media to a tee, keeping their expectations low, announcing breakthroughs at well-timed moments to get the best CNN coverage. He intentionally made very clear privately and publicly that the Contact Group was being sidelined, to be brought in on ceremonial occasions or to rubber-stamp agreements made. The line that the United States had picked up the pieces left by the inept and incompetent Europeans may have made the selling of the ultimate agreement and the commitment of ground troops easier to a still reluctant and skeptical Congress, but it was manifestly unfair to the European negotiators, particularly Lords Carrington and Owen and Carl Bildt, on whose efforts Holbrooke was building. The maps were largely based on the original work of Owen, Bildt, and the Contact Group; the 51/49 split had been accepted in principle on HMS *Invincible*. In downplaying the European role, Holbrooke was relying on the good will of the Europeans and their desperate need for an agreement that could be made to stick.

I had less cause than many to complain of being sidelined. Holbrooke on his frequent visits to Belgrade during the shuttle period regularly took the trouble to brief me, although he had to be pushed very hard to let us know what his mapmaking consisted of. The Foreign Office felt, reasonably, that if we were expected to provide a very substantial percentage of the ground troops, we should have a clear idea of what our areas of responsibility would be.

Although Holbrooke and I had our disagreements, they were usually carried out in very good humor. His basic tenet, that a prolonged bombing campaign followed by an extensive Croat land offensive would make the mapmaking at the final peace conference easier and punish the Serbs for their aggression and misdeeds, had logic on its side. The problem was Holbrooke took some care, initially at least, to conceal the second prong of his policy (the support for a Croatian offensive) from us, indeed perhaps from others in his own administration. Certainly it was bizarre that Contact Group permanent representatives at the UN in New York were discussing action in the Security Council to rein in the Croat offensive (which was clearly being undertaken with regular troops from Croatia and which threatened to prompt another huge refugee outflow toward Serbia from Banja Luka to add to the 170,000 plus who had fled from the Krajina to Serbia in early August) at the same time as Holbrooke was, by his own admission, urging Tudjman to continue his offensive until Prijedor, Sanski Most, and Bosanski Novi were captured.[1]

I had two problems with Holbrooke's approach beyond the confusion he was sowing among friends, allies, and colleagues alike. Firstly, in his desire to use the Croats as his magic stick to beat the Serbs, he did not seem to take adequate account of the misdeeds of the Croats, who were by no means the innocent, injured party they successfully claimed to be. If we were rightly condemning Serb atrocities, rampant nationalism, and the desire for Greater Serbia and consequent ethnic cleansing, then we should be wary of turning a blind eye to Croatian nationalism and Greater Croatia. Through indulging the Croats and helping their war machine through the transparent means of a group of recently retired U.S. generals who formed a company called IMS, the West was in danger of fostering a nationalism almost as toxic and as repugnant as that of the Serbs.

Secondly, Holbrooke's policies risked provoking huge increases in refugee numbers, which in turn could lead to a revanchism, sowing the seeds of future conflict and instability. It was this that led me to tell Holbrooke that a prolonged bombing campaign was not conducive to a lasting peace. In his account of the Bosnian war, Holbrooke represented my views incorrectly as being opposed to a bombing campaign per se.[2] Nor was I, as he suggested, romantically attached to Rebecca West's analysis of the Balkan peoples. Still less did I share the views she attributed to all "English persons of humanitarian and reformist disposition" of favoring one over the other, or as she put it another way, "All came back with a pet Balkan people established in their hearts as suffering and innocent, eternally the massacree and never the massacrer."[3] Prolonged exposure made most diplomats in Belgrade cynically aware of the ability of most parties to be duplicitous, meretricious, and manipulative despite certain honorable exceptions. But serving in Belgrade required me to explain to my government why the Serbs behaved as they did and to attempt to analyze and predict their often perverse and seemingly irrational behavior. The Foreign Office understood perfectly well what I was doing, but some others with whom they shared my telegrams appeared incapable of distinguishing explanation from exculpation. Holbrooke was not the only American to fall into the trap of seeing an analyst as an apologist.[4]

There is no need to rehearse the Dayton negotiations here. I was, in any case, not present, although a member of my staff was initially part of the British delegation until it became clear that the Europeans were largely at Dayton for decoration. But certainly it would be curmudgeonly not to acknowledge that without the incredible energy and determination of Richard Holbrooke in that period, and particularly at Dayton, agreement would not have been achieved. It was well worth the Europeans taking a back seat and trailing in his wake. Nor is it to deny the value of his contribution to peace to say that a little more generosity toward his allies might have created fewer bruised feelings. The three weeks of meetings at the Dayton air base brought about an agreement that was just about the best available at the time. Final agreement was barely secured. While it is tempting to imagine that the conference could have borne the extra weight of other complex, major issues like Kosovo, the reality was different. We need only remind ourselves that to reach agreement at Dayton, it proved necessary to leave the complex and thorny question of the corridor between eastern and western Bosnia at Brčko unresolved, to be adjudicated at a later stage.

Along with the other Contact Group heads of mission, I met the returning Serb delegation at Batajnica, the Belgrade military airport. I told Milošević, as he came off the plane, that I thought it was a very good agreement. He said he thought so too and praised the efforts of the British delegation to help ensure success. The Bosnian Serbs, Krajišnik and Koljević, trailed along at the end of the delegation looking bedraggled, crushed, and defeated. I imagine that they were not looking forward to having to explain away the maps agreed to at Dayton to Karadžić, Mladić, and the other colleagues in Pale. Milošević had deliberately kept the Bosnian Serbs in the dark over his negotiations. According to my staff members there, they cut a pathetic figure. Ignored by the United States, they were humiliated by Milošević, who did not even allow them to use the Serb delegation fax machine. On one occasion they were driven to ask to use Carl Bildt's fax to send a document to General Mladić. They were permitted by Milošević to see the final version of the map only ten minutes before their signatures were required on the Dayton document. Krajišnik fainted when he saw it and had not come round in time to sign the document. Koljević, with his elbow firmly guided by Milošević, did the necessary signature. At Belgrade airport, Milošević made one of his very rare public pronouncements, which then set the tone for the media blitz of the next few days to persuade the Serb people on both sides of the Drina that the deal was the very best that could have been expected and, of course, that without Milošević no such happy outcome could have been achieved.

As for the Dayton Accords, we have tried to make them work with all their imperfections—which is why so many thousands of troops were committed to the operation. It has proved to be a very long haul. Yet the real tragedy, with the benefit of hindsight, was the failure to secure agreement on and implementation of the Vance-Owen Peace Plan (VOPP), the best chance for a multiethnic Bosnia. Not only would the war have been ended nearly three years earlier, with so many fewer casualties, atrocities, massacres, and, of course, refugees. But above all, while a civil war lasting six months is bad enough, the scars are likely to heal much more quickly than from one lasting nearly three and a half years.

CHAPTER 11

Independent Media and the Opposition

Although Bosnia was my main food and drink for the best part of two years, it was far from being my only concern. There was important work to be done in promoting and defending the work of the independent media, which was in a weak and oppressed condition, a regular feature of the problem of the "democratic deficit" found in all the former Yugoslav republics except Slovenia. Along with many other Western countries, we gave the independent media practical help and political support. We also multiplied contacts with the opposition and with the more liberal regime in Montenegro. All these measures were aimed at promoting a level democratic playing field in Serbia.

Our contacts with the opposition in Serbia were frequent and cordial. They also successfully got under Milošević's skin. His security apparatus clearly monitored all my calls and contacts. At one point, he asked me why I was seeing a couple of Vojvodina political leaders. I said that the correct question was why shouldn't I see them. I started to explain that the job of a diplomat was to meet and get to know all shades of political opinion, but Milošević's communist schooling was too deeply inculcated. His eyes glazed over. He seemed less sensitive about contacts with Belgrade opposition figures, from which I inferred that he regarded Vojvodina leaders like Kosovar Albanians as potential secessionists. It would be wrong, of course, to say that he was relaxed about contacts with the democratic opposition in Belgrade. Like all autocrats, Milošević wished political life to flow through his channels exclusively. In any case, I paid no attention to his views and continued to cultivate the whole range of the opposition with two exceptions. The most significant was Vojislav Šešelj, a self-confessed fascist and racist, leader of an infamous group of ethnic-cleansing paramilitaries during the Croatian and Bosnian wars and president and founder of the Radical Party—taking on the name of the party of the Serbian leader at the outbreak of the First World War, Nikola Pašić. It had always amazed me that the International Criminal Tribunal for Yugoslavia (ICTY) had not at that stage indicted Šešelj—there were enough harrowing accounts of the activities of his paramilitaries in, for example, places such as Zvornik on the Serbian-Bosnian border, which had been comprehensively ethnically cleansed.[1] Šešelj was known to have led his rabble in to battle himself, claiming that he had received his orders directly from Milošević. There is no reason to doubt this, though in Milošević's paper-averse autocracy, documentary proof is hard to come by.

Neither I nor any members of the embassy consequently had any contacts with Šešelj or his party, although some other Western embassies took a different view. I also declined to have any contact with a faction of the Sandžak Muslim nationalist party (SDA) whose leader, Sulejman Ugljanin, had issued a death threat against the moderate Sandžak Muslim leader Rasim Ljajić. Once the "fatwa" was withdrawn, I started to talk to Ugljanin and his group.

While contacts with the mainstream opposition were regular, they were not always particularly productive. The Serbian opposition kept on forming and reforming in different shapes like an amoeba and had much the same amorphous cutting edge, despite a good deal of prompting and pushing from Western embassies to encourage them to unite, bury their differences, and promote a single forceful leader. If Milošević were orchestrating their performance—and I had no doubt he gave them a helping hand—he could not have been more satisfied with the outcome. His usual tactics of bribery and threats, abetted by the petty jealousies and selfishness of leaders not prepared to subsume their own ambitions in the common cause of creating a decent normal democratic state in Serbia, frequently snatched opposition defeat from what looked like the jaws of victory, most notably after the winter of discontent of 1996–97.

It would be wrong, however, to be overcritical of the opposition. They had in many ways an impossible task. They were chronically short of funds despite irregular and fitful Western financial support often held up by not entirely unjustified bureaucratic caution. Moreover, they were virtually invisible to the largest section of the Serbian population, never appearing in the official media unless it was to have their differences and squabbles played out on a wider stage. Among the less sophisticated parts of the electorate, the very idea of voting for the opposition still seemed a step too far. In Communist days, failing to vote for official candidates invariably brought unwelcome notice from the authorities. It was hard to believe that those days were entirely over. Indeed, the authorities probably had a very good idea of those who were less than enthusiastic about the Milošević regime. He had picked up all the reins of the Communist state security apparatus that in Tito's time was said to be so extensive that all the trees in the nomenklatura's favored suburb Dedinje were bugged.

Vuk Drašković, the charismatic but mercurial opposition leader, once told me a revealing story about his attempts to canvass support in the Serbian rural heartland. A villager had been pointed out to him as a fervent Drašković supporter, who was moreover very influential among his neighbors. Drašković approached him and was, in typical Serbian style, promptly invited home for a coffee and glass of rakija. Inside the house, Drašković was encouraged to see several posters of himself and his party. At the end of a convivial session, Drašković got up to leave, saying that he was so glad that he could count on the man's vote. He was dumbfounded to receive the reply, "Make no mistake about it, Mr. Drašković. As soon as you are in power, I shall vote for you!" The story was, I am sure, true and illustrates the extent to which the rural society still retains such an exaggerated respect and fear for those who currently hold the levers of power. The problem for the opposition remained how to break the vicious circle. In the absence of a strong leader and given the factionalism, it was hard to see any hopeful prospects in the short term. We looked in vain to see whether the monolithic government structure would throw up an opposition figure. But Milošević was too smart for that. Having stabbed his own political mentor, Ivan Stambolić, in the back and deposed him in 1987, Milošević was ever alert to the threat from a promising figure from within the party hierarchy—not that I could detect many candidates.

If the opposition was a frequent source of disappointment and almost despair to Western governments, the independent media were a more promising target for our attentions. The importance of helping the media had been widely recognized some time before my arrival in Belgrade. But quite often hare-brained schemes were proposed and implemented that wasted a good deal of taxpayers' money with no positive result. One such ill-conceived stunt was the pirate radio station, Radio Brod, which was moored in the Adriatic and was meant to beam objective news to former Yugoslavia. Regrettably the transmitter was unable to cope with the mountainous terrain in Bosnia and Montenegro. Its audibility was consequently so poor that it could be heard by only a handful of people in Yugoslavia and by no one in Belgrade.

Milošević's approach to the media was entirely Leninist, tempered by a wish to give a superficial impression of press freedom to ward off the most severe criticisms from the international community. The Information Ministry was therefore able to say with perfect accuracy that Serbia had over three hundred radio stations and several thousand newspapers or magazines. What the Information Ministry failed to add was that 99 percent of these media outlets had minute coverage and in the case of the radio or television stations carried no news at all. In Belgrade, for instance, we were able to receive more terrestrial channels than in London, but most of them carried nothing but old films and turbo-folk music. The only "independent" television station in Belgrade, Studio B, had a checkered career and a poor signal. For some time it took a genuinely critical attitude to the government but was then taken over through the thinly disguised ruse of a court case over ownership. As its ownership was finally legally vested in the Belgrade City Council, when the opposition won the local elections of November 1996 and took power in Belgrade the following spring, there were high hopes that Studio B might become its old self again. However, when Drašković's party ousted the Democrat leader Zoran Djindjić from the position of city mayor and went into coalition with government forces, Studio B became effectively a visual house magazine for Drašković's party. While this may seem very depressing to outsiders, it was anything but unusual in the Balkans of the 1990s. A frequently expressed view was, "They had their hands on the levers of power and influence for many years; now we have control: we must use it to our full advantage."

The main opposition newspaper in my early years was *Borba*. It had come a long way from its foundation as the Communist Party newspaper *Borba* in the 1940s under the editorship of the veteran partisan leader, and later dissident, Milovan Djilas. I gave a lengthy interview to the editorial board of *Borba* in December 1995, immediately after the Dayton Agreement. The following day the newspaper was taken over by the government, again quoting obscure and patently false questions of ownership.

When I raised the matter with Milošević, he claimed with a straight face that it was a matter for the courts and not for the government—ever maintaining the fiction that the judiciary was genuinely independent—adding elliptically that the managing editor, Branislav Milošević (no relation), was an old supporter of Milošević's predecessor as Serbian president, Ivan Stambolić.

It was typical of Milošević to decline to engage in a genuine discussion of these matters. He would claim to know nothing of the details nor to have any role in the decision-making process. As it is not possible for a diplomat accredited to a country to call the local president a liar to his face, it was necessary to find a blander formula. "All the reports I have read suggest otherwise . . . you must be misinformed by your subordinates, Mr. President . . . I can quote you chapter and verse . . . etc." We went through this stately minuet over the role of the media several times. Milošević always claimed that the media were free to criticize him and duly did so. This was true up to a point. No attempt was made to prevent the publication of tiny circulation, even scurrilous, magazines that often carried offensive cartoons and articles that would certainly have been the subject of libel cases in most Western countries. But these had little or no influence as they had restricted access to newsprint and could not afford to sell their product at a sufficiently low price to ensure wide circulation.

Nearly all the local radio stations that wished to have a trouble-free life either carried no news at all or simply relayed broadcasts from Radio Television of Serbia (RTS), the state network. Those who tried to provide a genuine news service found themselves frequently under enormous pressure and had their requests for licenses refused or simply unanswered. The vast majority of the opposition or independent electronic media was therefore obliged to operate illegally. Against this depressing background, one beacon shone out: Radio B92 was an outstanding exception to the otherwise rather dismal scene. We regularly provided them with practical support and kept in close touch with their key management. After coming close to extinction during the street demonstrations (see chapter 13), they bounced back to set up a network of independent stations, which gave some genuine hope for the future of the independent media.

The regime in the immediate post-Dayton period had the opportunity to come in from the cold. But the realization that sanctions relief granted after the Dayton Agreement did not mean instant normalization and readmission of the Federal Republic of Yugoslavia to international organizations nor access to international financial institutions led instead to an orientation away from integration with Europe and toward self-isolation.

I sent a telegram to the Foreign Office at the time asking the question "What do we want from Milošević?" I pointed out that Western attention was very firmly focused on Bosnia. While the problems of Kosovo and the general lack of democracy in the FRY were understood, they were generally seen as isolated from the broader picture. Milošević, on the other hand, felt short-changed by Dayton; his cooperation in bringing the Bosnian Serbs on side had brought the suspension of sanctions but no access to frozen funds nor any new international investment or finance.

An "outer wall" of sanctions had been put in place by the United States—partly to appease the Albanian lobby (very influential in New York), who were incensed at Dayton's failure to address the Kosovo issue—as soon as the UN wall had been dismantled. As a result Milošević saw the West as hostile: offering little, promising nothing, and making a series of demands that he saw as impinging on Serb internal affairs and sovereignty and (crucially from his point of view), if accepted, threatening his hold on power. Under the baleful influence of his Marxist wife and other neo-Communist advisers, he began turning the FRY toward the East. The models held up were China and North Korea. He flirted with the Communist opposition in Russia; domestically he shifted his power base to left-wingers and tightened his control within the party by removing those whose stance might be interpreted as too independent; and he cracked down further on the media and removed the main pillar of economic sanity in the establishment, Dragoslav Avramović, the governor of the central bank, a former World Bank economist, and member of the Brandt Commission, only weeks after he had visited London for talks that I had arranged with the governor of the Bank of England.

If nothing was done to redirect Milošević, I predicted that two serious negative consequences would flow. Firstly, Serbia would continue to polarize politically, with the extreme right wing, whose support was holding up well, becoming more radical. Secondly, Milošević would not be prepared to negotiate seriously over Kosovo; his failure to do so would, I said, create dangerous pressure there. Both developments affected Western interests. Serbia's known capacity for mischief making and destabilization, which went well beyond its immediate borders, required us to make a determined effort to point the FRY in a stable Western direction.

I recommended that we should impress on Milošević the logic of orienting Serbia and Yugoslavia toward the West by a program of democratization within Serbia and autonomy for Kosovo. I thought we should discuss among leading allies how to provide Milošević with a clear road map that would lead the FRY to the West. We would have to be prepared to say that a pluralistic liberal FRY that had provided a solution to Kosovo would not be denied access to European institutions.

My telegram aroused some interest in London, but the difficulties of getting a coordinated approach among allies and partners meant that it was never effectively acted on. The Americans were allergic to any joint initiative with the Europeans over Kosovo. Indeed, they declined to cooperate with Carl Bildt's minority experts, Martin Lutz and David Austin, and appeared strangely reluctant to launch any plan of their own. They clearly felt sensitive to the Albanians' charge that their interests had been forgotten at Dayton and limited their activity to continuing strong criticism of Serb repression in the province, the opening of a U.S. information center in Priština (which came to be viewed by the Kosovar Albanians as a kind of embassy), and sharp comments to their European partners about the folly of recognizing the Federal Republic of Yugoslavia. As far as the UK and most of the other Europeans were concerned, recognition of the FRY carried no seal of approval; it was merely a recognition of facts on the ground and of international borders. The nearest we Europeans came to providing Milošević with a road map came in a document eventually approved and issued many months later by the European Union entitled "The Regional Approach," which had all the nuances and subtleties to delight a European bureaucrat but none of the broad-brush deals that would have been likely to appeal to Milošević.

While the bureaucratic processes were in progress, Milošević had at least taken one positive step forward, which was to recognize the Former Yugoslav Republic of Macedonia (FYROM). This was the first of the former Socialist Federal Republic of Yugoslavia (SFRY) republics to be recognized by the third Yugoslavia, and it in turn triggered European Union Member States' recognition of the Federal Republic of Yugoslavia, with its two republics of Serbia and Montenegro.

Recognition involved my re-badging—from chargé d'affaires to ambassador—and the formal process of seeking the Yugoslav government's approval for my appointment even though I had already been in charge of the embassy for two years. Thereafter came the ceremony of presenting my credentials to the then head of state, Zoran Lilić, widely dismissed as a nonentity. I had only returned from the White Palace, as the FRY president's residence was known, some twenty minutes previously when I was asked to go to Milošević's office to hand over a message from the Foreign Secretary to Milošević about the removal of Karadžić and Mladić from office and the need to make early progress on Kosovo. The Foreign Office felt that the formal opening of full diplomatic relations was a good opportunity to press these matters.

Milošević read the message carefully but did not immediately react. I added that we wanted him to use his full weight and influence to get Karadžić to stand down. Could Milošević not say to him that his continuation in office was deeply damaging to Serbs generally? Milošević scoffed at the idea that Karadžić was susceptible to appeals to his better nature or to his patriotism. Milošević said that he did not expect Mladić to be a problem. He thought he would retire or be stood down quite soon. On Kosovo, Milošević said that he was preparing to move ahead on education. If attempts to reincorporate the Albanians into the state system were successful, he thought it should prove possible to move on to more sensitive areas. After my standard speech on the deplorable lack of human rights in Kosovo, I urged Milošević to restore some element of trust there by some confidence-building measures such as the release of political prisoners. He could transform the political climate by announcing an amnesty. Milošević said that he would think very carefully about it. If he did, that was all he did.

The Foreign Secretary's message was reinforced by representations I was asked to make on behalf of the High Representative for Bosnia, Carl Bildt (who had exchanged the role of EU representative for the Dayton Agreement–created position of High Representative for Bosnia), about Karadžić's illegal dismissal of the prime minister of the Republika Srpska. The dismissal had no legal validity, Bildt's message read, as Karadžić should not be in office anyway. Karadžić was, in effect, attempting a coup d'état. We looked to Milošević to take action. Milošević began with a curious digression. He thought I should be spending 90 percent of my time on commercial rather than political matters. I made the obvious reply that I was forced to spend 90 percent of my time on political issues, most of which only he could solve. Milošević continued with one of his serpentine logic-chopping exercises in which he demonstrated that the dismissal of the Bosnian Serbs' prime minister by Karadžić was, in fact, a "good thing" as it demonstrated the fundamental weakness of Karadžić's position and his paranoia over anyone who was perceived to take his instructions from Belgrade.

Nobody was much taken in by the protestations of Karadžić's weakness—at least not for any length of time. Pressure quickly mounted for further action to force Karadžić off the public stage, if he could not be physically removed to The Hague. At a meeting in June 1996, three months before the first post-Dayton elections, I called on Milošević again to discuss the situation in Bosnia and specifically to urge him to move further against Karadžić. The media was one significant area where Karadžić's influence was wholly poisonous. Talk was starting to emerge of sanctions being reimposed on the FRY if Karadžić and Mladić were not forced out of office as Milošević had promised to do at Dayton. Milošević responded by alluding to plans actively underway to force the Bosnian Serb leadership to appoint one of the two Bosnian Serb vice presidents, Biljana Plavšić, as acting president. "I will squeeze them violently" was his colorful if vague phrase. He hoped to bring about this change by the end of June.

Meanwhile, we had a separate bone to pick with Milošević over General Mladić, who had outrageously appeared in public in Belgrade to attend the funeral of a fellow general of the VRS. Milošević said that he had not even known that Mladić was coming. But even if he had, a funeral was a sacred event in Serbian culture and could not be interfered with. I said that the international community felt humiliated and insulted by Mladić's freedom to come to Belgrade and strut around, thumbing his nose at the War Crimes Tribunal (ICTY). Milošević said that it would not be happening again. (In fact, it recurred about a year later when Mladić secretly attended the wedding of his son.)

We also had a prickly exchange over the independent media, as a local radio station had just been taken over by the authorities. Milošević asked me whether I seriously believed that he had the time and energy to focus on the daily activities of every media outlet. The courts were often independently issuing judgments on the complicated question of ownership. The government was not involved. I said that the impression given was very different. This was not an isolated case. The opposition paper *Borba* and the independent TV station Studio B had been taken over, and the Open Society Foundation known in Serbia as the Soros Foundation was currently deregistered. I had argued the case for reregistration previously with him, his foreign minister, and even his wife. What were the prospects? Milošević said that he had not followed the question in detail, but he thought Soros would be reregistered soon. This at least happened. Sonja Licht, the veteran human rights campaigner and head of the Soros Foundation in Yugoslavia, was duly grateful.

As a reaction to my criticisms of his policies, Milošević derided my relationship with Vuk Drašković, whom he described as a third-rate politician who had been a strong nationalist in his early days. I said that he had not been alone in holding such views at that time. (My point was deliberately not taken.) Nevertheless, Drašković was now a very strong supporter of the peace process and of the Dayton Agreement. I pointed out to Milošević that I had probably seen him more often than I had seen Drašković in the current year. Milošević said that that reflected their relative importance. I said that in my experience in previous posts it was always easier to see the opposition as they tended to have time on their hands. It was, I repeated, my job to meet all shades of political leader on a regular basis and to avoid as far as possible being used or manipulated by any side, hence my decision not to attend any party congresses or conferences in the run-up to the federal elections, due before the end of the year. This was a depressing position to have to take. In any normal functioning democracy, it would be entirely appropriate for an ambassador to attend the party congresses of the leading political parties.

CHAPTER 12
The High Representative's Delegate

In addition to my other responsibilities, I became the High Representative for Bosnia's informal delegate in Belgrade. This involved a good deal of fetching and carrying of messages on areas of implementation of the Dayton Agreement including the surrender of war criminals, the withdrawal from public life of Karadžić, arms control, and the incompatibilities between various bilateral agreements signed by the FRY and Republika Srpska and their obligations to the state of Bosnia under the Dayton accords. I usually set up Carl Bildt's meetings with Milošević and acted as counselor cum note taker.

I enjoyed very much working with Carl Bildt. He had a breadth of vision, a questioning and very quick mind, and a formidable intellectual integrity. He brooked no bullshit or bureaucratic bungling. Allied to his intellectual talents were a persistence and determination to achieve results and a remarkable tolerance for the sniping and the backbiting (as often as not from one's allies) that were such a frequent feature of life as an international negotiator in Bosnia and throughout former Yugoslavia.

Bildt and I paid several visits to Milošević in the run-up to the Bosnian elections. Bildt was determined to force Karadžić out of office and off the public stage. Karadžić at one point had agreed to stand down and to be neither seen nor heard in public. The undertakings had all been violated. In early July, Bildt told Milošević (who was, of course, aware of it from his own sources) that Pale TV was almost a parody of a real television station. It carried hours of Karadžić, described as the president of the Republika Srpska, making speeches, with the occasional light relief of scantily clad turbo-folk singers. The transfer of power that was supposed to have been made to allow his vice president, Biljana Plavšić, to assume the title of acting president had gone unreported. Indeed, said Bildt, it was a secret in the Republika Srpska that Plavšić had taken over power. Pale TV propaganda was a disgrace that would have embarrassed Stalin. Milošević, who looked bemused by the reference to Stalin's embarrassment at propaganda on television, maintained that while he did not have military weapons at his disposal to take out Pale TV, he would use other unspecified means if the violations continued. I added that the image given by the Pale clique was one of hoodwinking the international negotiators. Moreover, Karadžić's negative influence persisted in poisoning the atmosphere throughout the Bosnian Serb entity. The Bosnian Serb police near Srebrenica had prevented a Finnish group of forensic scientists from collecting bodies of Muslim men who had been murdered fleeing from the Srebrenica massacre in July 1995. Milošević maintained that he would insist at his meeting with Plavšić the next day that she should ensure that the Bosnian Serb undertakings about Karadžić's withdrawal should be honored in letter and spirit. (Karadžić at this time had had the effrontery to send by fax a condolence letter on the death of Princess Diana on letterhead that clearly stated "President of Republika Srpska"!)

Bildt had to leave Belgrade at this point, but Milošević asked me to call immediately after his meeting with Plavšić the following afternoon. Milošević claimed that Plavšić had promised to issue a statement assuming full powers and promising to work for full implementation of the Dayton Agreement. She would, moreover, be the candidate of the SDS party (Serb nationalist party, Karadžić's own creation) for president of the Republika Srpska at the forthcoming Bosnian elections. Plavšić, continued Milošević, had volunteered that she felt very uncomfortable about the noncompliance with earlier undertakings. She had assured Milošević that Karadžić would not now appear on TV or radio, although they could not help it if somebody mentioned his name, for example, during a phone-in program. Milošević concluded that he thought this had covered all the points he had discussed with Bildt and me the previous day. I said that there was still the possible problem of Karadžić being the president of the SDS party. Milošević replied that this would not be mentioned in public either. In a tone of exasperation, he said that he had done as he had promised in removing Karadžić from power. Short of having him killed (and he added, "I am not the Sheriff of Kansas City"), there was nothing else he could do.

After a short respite, however, Karadžić's position as party president continued to be offensively highlighted, which brought in the Americans. Reenter Holbrooke. He arrived with an impressive document detailing every violation by the Bosnian Serbs of aspects of the Dayton Agreement and threatening to block the final lifting of sanctions due to come into effect after the Bosnian elections had been held in September. After one of their by now legendary and epic abusive matches, Milošević forced Karadžić's resignation as party leader, thus ensuring his SDS party would be able to take part in the elections. Unsurprisingly, like all the nationalist parties standing in Bosnia, they did rather well. Milošević's sister socialist party, by contrast, did not. He had the gall consequently to complain to me about the lack of access to the media from which parties in opposition to Karadžić's SDS suffered!

Shortly before the Bosnian elections took place there came some rare good news with the announcement of the signing of an agreement on education in Kosovo by both Milošević and the Kosovo Albanian leader, Ibrahim Rugova, brokered by the indefatigable papal emissary Monsignor Vincenzo Paglia, spiritual leader of the lay Catholic Sant'Egidio community. The community had been involved in mediating conflict resolution in many parts of the world including, and most successfully with, the opposing sides in the Mozambique civil war. This seemed temporarily to offer the prospect of a continuing process that, if it went well, could defuse the potential time bomb of Kosovo. Unfortunately, progress on Kosovo through the education agreement proved to be a chimera.

One last question in the run-up to the Bosnian elections that generated a good deal of heat and light was the timing of the final lifting of sanctions. At Dayton it had been agreed that sanctions would be suspended with the initialing of the agreement and would be finally lifted ten days after the first post-Dayton elections in Bosnia were deemed to be free and fair. Milošević grew increasingly agitated in the period immediately before the Bosnian elections when it became clear that the international community, and the United States in particular, believed that the clock started ticking on the ten-day postelection period after the count and after the elections had been verified by the election supervisors, the Organisation for Security and Co-operation in Europe, as being free and fair. When Bildt and I saw Milošević and Foreign Minister Milan Milutinović three days before the elections, we pointed out that the ten-day countdown started around September 25, during which time there would be agreement on a new Security Council Resolution formally lifting sanctions.

Milošević reacted angrily, saying there was no need whatsoever for any further Security Council resolution. He and Warren Christopher had agreed at Dayton that there should be an irrevocable decision on the lifting of sanctions provided the Dayton requirements were met. They had originally discussed the possibility of sanctions being lifted after withdrawal of forces from the zones of separation, but the Americans had wanted to have it later. Milošević said that he had agreed, provided there was an absolutely clear-cut deadline. This had been agreed as ten days after the occurrence of the first elections. I intervened to say that elections could not be taken to mean just the casting of votes. There had to be a count and the announcement of a result. This was bound to take several days in Bosnia, given the unusual—indeed, unique—circumstances in which the poll was taking place, including refugee and out-of-country voting.

Milošević said that, as far as Bosnia was concerned, the elections were taking place on September 14, just as the Yugoslav federal elections were taking place on November 3 (an occasion for a quick reference to my frequent contacts with "that psychopath Drašković, who should be locked up"), and the U.S. presidential elections on November 5. That was the day that counted. If we were now trying to change the goal posts, the international community's reputation in Yugoslavia would be zero. We forbore from making the obvious riposte about his reputation in the international community. Milošević then claimed that in separate discussions with American negotiators in Geneva in recent weeks they had all agreed with his interpretation. Bildt and I ducked the obvious attempt to drive a wedge between us and the Americans, and we invited the Yugoslavs to discuss the question directly with the United States. Whatever the two of them could agree on would probably be acceptable to the rest of the international community.

While I had originally been puzzled over Milošević's anxiety to see sanctions lifted ten days after Bosnia's polling day, I realized from his reference to the Yugoslav federal elections that I had overlooked a core element in his election strategy. He had undoubtedly picked the date to ensure that his party and coalition could garner the maximum credit from the lifting of sanctions. His whole electoral timetable was predicated on the formal removal of sanctions and risked being upset if there was any serious delay. Although the lifting was duly delayed until ten days after the certification of the election results, Milošević still had sufficient time to cash in. The state media had a field day running endless interviews with the Belgrade man in the street praising the Great Helmsman's role in securing the lifting of the international community's "unfair" embargo.

It goes without saying that the state media never referred to the original sins for which sanctions were imposed nor, indeed, to the central role played by Milošević in the four and a half years of misery the Serbian people had endured. It was as though the prisoner, having been unfairly locked up for several years and finally released, was invited to reward the public prosecutor.

A couple of incidents from the election campaign demonstrate the pitfalls of diplomatic life in Belgrade at the time. A diplomat in Serbia never enjoyed immunity from the manipulation practiced by government and occasionally by the opposition, particularly during an election campaign. My U.S. opposite number and I received the treatment in equal measure. About a month before the elections I paid a commercial visit to southern Serbia to look at prospective partners for British business. This was an aspect of normal diplomatic life that had received very little attention from me during sanctions, but with their suspension and subsequent lifting the way was clear to promote the interests of British business. I decided to tour a series of factories in both the private and public sectors. The media were as usual present in force throughout, but I suppose it should have been no surprise that the state television news that evening chose to show me visiting only a state-owned plastics factory, claiming that this was proof positive of the West's endorsement of Milošević's economic policies. This was run together with a report of the visit (on the same day by bizarre coincidence) to the state steel works in Smederevo by my U.S. colleague, Dick Miles, with the same insinuation of Western support for Milošević. Naturally Dick and I had not coordinated our diaries in any way, but the unlucky conjuncture gave the state media chiefs an opening that they exploited to the full. "I wish to God I had never heard of the Smederevo steel works," moaned Dick the next time we met.

The opposition turned their hand to manipulation at about the same time. Their coalition, Zajedno, had adopted as their figurehead the former Central Bank governor, Dragoslav Avramović, who had been the architect of Yugoslavia's economic recovery from the rock bottom of the winter of 1993/94. As mentioned previously, he had been sacked by the regime for criticizing the government's policies and going beyond what they saw as his sphere of responsibility. I introduced Avramović (who still remained a close contact and source of great wisdom on the economy—and whom I regarded also as a friend) to a visiting under-secretary from the Foreign Office, who found him as impressive and lucid as I did. We listened to his ideas for government in the event of an opposition victory and wished him luck.

About a week later, Avramović abruptly stood down as Zajedno's leader, citing medical reasons. This was not entirely surprising as he was known to have suffered from major kidney problems for some time. However, the Belgrade rumor mill soon revealed that the real reason for Avramović's resignation lay in the pressure brought to bear on the former governor by the U.S. chargé d'affaires and the British and German ambassadors. The twisted logic ran as follows. With Avramović as their standard bearer, Zajedno now had a real chance of winning (Avramović was genuinely very popular with the Serbian masses). But the West felt they needed Milošević to implement Dayton. Therefore, the opposition must not be allowed to win. Their front-runner must accordingly be thwarted. A quiet word by Western ambassadors would persuade Avramović to see where the highest national and international interests lay.

The idea that Milošević's demise—physical or political—would be regarded as other than a godsend or unalloyed blessing in Western capitals was laughable. Not that anyone was inclined physically to bring about such a demise. But there would have been no tears. What anxieties existed about stability in the region would have quickly given way to relief at the end of a ten-year nightmare. Certainly the prospect of an Avramović-led coalition held few terrors. The prospect of an ultranationalist victory by the Radicals under Vojislav Šešelj was a real preoccupation, but at that time seemed far from likely.

Miles and I were appalled at the currency given to this preposterous story. While Avramović repeated like a mantra the medical grounds for his resignation, he was annoyingly coy about publicly ruling out or denying the rumors of Western pressure, leaning on him to pull out. Although I was instinctively opposed to issuing denials of every fatuous rumor to circulate in the Belgrade hothouse, the persistence of this particular tale was such that the Germans and the Americans felt obliged to issue public denials. I reluctantly followed suit.

The rumors eventually died down. It was many weeks later that we discovered the source to be the mischievous first lieutenant of opposition leader Vuk Drašković, Milan Božić, who finally admitted that he had put the rumor into circulation to provide an effective alibi in the event of a poor Zajedno coalition performance in the elections. Although autocracies in general foster conspiracy theories (and Serbia was no exception), it was a depressing comment on the Serb public that they could be credulous enough to think that the international community—whom they had long expected to meddle in their affairs—should have been attempting to manipulate their elections. It was also an indictment of the fragile state of democracy in Serbia that there was an assumption that any political or semipolitical figure, and particularly a representative of one of the "Great Powers," would not hesitate to behave in a way more redolent of Britain before the 1832 Reform Bill, given half a chance.

Nonetheless, it looked initially as though the long-suffering Yugoslav public would continue to kiss the hand that cuffed them. The federal elections gave a reasonably comfortable majority to the government coalition. The opposition briefly united in a heterogeneous coalition but in different configurations for the federal and the Serbian local elections that were being held at the same time (over two rounds in the latter case). While the federal election results were clear cut, the first round of the local elections was indecisive. When I called on Milošević between the two rounds, I delivered an invitation from the British government to attend the December London conference on Bosnia. Although it was principally aimed at foreign ministers, we attached importance to the three "Dayton" presidents, Tudjman, Izetbegović, and Milošević attending.

Milošević was at his most relaxed in commenting on the opposition's poor performance in the elections. The problem, he claimed, with no hint of irony, was that most of their leaders were or had been in the past nationalists whose time had passed. I said that those of us who had seen the elections at close hand had not regarded them as a model of Western democracy. The opposition had hardly had the chance to put their case to the general public. Milošević then attempted to argue that they had been given equal time with his party and in fact had drawn a more favorable position than his coalition in the last political broadcast before the elections, where the running order was decided by lottery.

I said that few people watched party political broadcasts in Britain. Opinion was crucially formed by the news and current affairs programs. In Serbia the opposition had been invisible as far as the daily news programs were concerned. Milošević said that the news had merely reflected government ministers going about their normal business, opening hospitals and schools, receiving visitors, and so on. I replied that in an electoral period in Britain, all news and current affairs programs had to observe a proper balance between the parties. Milošević looked at me as if I were from another planet. The tragicomedy of the government's manipulation of the media in Serbia was best illustrated by the pathetic attempts to show the real dynamism of the economy by footage of, for example, the Serbian prime minister opening a motorway that had already been opened by another minister some eighteen months previously. Obviously many people were fooled, but the intelligentsia of Belgrade treated the whole election campaign as a bad joke.

When conversation turned to Kosovo, Milošević as usual became quite agitated. I complained about the failure to implement the education agreement. I had raised with Ibrahim Rugova three weeks previously the need to press on with nominating his members of the Joint Commission. He had done so within forty-eight hours. The ball was now firmly in Milošević's court. Milošević then pursued his standard line about not allowing any third party, not even Monsignor Paglia, at the talks as it would permit Rugova to claim that he had successfully internationalized the issue. I said that Sant'Egidio was politically invisible and had no international persona. If Monsignor Paglia could facilitate by his presence the meeting of the Joint Commission, it was a tiny price to pay and would bring substantial benefit to Albanian schoolchildren and students who had been receiving their education in makeshift and inappropriate conditions for years.

We went on to discuss the possibility of a bilateral meeting between Rugova and Milošević. Milošević said he was ready; he had received word through Monsignor Paglia that Rugova was also prepared. In fact, by the time the bilateral meeting took place eighteen months later, the situation on the ground was about to disintegrate into full-scale fighting. Another example of Milošević's disastrous instinct for procrastination that enabled him to feel temporarily in control. An early meeting with Rugova, which, to preserve Rugova's credibility within the Kosovar community, would have had to involve a third party such as the Sant'Egidio community, could have headed off the catastrophe of spring and summer 1999.

CHAPTER 13

The Winter of Discontent

Milošević's imminent fall was predicted regularly during my time in Belgrade. But only at one point did I feel that he was creating the circumstances for his own early departure. As mentioned above, Milošević's coalition won a reasonably comfortable victory in the federal elections of November 1996, but when the second round of local elections was complete, the preliminary results showed that the democratic opposition coalition, Zajedno, an umbrella for several of the most significant and democratically inclined opposition parties, had gained control of most of the major cities of Serbia, including Niš and Belgrade.

This was something of a surprise given the outcome at the federal level, assisted by the disgracefully one-sided media campaign. The electorate in the cities, however, proved that they were more sophisticated than commentators had given them credit for, and while they apparently were prepared to vote for the ruling coalition at the federal level, they wished to punish the same politicians for their corruption and venality at the local level. The government reaction to this disaster was breathtaking. As the preliminary results indicated a monumental rejection of the government, Socialist party chiefs locally and centrally decided to reverse this process by blatant vote rigging, ballot box stuffing, and other manipulation of the results. Niš was a particularly egregious example, which came as no surprise to me.

The local Socialist party boss, Mile Ilić, was someone I had met some six months previously during an official visit to the city (largely on trade business) when I had called on all the official dignitaries and leaders of the main political parties. Ilić arranged for me to be ambushed in his office by the press, despite my insistence that I was planning to give a full press conference in my hotel later and had nothing I wished to say to the press at this stage. Undeterred, Ilić ushered in the Niš press en masse and proceeded to give them a tendentious account of our meeting. Despite my unwillingness to be dragged into a joint press conference with him, I felt obliged to correct the most blatant errors in his account and invited the press to meet me at my hotel later for a proper press conference. But I left Ilić's office angry at the manipulation that I knew would lead the state media into presenting what had happened as a joint press conference with only one party leader in Niš.

Fortunately Ilić's maladministration of the city was clearly well known to the local population despite the control he exerted over the Niš media. This undoubtedly played a major role in his electoral reverse. But Ilić, perhaps desperate to prove to Milošević that his stewardship of Niš was a positive one, reversed the election results, claiming major irregularities. This was true, but the irregularities were committed by Ilić's Socialists, not by the opposition. Although we raised the alarm immediately, the international election monitors had gone (they had stayed only for the first round and the federal elections poll two weeks previously). Foreign minister Milan Milutinović eventually agreed to meet a wide group of Western ambassadors the following Saturday to answer our concerns.

Milutinović painted a rosy picture. The story was blown out of proportion. Claims had been made of irregularities: as in any democracy (*sic*) they had to be investigated, any errors corrected, and the final results announced. Why, he said, all the fuss? This was a match in which the final whistle had not yet been blown. The claims of irregularities had affected only a limited number of results, and as if to refute our arguments absolutely, he pointed out that the capital Belgrade was now in the hands of the opposition.

The next day I heard on the independent radio B92 that demands to annul most of the results in Belgrade on the grounds of irregularities had now been lodged by the government coalition and accepted by the Electoral Commission. The opposition immediately denounced the annulment, appealed against it, but understandably declined to take part in any rerun election. What was the point, they said, as the government would simply keep annulling the results until they got the ones they wanted. I telephoned Milutinović to demand an explanation as soon as I heard the news. He claimed, and I believed him, to be completely uninformed. He asked for time to investigate and promised to phone back. When he did so later it was to say in a voice that even he could not find convincing that these were only technical questions on the voting procedures that would have to be addressed by the courts but that were most unlikely to affect the final results. I am sure Milutinović had as little conviction in what he was saying as I had belief in it. But I did believe his initial plea of ignorance. He would never have agreed to address the diplomatic corps on the Saturday had he known what was to happen the very next day. His credibility with the corps—never high—was significantly undermined.

I decided that, as usual in Serbia, to get a sentient reaction it would be necessary to go to Milošević. After the customary delay, I was received. Milošević initially attempted to take the wind out of my sails by saying that he was spending most of his time at present concentrating on the economy, which he believed could realistically grow at 13–14 percent in the next year without inflation. The secret, he confided, was to have no budget deficit. I congratulated him on this astonishing feat, which, if it could be achieved, would make him the envy of the world's finance ministers. I too wished to spend most of my time on economic and commercial matters. Unfortunately, I told Milošević, unlike him I found myself having to spend almost all my time at the moment on the political situation in the wake of the local elections fraud. The situation seemed to be very bad. The opposition had been denied victory in many important towns, particularly in Niš and Belgrade. In Belgrade even his Socialists' spokesman had initially conceded defeat. As for Niš, when I had visited it earlier that year, I had to say that of all the people I had met in public life in Serbia, the local Socialist Party chief Mile Ilić was the one of whom I had formed the lowest opinion. I believed him to be a crude manipulator, and I placed little or no credence in what he said. I advised Milošević to do likewise.

Milošević sighed, as if to say "So tell me something new!" Ilić was, he said, "my personal mistake." He had planned to get rid of him the previous year when he had published an autobiography that was more an autohagiography. Even Jesus Christ would have blushed, said Milošević, at the terms in which Ilić described himself. After Milošević had announced Ilić's sacking, however, a delegation of Socialists had come from Niš pleading for Ilić's political life, claiming that he was at heart a good man and a strong party supporter. Against his better judgment, Milošević said that he had given way, adding as an aside that whenever he had made mistakes, it had been against his better judgment. Ilić would, however, now be removed as soon as the election process was complete.

Milošević continued that in 96.5 percent of municipalities the election results were clear cut and undisputed. In only 3.5 percent of cases was there a necessity for a rerun. I pointed out that this 3.5 per cent of cases involved most of the big towns in almost all of which the opposition coalition had won. Milošević, painting a fantasy picture of Serbia as an advanced democracy, said that while in many countries it was the Ministry of the Interior that ran elections, in Serbia they were run by a multiparty Electoral Commission that could appeal to the courts in the case of disputes. The whole electoral process was out of the hands of the executive, and "to be perfectly honest"—always a prompt to be on full alert during Milošević's conversations—he had not followed the details of the local elections very closely. He had found it humiliating when the Americans had suggested to him that he should use the Serbian courts to reverse the decisions of the Electoral Commission. The courts were independent, and their members were elected for life.

I said that I wanted to speak very frankly. It did not really matter whether I believed anything or everything of what he had just told me. The political reality had moved on. The overwhelming perception inside and outside the country was that electoral fraud had taken place. We had seen detailed allegations that the minutes of the Electoral Commission in Niš had been fraudulently altered. I was not in a position to judge the accuracy of these allegations. Nor did I doubt that Ilić would have informed Milošević that everything was above board and had been conducted according to legal requirements. But did he really expect Ilić to come to him and confess that he had messed up in Niš and that the opposition had won? Ilić was not the sort of man to tell the truth when a lie would do. Moreover, he knew that his political skin was at risk.

I told Milošević that he had to accept that he could not change the perception that fraud had taken place; no number of decisions by the Serbian Supreme Court would cut any ice. The only adjudication that would carry any weight would be an outside assessment, perhaps by independent legal experts from Western countries who would be empowered to look at all the data and to judge whether they could detect any sign of irregularities.

Milošević could, of course, I continued, choose to say that all this was none of my affair. But I believed I had a responsibility to tell him bluntly that Serbia now was at a crossroads and had to choose whether it was going to turn in on itself or look outward. If Serbia wanted to develop a relationship with the European Union, he would have to take urgent measures to break out of the current impasse, in order to restore Western faith in the possibility of peaceful change of government at any level in Serbia. The present situation, unless reversed, would cause enormous damage to Serbia's relations with the EU, which was to have taken a decision in a few days to incorporate the Federal Republic of Yugoslavia into its autonomous tariff regime. In the light of the current situation, there had been agreement only in principle on the desirability of its inclusion, while leaving open the timing. Milošević had to decide what was more important for him: that his Socialist Party should run places like Niš; or that Serbia should have good relations with the EU.

Milošević said that there was no comparison. Serbia needed Europe and the EU, in particular. He agreed that the present situation was very bad. He preferred to lose honestly than to win in a dirty fashion (*sic*). He would undertake to do two things: he would reexamine the whole question of the voting in Niš and Belgrade, not relying on the word of people like Ilić; and he would seriously consider my idea of inviting in international legal experts. This could be a way out of the current impasse.

A sterile exchange about the size of the demonstrations followed. The police had assured him, he said, that even on the day of the largest demonstrations, there had never been more than ten to twelve thousand people. I said that I was no expert on crowd numbers. Again it did not really matter whether there were two thousand or two hundred thousand in reality. The perception had gained hold that there were a hundred thousand present. He would have to live with it. Milošević asked why everybody believed the opposition's lies. I said that one reason why the opposition's version of events had taken hold was that the government's spokesmen and the state authorities had been so inept and lacking in transparency. Reuters had told me that when they had telephoned the Electoral

Commission for results, they were told that the results would only be given to Tanjug, the state news agency. Why only to Tanjug? Was this the mark of an open democratic society? In the same vein I characterized *Politika*'s coverage of the street demonstrations as a disgrace. The front pages were covered with details of visits of Greek Socialist youth leaders or the Israeli prime minister's visit to the Occupied Territories. Nothing could be found about the demonstrations. I asked Milošević to reflect carefully on what I had said and in particular to let me know his thoughts on my suggestion of a panel of international legal experts. Milošević brought the meeting to a close by promising to do so, adding ruefully that we had had a very frank exchange. He would ponder further. Meanwhile I reflected wryly on the surrealist image of a soft-hearted Milošević, a man who had cut off more people at the legs politically than Procrustes, acting against his better judgment in reinstating a worthless crook like Ilić.

A few days later, a group from the leadership of the democratic opposition approached me to see whether I could arrange a meeting with Milošević to try to find an accommodation. They made clear that the massive street demonstrations that had almost spontaneously filled Belgrade since the election fraud was perpetrated did not have as their aim the overthrow of Milošević, whatever the rhetoric from some quarters implied. They simply wanted the restoration of the election victories that they had gained. I agreed to pass on the request, which I did in a letter to Milošević in the interests of speed. If the two sides could meet, agree on the restoration of the election results, and begin a dialogue, it could mark the beginning of a more normal democratic political life in Serbia, something that up till then was entirely lacking.

I received no reply to my letter, nor was there any sign publicly that the two sides would meet. It was some months later when it emerged that Milošević had met secretly with Zoran Djindjić, the president of the Democratic Party and one of the three leaders of the Zajedno coalition—and later prime minister and assassinated in office. Meanwhile other members of the opposition who were opposed to meetings with Milošević spun their own line to the press. According to this fantasy, the idea of a dialogue between Milošević and the opposition was being proposed by Western diplomats to throw Milošević a lifeline with the aim of maintaining him in power, by implication to keep the Dayton Agreement alive.

As the proposal for a dialogue had come from elements of the opposition themselves, and as I had acted purely as a nonparticipating conduit, I was distinctly irritated but not surprised at this line of mendacious briefing. I regretted having allowed myself to be used as a conduit, as some members of the opposition and media in Serbia never accepted and never believed that Milošević was far from being the pet of the West. His role in securing agreement at Dayton was indispensable, but the Dayton Agreement has been sustained by all his successors. Despite inherent weaknesses, its failings are most conspicuously due to the parties within Bosnia. Unfortunately both politics and the media's perception of politics were at an immature stage of development for which the regime, as the main beneficiary of this retarded state, was very largely to blame.

The street demonstrations continued unabated. Original twists were provided by the leaders of both the student and the main political demonstrations. Trash can lids were drummed to drown out the main evening news on state television; cars were driven to the city center to have a collective breakdown with hoods raised to bring Belgrade to a halt; unflattering effigies of Milošević and his wife were dragged in floats through the main pedestrianized area of Belgrade. And every day the leaders of the Zajedno coalition maintained the crowd's enthusiasm, good humor, and control during a winter of discontent, which finally emerged in a Belgrade spring of hope for real democratic change.

Although the results in Niš were indeed reviewed and partially restored, and Ilić was sacked from his job and expelled from the party, the overall electoral fraud was clearly a long way from being reversed. Armed with a stiff message from the Foreign Secretary, I returned to the charge with Milošević. This was by some measure the most difficult meeting I had with him. The prospects for a successful meeting had in any case been substantially soured by the regime's attempts to take B92, the leading independent radio station, off the air the previous week. Within an hour of hearing from the embassy press attaché, Julian Braithwaite, that it had been shut down, I had driven to the studios of B92 to offer my support in person to Veran Matić and Saša Mirković, the leading luminaries. On my way out I was approached for a statement by other media that were still on the air and a selection of the foreign press. Asked for my reactions, I said that we regarded it as a very negative, retrogressive step, a denial of press freedom that could only be damaging to Serbia and its people. I promised to raise the matter at the highest level, praised peaceful demonstrations, and called for maximum restraint on all sides and the avoidance of violence. When I returned to the embassy I spoke to Carl Bildt, the High Representative for Bosnia, who was in London for the conference on Bosnia, which was about to start, and asked him to raise it publicly and privately with the Yugoslav foreign minister, Milan Milutinović. Bildt did so to very good effect. Within a day B92 was back on the air.

When I saw Milošević, I began by saying that the temporary disappearance of B92 had been another ill-judged and inept performance by the Serbian authorities that had further alienated the world community. Milošević claimed that it was all a technical problem. At no stage had it been off the air. I said that he was badly misinformed. I had tuned in to B92 to find that there was no broadcast. Milošević replied that he had been assured by his experts that the problem was technical and that they had even helped B92 to repair it. I said that while he might believe that, nobody else, not even for a moment, would believe that the regime would help B92 overcome their technical problems. The idea was laughable.

Milošević countered by saying that he did not know why the West should be so badly informed about the election saga. Only a small percentage of results had been disputed, and after a rerun the opposition had won some and the government others. The opposition now ran Kragujevac, Novi Sad, Čačak, and other important towns. He claimed with a straight face that he had been glad to hear the first reports of the opposition victory in Belgrade. He thought that this would put his party in the city on their mettle. But the election process had to take its course, and the final result came only when the referee blew his whistle and all disputes and complaints had been adjudicated. (Other insider accounts painted a very different picture of Milošević in the blackest of moods, shouting that he was not prepared to live in a city run by the opposition.)

I said that we could argue about this all night. Nobody believed that the results in Belgrade and Niš were other than fixed. Milošević said that the powers of local councils were very limited. All the more reason, I replied, to let the opposition run them. There then followed a futile discussion on the limitations of his presidential power. I said that that statement would not wash either. Was he seriously trying to pretend that he was not all powerful within the regime? He claimed that the judges—none of whom he had met for two years—were above the executive and could not be influenced. I said that it was not my job to suggest that the executive should override the judiciary. I was simply saying that there was a political problem that he had to sort out politically and that would not go away as far as the international community was concerned.

At this point Milošević's mood turned ugly. He flared up when I made a reference to the demonstrators. They were, he claimed, being manipulated by the Bosnian Serb leadership. Completely untrue, I said. I had spoken to many of them; never had the word "Bosnia" crossed their lips. The police, he went on, came to his office begging to be allowed to sweep the demonstrators away. A pity, I said, because I was about to congratulate him on their professionalism and restraint to date. He warned that he could crush the demonstrators at a stroke. Indeed, he was under pressure from Kosovo Serbs ("the hard men") to allow them to come to Belgrade in a counterdemonstration. If they came they would soon crack a few heads. He was protecting the demonstrators from their wrath, but there was a limit to his patience. If the demonstrators resorted to violence, the police response would be swift and decisive.

I said that I could only warn him most solemnly that any action that was seen as an infringement of the right of peaceful demonstration would attract a virulently hostile Western reaction and would set back Yugoslav integration into the international community by many years.

During this point of the conversation, the noise of that day's demonstrations could be clearly heard outside his window, which no doubt contributed (as did his substantial whisky intake) to his mounting anger. He claimed that the number of demonstrators was far below the figures quoted in the international media. He went to great pains to explain how scientific assessments of actual numbers could be made by enlarging television pictures of the demonstrations. I was never sure where the figures for demonstrators came from or whether Milošević was right in claiming that it could be scientifically gauged. One international journalist told me that the numbers of demonstrators was deliberately kept high and exaggerated to persuade foreign editors that the story was still a runner and worth keeping correspondents and crews in the field. Every day there would be a general consultation, and the highest figure would usually become the accepted standard. My own defense attaché carried out his own scientific survey daily and regularly reported figures about a third of those adopted by the international press corps. Whatever the truth of the matter, I saw no need to give Milošević any satisfaction on this point. I told him again that the actual numbers did not matter. The perception abroad was that a very significant number of people were protesting on a daily basis against what they rightly saw as an infringement of a basic human right, free and fair elections.

In an even more agitated state and with frequent obscenities, he went on, "If you are here to represent your country, then you are welcome; but if you are here to settle the affairs of Serbia, you are not." He then added, "Believe me, if I were not here in charge, it would go very badly for Serbia." I avoided the obvious rejoinder. I was already on pretty thin ice. "Certainly," I replied, "Serbia would be a very different place in your absence." I then added that I would try to explain why I was in Belgrade. I was trying to promote overall British interests in the region—bringing Yugoslavia into a closer relationship with Europe by encouraging the nation to match up to the democratic norms that modern Europe demanded. I had asked him to choose in our previous conversation between Europe and running the local government. He repeated the overriding importance of the European Union, but he could not accept blackmail. I said that there was no blackmail. The wound was self-inflicted. We wanted to maintain a dialogue, but it could not be an open-ended commitment. The present circumstances were making it impossible to help the Federal Republic normalize—indeed, the process was going into reverse.

As I left, I asked him to reflect very carefully on what I had said and to calculate what on balance over the last two and half years would have been better for him—following my advice or that of his closest advisers (coded language for his wife). He replied, tight-lipped, that he always thought carefully about what I had said. I concluded, "It has never been more important to do so than now."

In commenting to the Foreign Office on this extraordinary exchange, I said that Milošević was behaving like a cornered and wounded animal. Whether he seriously believed that he was the offended party or whether it was all make-believe was almost irrelevant. He was in his present mood fully capable of acting irrationally and against his own and his country's best interests. I concluded that it was important to maintain a dialogue. A pressure cooker approach in his present dangerous mood could lead to violent explosions elsewhere (for example, in Kosovo) to distract attention from the events in Serbia proper.

We both had time to reflect carefully about the contents of our exchange. I was given the Zimmerman treatment.[1] I had been blacklisted. I was not received for five months, having crossed the Rubicon between diplomatic candor and outright interference, in his eyes. It was to be late April 1997 before I saw him again and then only briefly at the federal president's reception for Constitution Day. It was, diplomatic corps excepted, very much a gathering of the great and the bad. All ministers were on parade, as were the federal and republican presidents and their prime ministers. Milošević was all smiles, regretted that he had not seen me for some time—as though it had all been a question of congested diaries—and suggested that we should meet as soon as he got back from a few days holiday over "our Orthodox Easter" (interesting timing for a convinced atheist).

Shortly after my stormy meeting with Milošević, Foreign Minister Milutinović, in a modest gesture toward the international community, invited the former Spanish prime minister Felipe González to head a delegation from the Organization for Security and Co-operation in Europe (OSCE) to investigate the crisis over the election results and to recommend ways to resolve it. His lightning visit just before Christmas 1996 left the authorities in no doubt about what to do: reverse the electoral fraud, open up the state media, reform the judiciary, and begin a genuine democratic dialogue with the opposition. As the initiative to bring in the OSCE belonged to Milutinović, so it was natural that he should be blamed for what Milošević and his hard-line cronies saw as a disaster. It was hard to know how else they thought Gonzalez would have reacted to the situation he found. But they were clearly furious. Yet again, as they saw it, outside bodies had come to Yugoslavia, and to Serbia in particular, to meddle, to fail to understand, and to pursue their own agenda.

In high dudgeon with the international community, Milošević retreated further and further into his laager and away from all advice likely to point the way out of the impasse. His sources of counsel came increasingly from the hardliners in and around his wife's circle. The demonstrations continued. Milošević tried unsuccessfully to settle with the students (a classic Tito ploy) and to ignore the main demonstrators. Eventually after about one hundred days of demonstrations and with a last flourish of police brutality, Milošević caved in and introduced what he called a *lex specialis*. Circumventing the legal niceties, he had finally produced a political solution to the crisis his associates had created for him. As it was done in the most begrudging way, it earned him minimum political credit with the opposition within the country and with the democratic world outside. He had rarely looked weaker.

Just then, however, the opposition came to his rescue. Having been feted round Europe (including a slightly problematic visit to London, where Zoran Djindjić hoped to be lionized on his own), the Zajedno leaders forsook their whistles and trash can lids and set off for a meeting with Madeleine Albright in New York. When they returned, their fragile unity was finally fractured. Djindjić was forced to admit after initial denials that he had held a secret meeting with Milošević some weeks earlier; Vuk Drašković became increasingly mistrustful of his coalition allies and, in particular, queried Djindjić's commitment to support his (Drašković's) candidacy for the Serbian presidency—a post that Milošević had to relinquish by the year's end. And even the saintly Vesna Pešić of the tiny Civic Alliance wearied of Drašković's tactics of imposing deadlines and ultimatums on his coalition partners.

So Milošević's ship of state, having been apparently holed beneath the waterline, was able to right itself and sail on into more serene waters, at least temporarily. Zajedno had disillusioned their hundreds of thousands of supporters who had braved the elements throughout the winter for three months. It also disappointed the hopes of many in the West, who saw in the demonstrations the prospect of a real revolution in the political landscape of Serbia, a revolution that could bring Serbia out of the permafrost of isolation to which the actions of the Milošević years had consigned it.

Although the election crisis was behind us, the new situation posed at least as many problems. Egged on by his wife's Marxist dialectic, Milošević continually strove to promote conflict and chaos among enemies but occasionally among his ostensible friends as well. The question we had continually asked ourselves—was Milošević capable of genuine democratic and economic reform?—now seemed to have been answered definitively in the negative. But what did he actually want? Any analysis of his motivation had to begin from the premise that his makeup was intrinsically flawed. Roosevelt famously, if risibly, assessed Stalin as having some of the attributes of a Christian gentleman, perhaps because he had originally trained for the priesthood. Even though Milošević's father had actually become an Orthodox priest, nobody was inclined to see shades of a Christian gentleman in Milošević. He was both deficient in Christian values and obsessed with the need to retain power at all costs, thus lacking the first fundamental attribute of a democrat. He was not prepared to accept the verdict of the ballot box. Being out of power for Milošević imperiled his future and, given the attentions of the International Criminal Tribunal, his freedom.

But it was too simplistic to think of Milošević as merely an old Communist who had grafted on some nationalist body armor to protect himself from political attacks from the right. His comment that Serbia would be in a bad way without him was almost certainly the very opposite of the truth, but it certainly seemed obvious to me that without Milošević his Socialist Party would fall apart.[2] It resembled more a collection of satellites circling around a sun (a particularly inapposite metaphor for Milošević) motivated by no consistent ideology and powered by his patronage. The nationalist wing had been out of favor in the recent past but was poised to make something of a comeback to ward off the threat from the ultranationalist Radicals. There was no threat from the left. The Yugoslav United Left (JUL), led by Mirjana Marković, Milošević's wife, and formed in 1994 by merging nineteen left-wing parties (principally the remnants of the true Marxists in the old League of Communists of Yugoslavia), filled that gap. JUL declared itself to be a party of all those "left-wing and progressive forces that believed that the general interest always comes above private interest." Thanks to its leader, JUL had enjoyed influence out of all proportion to its public support, but following the street demonstrations of the winter, a decision appeared to have been taken to lower JUL's flag.

It was equally clear that Milošević's attachments to the Dayton Agreement process was, as it always had been, regulated by what he believed he could get out of it. He had evidently concluded that the Americans were committed to preventing any concessions to him and would do their best to discourage others from doing so. With the lifting of UN sanctions, the penalties for him in behaving badly were in any case much reduced. It was therefore a question of making it worth his while if we wanted his active rather than grudging support for Dayton. Apart from Bosnia, it was equally obvious that whether he chose to address fundamental questions of reform, political and economic, of human rights (notably in Kosovo), and of democratization would depend on the game from his perspective being worth the candle. This argued for a policy of constructive engagement, as I recommended to the Foreign Office at the time, rather than containment, however distasteful this prospect was for Western governments. It looked highly improbable that Milošević would ever get around to trading in expediency for conviction or follow the example of Anwar Sadat and actually get a taste for a role as peacemaker and international statesman. Moreover, his card was too heavily marked for him ever to get the benefit of the doubt in many capitals. But as he was a man only marginally older than Tito in 1945, it was wishful thinking to plan on the basis that he would soon be off the scene.

CHAPTER 14

Bildt's Farewell and the B92 Saga

After Milošević's Orthodox Easter break, I was duly invited to call. I had some Bosnia-related business to conduct on behalf of the High Representative, Carl Bildt, but most of the discussion was on Kosovo. I argued at some length in favor of Milošević's allowing the EU to open an information office in Kosovo. I pointed up the anomaly that the United States was allowed to have an office there while continuing to enforce a unilateral trade embargo against Serbia while the EU, which had recently granted autonomous trade preferences to Yugoslavia, was kept out. Milošević maintained that the U.S. Information Office flowed from an old cultural agreement between the former Yugoslavia and the United States. No such agreement existed with the European Union. I said that this was essentially casuistry. Was he prepared to accept an EU office in Priština if the EU as a whole upgraded their diplomatic relations with Yugoslavia? Milošević said that he would have to think about it. He did not rule it out. I said that I could not see how it was a matter of principle given the presence in Priština of the U.S. office. I was putting forward on a personal basis a deal that had something to offer him in exchange. Moreover he had frequently told me that the long-term OSCE missions had provided balanced and objective reporting of the situation in Kosovo. If the situation there was as normal as he liked to maintain, he ought to welcome objective reporting of that fact. This remained one of the "if only" questions. A deal in such clear-cut terms was never formally put on offer by the EU, and Milošević's attention wandered elsewhere.

Nevertheless, by contrast with our showdown during the demonstrations, this, like most of my final conversations with Milošević, was a tame affair: the chemistry had altered. There were no fireworks, no histrionics. The general mood tended to be subdued. There was much complaining and griping about Holbrooke and the United States, who had, he claimed, "double-crossed" him. He was very proud of his command of this idiom and asked whether I was familiar with it. I explained that it was a well-worn phrase on both sides of the Atlantic. He had been promised at Dayton, he maintained, full normalization and had seen instead an outer wall of sanctions erected. On closer inquiry it emerged that—in Milošević's account—Holbrooke had given a "best endeavors" undertaking to see what he could do within the administration and with Congress about normalization. Nothing more concrete and certainly nothing in writing.

It was something of a relief, therefore, to accompany Carl Bildt on his farewell call on Milošević and to see some sparks struck again. Carl went straight on to the attack, complaining of the Bosnian Serbs' delaying tactics in failing to ratify the package of legislative proposals that would enable the Bosnian central government to start working effectively. He laid the blame for the problem squarely on Karadžić and Krajišnik. When Milošević said that Karadžić had been on an enforced holiday for the last twelve months, Bildt quickly contradicted him. On the contrary, Karadžić was active and had been in Belgrade. Milošević claimed that Bildt had been misinformed, or perhaps deceived. Bildt insisted that Milošević call Krajišnik to Belgrade to force him to accept the laws and appendixes as soon as possible to allow a donors' conference to go ahead. Milošević was distinctly unenthusiastic. Bildt offered to supply Milošević through me the following day with some additional arguments that Milošević could deploy with Krajišnik and that would underline that failure to endorse the package would lead to very real losses of World Bank and other international projects. Milošević finally agreed to summon Krajišnik to Belgrade in two days. He hoped to see results by the next day.

The farewell lunch that followed concluded with some reflections on the calamitous events of summer 1995 and in particular the atrocities committed by the Bosnian Serbs in Srebrenica. Bildt provoked Milošević, saying it was difficult to avoid the conclusion that a green light had been given from Belgrade. When Milošević bridled, Bildt said that he had in mind the Yugoslav army's green light. Milošević, still prickly, said that Mladić's actions had been criticized in military circles in Belgrade, as the general feeling was that he should have been giving higher priority to events in western Bosnia. But Bildt had accurately touched a raw nerve. There may well have been involvement of the Yugoslav army and Serbian paramilitaries in the attack on Srebrenica. If the Yugoslav army was now criticizing Mladić, it could only be with the perfect vision of hindsight, but it was more likely that they either colluded in the attack or participated in it.[1] My defense attaché never picked up any criticism of Mladić on the grounds of mistaken priorities at the time, nor, of course, any criticism of Mladić's atrocities in Srebrenica. It was as though they had never taken place.

My last months in Belgrade were overshadowed mainly by Kosovo but also by the threat to the network of independent radio stations set up at the instigation of B92 with considerable help from the BBC and from the British embassy. At the beginning of 1997 at the height of the demonstrations, I had convened a lunch with Veran Matić and Saša Mirković of B92 to ask them how we could put our help to them on a higher footing. Our previous most practical help to B92 came through bringing in funds for the station through Budapest under diplomatic cover. One of my diplomatic staff would travel up to Hungary or Austria, pick up the cash for B92, and then bring it back into Yugoslavia, thus avoiding the risk that Milošević would find a way of confiscating funds coming from abroad to help B92. Now with the increased focus on democracy in Serbia with the end of the war in Bosnia, it meant that we expected to be able to access increased funds. B92 asked for time to think about it and quickly came back with a well-thought-out plan to bring their news service by satellite to a chain of similarly independent radio stations throughout Serbia and ultimately Montenegro and Republika Srpska. We, the BBC, and B92 worked on this plan for many months. My press attaché, Julian Braithwaite, was particularly deeply involved, and by the summer B92 was ready to launch the program. When the BBC insisted on an enciphered signal, this involved us in providing decoders for each of the independent members of the chain. As the authorities would certainly have confiscated them if they had been delivered through normal postal channels, I arranged for them to be imported under diplomatic privilege. I then technically loaned the equipment to B92 and to the network members free of charge. As they remained the embassy's property and could be reclaimed at any time, I hoped thereby to avoid the threat of their being confiscated by the authorities.

The chain became something of a runaway success, the downside of which was the attention it began to incur from the Serbian customs and telecommunications authorities. B92 was asked to provide details of how and when the decoders were imported. I wrote to the head of Customs, Mihalj Kertes, a particularly close Milošević crony, to explain that the goods were the property of the British embassy and were on free loan to the radio stations. I thought that this would satisfy the authorities, and so, for a time, it seemed to. Through a friendly ministerial contact, Danko Djunić, however, I heard a few weeks later that Milošević was furious and looking to disrupt the network at whatever the cost. My egregious interference in the strategic plan to keep the Yugoslav media muzzled had been raised in Cabinet, and suggestions were made that I should be declared persona non grata—in other words, expelled.

The helpful advance warning allowed the Foreign Office and me to prepare our defense, in consultation with B92. When the anticipated summons from a senior official in the Foreign Ministry came very early one morning as I was having breakfast, he claimed that I had broken the terms of the Vienna Convention on diplomatic relations between states by importing decoders that I had then passed on to the independent media without paying customs dues. I denied that I had broken any article of the Convention. I had imported property that remained the embassy's. The accusation was nothing but a thinly disguised attempt at censorship, curbing what limited press freedom existed in Serbia. If the government persisted, I would do my personal best to ensure that the FRY's trade preferences with the European Union were revoked. My interlocutor said that the offending decoders must be withdrawn within forty-eight hours. I said that this was preposterous. It would not be physically possible to assemble and re-export them in that time scale even if I accepted that we were obliged to do so, which I did not. I demanded that he pass on my comments, particularly about the threat to trade preferences, to Foreign Minister Milutinović urgently. Reflecting the views of the Foreign Office lawyers, I added that if, on the other hand, the Yugoslav government was merely worried about the loss of customs revenue from decoders that, while remaining British embassy property, were being used by others, I was prepared to consider payment of the customs dues. The senior official repeated his script, which clearly left no room for individual initiative.

I left to consult B92 about the next step. They were adamant that if the government insisted, they would prefer the decoders to be removed from the studios and either stored by the embassy or reexported. What they did not want was an opportunity or opening created for the authorities to raid their premises to remove the decoders, which would inevitably result in a good deal of deliberate collateral damage. Some of my colleagues in London and Washington believed they should second-guess B92. We should insist, they said, that the decoders stay in place and defy the authorities to remove them. I did not believe it was right to expose the radio networks against their clearly expressed wishes. We were not the ones likely to suffer the damage and intrusion of government raids. Fortunately our bluff worked; the next morning while I was again having breakfast, I was telephoned by the senior official and asked to call again. This time he said that if we agreed to pay the customs dues, that would be the end of the matter, as far as the government was concerned. Clearly the prospect of the withdrawal of trade concessions had swung the argument. And, incidentally, I never heard anything more about customs fees. I did, however, hear from the Foreign Office lawyers that I had been acting against diplomatic conventions in passing on equipment imported under diplomatic privilege (even on loan) to third parties. Such equipment had to be used for diplomatic purposes only. I decided that far from giving any satisfaction to the FRY authorities, it was best simply to ignore this advice. I never heard anything more about that either.

With the prospect of a premature departure removed, I prepared to spend my last weeks focusing as much as possible on Kosovo, where the situation was beginning rapidly to deteriorate.

CHAPTER 15
Kosovo

Kosovo had been a crisis waiting to happen. In a sense it has been waiting to happen since October 1912, when Serbian soldiers reoccupied Kosovo in the First Balkan War after more than five hundred years of Ottoman rule. The battle of Kosovo of 1389 was a major turning point in Serbian history, though as Noel Malcolm points out, it was not the decisive factor in destroying the medieval Serbian empire, nor did it lead to the yoke of Ottoman rule overnight.[1] But as he also correctly underlines, even if the earlier Turkish victory at Marica in 1371 was arguably the more decisive battle in the overall Ottoman conquest of the Balkans, the battle of Kosovo Polje "has become a totem or talisman of Serbian identity, so that this event has a status unlike that of anything else in the history of the Serbs."[2] In 1939, the Serbian Orthodox bishop Emilijan of Timok said on the 550th anniversary of the death of Prince Lazar of Serbia at the battle of Kosovo, "Beside the name of Christ, no other name is more beautiful or more sacred."[3]

"Those who quote history do so because they believe history—or their version of it—is on their side," says Professor Roy Foster, reminding us that Daniel O'Connell, speaking in the House of Commons on the repeal of the Union between Britain and Ireland in 1834, prefaced his remarks by saying, "I shall be as brief as I can upon this subject."[4] But O'Connell persisted in giving a lecture on Irish history from 1172, which took up forty-six columns of Hansard, the parliamentary record, before approaching the present day. The Serbs will, if you allow them, talk at similar length on the events down the years since 1389 before addressing the present reality. The reality, of course, is that present-day Kosovo is occupied largely by Albanians—a little short of 90 percent of the population by most objective assessments.

The events of the fourteenth century can be discussed at length by historians, with revisionists contradicting the orthodox while the revisionists themselves may merely be repeating previously orthodox versions, and so on down through the palimpsest of historiography. The twentieth-century history of Kosovo is less open to interpretation and revisionist theories. The capture of Kosovo by the Serbian army in the First Balkan War in 1912 may have been the culmination of a dream for the Serbs, but it was a nightmare for the Albanians. The war correspondent for the Ukrainian newspaper *Kievskaia Mysl*, Leon Trotsky, a man not noted for his squeamishness, professed himself shocked by the atrocities committed in that war by the Serbs and Bulgarians. In his book *The Balkan Wars* he describes the entry into Kosovo as told by a Serbian officer: "the horrors actually began as soon as we crossed into Kosovo. Entire Albanian villages had been turned into pillars of fire.... The picture was repeated the whole way to Skopje. There the Serbs broke into Turkish and Albanian houses and performed the same task in every case: plundering and killing."[5] Edith Durham was forbidden to visit Prizren by the authorities because they did not wish her or the British military attaché to see the mutilations of noses and lips that had been carried out on captured Ottoman soldiers. The aim of the brutality, as the Carnegie International Commission on the Balkans found in 1914, was "the entire transformation of the ethnic character of regions inhabited exclusively by Albanians."[6] This would strengthen the Serb case when the Great Powers met to discuss territorial changes again as they had done previously in 1878.

The London Conference of Ambassadors (of the Six Great Powers of the time) in 1912–13, called to settle the boundaries of the region after the First Balkan War, ended up by satisfying nobody. The Serbs failed to get an outlet to the sea; Montenegro had to give up the strategically valuable city of Scutari, which they had besieged for months and finally captured; Greece was forced to renounce its claim to southern Albania; while the Albanian state, which was created at the conference, left more than half of the total Albanian opposition outside its borders largely in Kosovo and thus under Serbian sovereignty. This unsatisfactory compromise was a result of the overriding concern of the Great Powers to reach a settlement that kept the Powers away from each other's throats. Sir Edward Grey, who had played the mediating role between the pro-Albanian (or, perhaps more precisely, anti-Serb) position of Austria-Hungary and the Russians, who were openly supporting their fellow Orthodox brothers, Serbia and Greece, accepted nevertheless that "many criticisms could be raised of the border agreement by anyone who knew Albania and viewed the issue from that country's standpoint." The agreement that headed off a major confrontation between Russia and Austria-Hungary merely bought a few months' respite as the events of summer 1914 finally provoked the cataclysm. But the legacy of injustice and the unfairness of the frontier survives to the present day. In his bitter parting words, Isa Boletini, the leader of the Albanian delegation to the Ambassadors' Conference, threatened, "When spring comes, we will manure the plains of Kosovo with the bones of Serbs, for we Albanians have suffered too much to forget."[7]

The Serbs' war of liberation—seen by the Albanians as an act of colonization and oppression—was quickly negated by the Serb reverses in the First World War. By 1915, Serb armies were withdrawing from Kosovo in an epic and tragic march to the Adriatic, whence the survivors were embarked for Corfu and ultimately for reinsertion in the celebrated Salonika campaign. The Serbs lost an estimated one hundred thousand troops on the journey to the Adriatic through Kosovo and Albania. Relatively few losses, however, could be ascribed to Albanian attacks on the retreating army, although they were not averse to extorting money for free passage. Those who could not pay were left behind to die. For the remainder of the war Kosovo was divided up into various occupation zones, and the Austro-Hungarian authorities promoted the opening of hundreds of Albanian language schools in a determined effort to minimize the Serb presence in the region. A month before the Armistice of November 1918, Serb (together with French) troops reentered Kosovo with predictably awful results for the Albanian civilian population. In turn, guerrilla warfare against the Serbs was carried on by Albanian rebels known as kaçaks (from a Turkish word meaning "fugitive"). Their "armed resistance spread in many parts of northern and Western Kosovo in the early months of 1919. Serb reprisals were extremely severe."[8] The rebellion continued in varying degrees of intensity until the late 1920s.

The peace treaties of 1919/20 gave no satisfaction to the Albanian population of Kosovo. Yugoslavia was recognized as a specifically Slav state, "the Kingdom of Serbs, Croats and Slovenes." And this despite the evidence of the 1921 census, according to which 64 percent of the inhabitants of Kosovo were Albanians and more than four hundred thousand Albanians were to be found in a Yugoslav population of twelve million. The remainder of the interwar period saw a strong focus by the Serbs on assimilation through the Serb language. Moreover, the colonization process was underpinned by successive settlement programs affording generous land allotments, building of settlements, houses, schools, and churches at the expense of the Albanians. This process was complemented by the state's official encouragement to the Albanians to emigrate. A more vigorous campaign of encouraged immigration faltered as the Second World War intervened.

The German invasion and dismemberment of Yugoslavia in April 1941 led to the larger part of Kosovo being incorporated into Italian-occupied Albania the following month. The Italians played on the Albanians' desire for unification of the nation in one state, encouraging the Albanian language and allowing the flying of the Albanian flag throughout the area of Kosovo under their control. While the Albanians were largely collaborating with the Italians and Germans, the Serbs and Montenegrins in many cases faced the option of leaving Kosovo or being forced to labor in the mines. Those who avoided this Hobson's choice overwhelmingly favored the Chetnik resistance led by Draža Mihailović. Partisan resistance was originally on a very small scale and eventually owed what success it had to the growing strength of the Communist Party of Albania, whose party secretary, Enver Hoxha, ruled postwar Albania with an uncompromising Marxist-Leninist rod of iron for nearly fifty years.

Anti-Axis Albanians in Kosovo were still largely reluctant to join the Partisan Communist movement despite the formation of a Balkan general staff after meetings between Hoxha and one of the most gifted Partisan generals, Montenegrin Svetozar Vukmanović-Tempo. To gain Albanian support it was stated explicitly that the postwar Yugoslavia would be "a country of free people and there will therefore be no place in it for national subjugation of the Albanian minority."[9] The Yugoslav and Albanian Communists eventually agreed that the question of the future borders should not be addressed during the war. The overriding priority, as Hoxha put it, was that "Kosovo Albanians should fight fascism within the framework of Yugoslavia. . . . The problem of Kosovo will be resolved after the war by the two sister parties and the Albanian people themselves."[10] Vukmanović-Tempo stated in similar terms that the question of the future borders would "be resolved by brotherly agreement . . . on the basis of the right of self-determination of nations. How the borders will be drawn will depend on the evolution of the political situation in Yugoslavia and Albania."[11] These assurances did not prove entirely convincing to the Albanians, and with the likelihood of an Allied victory they expressed the hope that the Allies would organize a plebiscite to allow the population of Kosovo to make their own determination.

In the meantime Albanian attacks on Serbs and Montenegrins in Kosovo continued into the spring of 1944, prompting the emigration of up to ten thousand Serb and Montenegrin families mostly to Serbia. However, by the end of November with the withdrawal of the Germans from Greece through Kosovo, the whole of the territory was liberated by the Partisans. The customary appalling score settling followed.

The political chemistry between Tito and Hoxha—a master-servant relationship in Noel Malcolm's phrase[12]—took place against the background of proposals pushed forward by Tito. These proposals, presented to Stalin in Moscow by Milovan Djilas, aimed at the creation of a Balkan federation to include Yugoslavia and Albania, whereby Kosovo and Albania would be united. Stalin's reaction was predictably crude. "'We have no special interest in Albania. We agree to Yugoslavia swallowing Albania! . . .' At this he gathered together the fingers of his right hand and, bringing them to his mouth, he made as if to swallow them."[13] At a later meeting, however, he expressed himself as more interested in a Yugoslav-Bulgarian federation first. "A federation between Yugoslavia, Bulgaria and Albania. . . . This is a federation that should be created and the sooner the better. Right away if possible, tomorrow. . . . Agree on it immediately." When the leading Yugoslav party ideologue, Edvard Kardelj, observed to Stalin that a Yugoslav-Albanian federation was already in the making, Stalin was firm: "no, first a federation between Bulgaria and Yugoslavia, and then both with Albania."[14] These proposals were effectively buried by Tito's growing split with Stalin and by Hoxha's decision after the decisive rupture in 1948 to throw in his lot with Moscow. Had the federation idea prospered, it seems highly probable that Kosovo would have been part of a federal unit—a separate republic with Albania within the larger federation.

When I first visited Kosovo in early 1994 with Douglas Hogg, I was struck by the warm memories still retained of Tito. His portrait could frequently be seen in shops, a phenomenon also found in the Sandžak and in Sarajevo. But, as Noel Malcolm underlines, the Tito years were very far from being a period of unqualified Yugoslav concessions to Albanian aspirations. "The first two decades of Communist rule were particularly harsh, and the dominance of Serbs and Montenegrins in the Party and State security apparatus meant that the Albanians there still had very much a second-class position. The resentment created by this initial imbalance of power set up an oscillating dynamic of reaction and counterreaction—Albanian reaction to the Slavs after 1966, and Slavs counterreaction in the 1980's—which made Kosovo's internal politics all the more bitter and intractable."[15]

The question of what status Kosovo should enjoy within Yugoslavia was also a major topic in the immediate postwar discussions by the Yugoslav Communist Party. At a meeting in Prizren in July 1945, a resolution was passed providing for Kosovo to become a constituent part of Serbia and through Serbia with Yugoslavia. The following month, legislation was passed formally creating the autonomous provinces of Kosovo and Vojvodina. Some saw, in the attempts to subdivide large areas of Serbia, the elaboration of a policy to reduce Serbia's overweening influence within Yugoslavia as a whole—the "weak Serbia: strong Yugoslavia" thesis based on the Leninist doctrine for resolving nationality questions in multinational states. (No other republic experienced the creation of autonomous provinces within its territory, despite the attempts by Moša Pijade, a leading Partisan, to persuade the Central Committee of the merits of creating autonomous Serb regions within Croatia and the original plan to make Bosnia an autonomous region of Serbia.[16]) Others saw in the creation of the Kosovo province the kernel of the old idea to bring Albania into a Balkan federation, which Tito would undoubtedly have expected to lead. As we have seen, the split between Moscow and Belgrade buried the idea of a Balkan federation, with Albania and Bulgaria becoming, in fact, two of the most loyal satellites of Moscow.

In the late 1940s and 1950s, the strong hand of central administration, as exercised particularly by Aleksander Ranković, variously federal interior minister, vice president of Serbia, and security chief, led to frequent and extensive purges of those suspected of being pro-Moscow or pro-Hoxha among the ranks of the Albanian Communists in Kosovo. (Hoxha and his media, in turn, reported extensively on the persecution of Albanians in Yugoslavia who were encouraged to revolt against Tito.) On the other hand, the Yugoslav government kicks were matched by some kindness in the field of education and culture. There was an enormous deficit to overcome, as the 1948 census showed over 73 percent of the Yugoslav Albanians to be illiterate. New Albanian language schools were opened; there was a drive to train new school teachers because there was a desperate shortage; and numerous cultural societies, theaters, and reading rooms were set up in the early postwar years.

This limited cultural flowering, however, was not extended to the freedom to display the Albanian national flag. In 1956 the display of Albanian flags all over government buildings and schools led to a strong response from the security police, who stepped up the sporadic campaign to pressurize Albanians to emigrate, mostly to Turkey. Harassment increased, and given the authorities' apparent expectation that every household would possess a weapon, many Albanians ensured that they had one in order to have something to hand over. Economically, although Kosovo received substantial investment funds, as its growth rates were lower than those in any other part of Yugoslavia, it became relatively poorer and poorer. The 1963 constitution led to a downgrading in Kosovo's status, transferring from the federal government to the Republic of Serbia (and indeed to all the republics) "the right to establish autonomous provinces in areas with distinctive national characteristics." Kosovo therefore became a "socio-political community within the Republic" of Serbia. However, with the removal of Ranković in 1966 (after it was revealed that he arranged for the bugging of Tito's conversations and, moreover, was actively opposed to Tito's decentralization policy), the situation in Kosovo began to ease.

Tito paid his first ever visit to Kosovo the year after Ranković's disgrace, an event that marked a significant turnaround in the authorities' attitude to Kosovo. The more favored policy toward Albanians may have ignited some signs of affection for Tito, but it also raised national awareness. This was fostered by a marked thaw in Yugoslav-Albanian relations in the wake of the Soviet invasion of Czechoslovakia, an event that worried both leaders. In 1968 the constitution was amended to restore Kosovo and Vojvodina to their position in both the federal and republican structures. However, toward the end of that year disappointment at the failure to secure improved autonomy if not republican status for the region led to major demonstrations, in which several policemen and students were seriously injured and one Albanian killed. In neighboring Macedonia, there were calls for the Albanian areas to join with Kosovo to form an Albanian Republic within Yugoslavia. The Albanians in Kosovo at least secured the right to fly the Albanian flag, a concession that would have been unthinkable under Ranković, and that did nothing to assuage the increasing fears of the Kosovo Serbs at the direction Tito's policies were taking.

The measures that had been taken to improve education gradually brought an increase in the percentage of Albanians holding significant posts in the state and security structures. For the Serbs, used to being top dogs, finding that the majority of policemen were now Albanian came as a shock and became one of the key factors in the events leading to the rise of Milošević to power.

These were, however, still early days. Albanian successes in turning around the oppressive situation under Ranković were crowned by the 1974 constitution, the last of the three that Tito introduced and the one that Milošević once described to then UK foreign secretary Malcolm Rifkind at a dinner in Belgrade as Tito's greatest mistake, the solvent that broke up Yugoslavia. The two autonomous provinces of Kosovo and Vojvodina now received a status almost commensurate with the six republics. Although they continued to be part of Serbia, they were fully represented on the Federal Presidency and frequently took pleasure in voting with other republics against the Serb representative. Having their right to promulgate their own constitutions rather than having such documents promulgated for them by the Serbian Assembly gave them the status of a federal unit. To have gone any further would have created a major crisis within Serbia proper, and it was not a step on which Tito, even freed from the pro-Serb influence of Ranković, would have lightly embarked. The theoretical reason to draw the line at republican status was the Leninist distinction between nations and nationalities. Only a nation could form a potential state-creating unit, that is, a republic. A nationality having a mother state outside Yugoslavia (e.g., Hungary for the Hungarians of Vojvodina and Albania for the Albanians in Kosovo and Macedonia) could only aspire to being a nationality.

The 1974 constitution is frequently harked back to by those who see it as the model of a modern form of autonomy. Certainly at its time it was said to be the most decentralized constitution in Europe, only to be exceeded subsequently by the post-Franco Spanish constitution. But while it caused substantial disquiet among the Serbs, it aroused expectations and disappointment in equal measure among the Kosovo Albanians. In 1981 a trivial incident at the University of Priština involving a cockroach in the soup of a student led to massive protests that quickly escalated from demands for better living conditions for students to calls for a Kosovo Republic. The Yugoslav army and tanks were finally sent to the streets, and security police were brought in from all over the country, culminating in the declaration of a state of emergency. Officially only nine people were killed, although local hearsay (probably exaggerated) put the number of dead at more than a thousand.[17] Whatever the correct figure, hundreds of Albanians were sentenced in the trials that followed—some to a few months in prison, others up to fifteen years. The classic Communist purge followed with the president of the League of Communists in Kosovo, Mahmut Bakalli, being expelled from the party Presidium. A new leader was promoted, a leader of the Young Communists and a protégé of Tito, Azem Vllasi. But while the authorities concentrated on political measures to resolve the situation, the primary cause, the economic and social problems of Kosovo, was left unaddressed. The unemployment level was the highest in the country, and despite reforms, Serbs and Montenegrins held a disproportionately high percentage of jobs in the swollen public sector. Meanwhile Serbs and Albanians continued to trade accusations and insults. Both sides were accused by the seriously alarmed government in Belgrade of nationalist tendencies, and increasingly strident Serb claims were made of aggression against Serb men and rape of Serb women. Objective evidence was, as usual, hard to come by, though it seems clear that most of the Serb claims were greatly exaggerated, while not wholly unfounded. But however concrete and objective the evidence suggesting that the situation was not as bad as was claimed, it is unlikely that it would have cooled the increasingly heated level of comment and debate.

In 1986 a draft memorandum drawn up by leading figures in the Serbian Academy of Sciences and Arts, inspired by the thoughts of the nationalist writer Dobrica Čosić but drafted by a working group under the chairmanship of academician Antonije Isaković, brought together in one document most of the Serb grievances, real and imaginary. The document, although only a draft and not released in full until three years later, created a sensation when it was partially leaked in September of that year. It was quickly condemned by the Serbian president, Ivan Stambolić, and the head of the Belgrade Party Committee, Dragiša Pavlović. Although the Serbian Party Central Committee also condemned the document, no public denunciation was issued, at the insistence of the general secretary of the Serbian League of Communists, one Slobodan Milošević.

The memorandum is widely credited with being the starting point of the rebirth of Serbian nationalism. It was, in fact, nothing of the sort. If the memorandum had never existed, it is highly unlikely that events would have developed differently. Nor did it exist in isolation. Academics and intellectuals on both sides were regularly putting forward ideas and opinions that were inflaming the already fragile situation. Indeed earlier that year, 216 leading academics had presented a petition to the Yugoslav Assembly complaining of the "genocide" to which the Serbs in Kosovo were subjected. When some six months after the leak of the memorandum the more militant Kosovo Serbs asked Stambolić to address them in the town of Kosovo Polje, a stone's throw from the site of the famous battle, Stambolić ducked out and sent his trusted protégé, Milošević, instead. The rest, as they say, is history.

Having, as we have seen, defenestrated his patron, Stambolić, in the aftermath of the notorious Eighth Plenum, Milošević moved quickly to strengthen his position nationally, first by bringing the two autonomous provinces under tight Serbian control. He organized a series of protests and demonstrations, using the Committee for the Protection of Kosovo Serbs and Montenegrins headed by Miroslav Šoljević—a main organizer of the protest meeting in Kosovo

Polje addressed by Milošević in April 1987—as his stalking horse. Within less than a year there had been close to a hundred demonstrations involving around five million people.

In December 1988 Milošević addressed nearly one million supporters in Belgrade, calling for the ending of Albanian terror in Kosovo and the continuation of his reform process. Milošević at this stage liked to cloak his nationalist program with the respectable veneer of an "antibureaucratic" revolution. At the same time Milošević removed from the Kosovo leadership his main Albanian adversary, Azem Vllasi, and substituted a stooge, riding out the inevitable demonstrations and banning future ones. When the ban was flouted, the continuing strikes and protests gave Milošević the excuse to introduce emergency measures and to arrest Vllasi, who was accused of "criminal acts." Under the threat and intimidation of Serbian arms and tanks, the provincial assembly of Kosovo voted in March 1989 to accept constitutional amendments (passed by the Serbian Assembly a month earlier) that considerably reduced the status and powers of the autonomous provinces. Milošević was careful to ensure, however, that the provinces still retained their separate and quasi-republican status at the federal level, thus allowing Milošević, through his placemen now installed in Kosovo, Vojvodina, and the Republic of Montenegro, to control half of the eight seats on the federal Presidency.

While Milošević was thus engaged in a centripetal strategy to bring all the republics gradually under his control, his policies were weakening the only genuine central political body, the federal government, and convincing the leaders of the other republics—some of whom needed no persuasion—that, faced with Milošević's bullying and strong-arm tactics, they had no future in Yugoslavia. It was Milošević himself who sprinkled fertilizer on the seeds of secession, which in Slovenia and Croatia had already been sown.

The next few years saw a return to the colonialist policies of the post–First World War era with renewed attempts made at enforced emigration, the enactment of property laws that discriminated against Albanians, and the dismissal of the vast majority of Albanians working in the state sector. When the Serbian Parliament finally dissolved the Kosovo Assembly and its government in July 1989, the Albanians responded by proclaiming a Republic of Kosovo and in 1990 held an underground referendum in which 99 percent of those who voted were said to have declared themselves in favor of a sovereign independent Kosovo.

In December 1989 the LDK, the Democratic League of Kosovo, was formed, electing the president of the Association of Albanian writers, Dr. Ibrahim Rugova, as its leader. More of a movement than a party, the LDK and Rugova thereafter became the dominant forces in Albanian political life in Kosovo. Rugova, who was frequently dubbed the Kosovo Gandhi and who wore a trademark scarf round his neck on all public occasions, sought to follow Gandhi's principles of peaceful resistance to the relentless Serb oppression. He sought at the same time to use every opportunity to internationalize the Kosovo issue and to resist the international community's insistence that even with the breakup of the old Yugoslavia (SFRY), Kosovo should remain part of Serbia and consequently of the new Yugoslavia.

I met Rugova many times over my four years in Yugoslavia. The conversation tended to be circular and repetitive. Rugova would describe how bad the repression currently was and give me graphic illustrations. He would then ask for international help and recognition of the independence of Kosovo, perhaps as a first step going through the transitional process of UN trusteeship. I would praise Rugova's restraint in the face of huge provocation but urge him, as a good democrat, to take part in normal political life. The LDK and other Albanian parties would be able to exercise considerable influence in local, republican, and federal government if they took part in the elections. Rugova would explain that to take part in elections would compromise his rigid position on nonrecognition of the Serbian state. I would explain why the international community could not agree to support Kosovo's independence but promised that we would continue to work on Milošević to remove the repression and restore autonomy to the province.

The word "autonomy" was not, in fact, one I used often, as it carried unfortunate resonances for both Serbs and Albanians. For the Albanians it was by definition not independence and therefore inadequate; for the Serbs it was a reminder of the status the autonomous provinces enjoyed under the 1974 constitution, which they blamed for the breakup of Yugoslavia. The term of art that the UK and the United States favored was an "enhanced status." One of my American colleagues, when asked to define what was an acceptable level of autonomy or enhanced status, put it succinctly but bluntly: "It's like pornography. You'll know it when you see it."

Rugova was always exceptionally friendly and warm—kisses were invariably exchanged. We spoke in French as he did not wish to speak in Serbo-Croat, and we usually spent some time meeting on our own. After an hour or so, we would repair to his favorite restaurant, where his arrival was treated like a state visit. The guests and the staff would get to their feet as Rugova entered. He claimed that his security people insisted he sit in the same seat with his back to an outside wall.

It was never clear to me whether this was on grounds of physical security—to thwart any attempt at physical attack or assassination—or of technical security to prevent the bugging of his conversations. If the former, my own limited contact with security people suggested that best practice would dictate he should move seats rather than occupy a fixed regular position. On one occasion we had the clearest evidence that the restaurant was bugged. After a discussion at lunch over the exclusion of Albanians from sports facilities, we set off to visit a sport stadium run by the Serb authorities. Remarkably when we got there two of the first three practitioners in the stadium we were introduced to claimed to be Albanians. One looked suspiciously like a Serb to me. No doubt the strain of finding two or three compliant Albanians in such a compressed time scale was too much.

I was once asked by an Albanian journalist whether I found conversations with Rugova boring. I said that the question missed the point. I felt not boredom but a sense of frustration that despite countless rounds of talks we never seemed to be moving the agenda along. It was as though Rugova's academic background made him more rigid than conventional politicians. I could not detect his exit strategy if the situation remained deadlocked. Indeed, I could at a pinch have transposed my last conversations with my first. It would have been hard to tell the difference. There was nevertheless something touchingly dignified about Rugova's determination to avoid violence and his patient belief in the validity of his own strategy. I did not share his confidence in its wisdom. I believed he was being too passive and should have taken more risks, taking initiatives in proposing dialogue with the Serbs, preferably without preconditions, but on the understanding, negotiated if necessary by a third party, that if he agreed to face-to-face talks there should be an amnesty for those convicted of political offenses. I would happily have helped to broker such a meeting, but it was better to leave it to an organization such as the Community of Sant'Egidio, which had no international persona.

Another Kosovar figure, Adem Demaqi, who spent nearly thirty years as a political prisoner (hence his sobriquet of the Kosovo Mandela), was a marked contrast: a vibrant, dynamic personality, argumentative, quick tempered, and violent in gesture and language. Yet he reacted positively to many of my interventions, was prepared to see some merit in them, and hinted at flexibility in his position. Conversations with him were heady affairs: the language was powerful, his basilisk eye missed no detail of the arguments advanced, and the quick-wittedness of his reactions led to vigorous and spontaneous exchanges. There were no scripted speeches from Demaqi, but there were usually a few chain-rattling references to the imminent blood bath he graphically and confidently predicted if early progress on political status was not made. While it would have been perverse to enjoy our conversations, they were certainly highly stimulating. It was no surprise that Demaqi was later nominated by the Kosovo Liberation Army (KLA), the paramilitary group that brought Rugova's peaceful resistance policy to an end, as their political voice.

Conversations with Milošević on Kosovo were by comparison with Rugova far from circular, more a study in parallel lines never converging. "Not your affair. Don't interfere!" would be a polite summary. I was able to see at first hand with Lord Owen and Thorvald Stoltenberg in early 1995 how neuralgic a topic it was for Milošević. Later that year at a meeting between Malcolm Rifkind and Milošević just before Dayton, the Foreign Secretary and I pressed Milošević hard on Kosovo and the need for political progress. Milošević replied that he had something in mind in terms of the creation of regional assemblies in areas where non-Serbs were a majority. We asked him about timing; he suggested that it would be soon. Despite regular reminders from me, Milošević was continually evasive.

Shortly after the Rifkind visit, however, I called in Rome on Monsignor Vincenzo Paglia of the Sant'Egidio community, a body that had been active in helping to bring some of the most intractable African civil wars to an end. Paglia was now involved in secret negotiations on a rapprochement between Serbs and Albanians in the field of education. Milošević described him to me as the pope's Kissinger. Indeed a remarkable figure, he had worked extensively on Albanian questions both at the fall of communism and in the lead-up to the Kosovo crisis. One of his aims besides working for a Serb-Albanian rapprochement in Kosovo was to thaw out and restore some warmth to relations between the Vatican and the Serbian Orthodox Church. Paglia had brought a message to Milošević from Pope John Paul II to say that he would very much welcome the prospect of visiting Serbia. I asked Milošević what the realistic chances were of a papal visit. Milošević said that he was working on the more moderate of the Orthodox bishops (almost a contradiction in terms), as any decision would have to be voted through by the bishops as a synod. The patriarch, Milošević added, was not altogether there and was heavily influenced by the last person he spoke to (not one of Milošević's failings unless it was his wife).

I kept in touch regularly with Monsignor Paglia, offering advice and support where I could and transmitting messages occasionally to the players. I felt an instant rapport with Paglia. He wore his priestly office lightly and was as much at home in a Trastevere restaurant as in the corridors of Vatican power. His range of contacts was wider than most Italian cabinet ministers. He dined privately with the pope and was frequently consulted by the Italian prime minister. He could be by turn patient and mercurial but acquired the respect of both sides for his patent integrity, sincerity, and conviction that an accord could be reached. Eventually his efforts culminated in the signature of the education agreement between Milošević and Rugova in September 1996, although an earlier attempt at an agreement was scuppered by premature leaks.

At the same time I urged Milošević to move quickly to implement the education agreement. Procedural problems that were at root political held up matters for many months. For instance, there was a prolonged wrangle over whether Monsignor Paglia should take part in the three plus three commission of implementation of the education agreement or whether he should just attend the introductory lunch. After a wholly disproportionate lengthy holdup it was agreed that he should be a full participant. The problem highlighted the way Milošević was most anxious to keep third parties out of the negotiations, while the Albanians, ever distrustful of the Serbs, were equally determined to ensure that talks took place in the presence of an objective outside body.

By the time I left in November 1997, the international community was still attempting to head off violent confrontation between the increasingly radicalized Albanian students and the Serb police while lending its full support to Monsignor Paglia's attempts to breathe life into the education agreement. Some of my last days in Yugoslavia were spent in Priština working on this apparently intractable problem with other diplomatic colleagues.

Why after so many years of uneasy standoff—a stalemate between Serbian muscle and Albanian numbers that maintained a fragile stability—did the undeclared truce finally collapse? Given the increasingly frequent Kosovo Liberation Army attacks on Serb security officials and their Albanian "collaborators" and the customary Serb overreaction with indiscriminate and wholly disproportionate attacks on civilians, was the outbreak of violence inevitable? Did Milošević believe or allow himself to believe that he could get away with a crackdown on "terrorists," as the KLA was described by Bob Gelbard, Bill Clinton's special envoy to the Balkans? Certainly no diplomat worth his salt in Belgrade failed to remind the government regularly of this time bomb with a fuse of an uncertain length. I also reminded London of Milošević's tendency as the high priest of chaos and conflict to stir up trouble in one area when he was faced with difficulties and reverses in another. It struck me that there was a moment of considerable danger during the street demonstrations of winter 1996–97 when the combustible situation in Kosovo could have "gone critical." But Milošević was never given a clear opening as the Kosovars were prudently restrained and realistic enough to know that the opposition in Serbia were unlikely to achieve power. If they did, they were even less likely to make major concessions to Kosovar aspirations. The Kosovars were moreover deeply concerned at the anarchy and chaos in the mother country across the border. In Albania, President Sali Berisha, married to a Kosovar, was forced to stand down in the wake of a pyramid selling scandal and the subsequent breakdown of law and order throughout the country.

There were, I believe, three reasons why the fuse finally burned down. After the Dayton conference there was a sense of disappointment, almost disbelief, among the Kosovar Albanians that their grievances were not being addressed. This was compounded by the recognition of the borders of the Federal Republic of Yugoslavia by most members of the international community in early 1996. The Albanians asked repeatedly why they should be the only prisoners left in the remnants of the old Yugoslav state. If even the Slavs could not live together and the Croats, Macedonians, and Bosnian Muslims had all been granted their exit visas from the old SFRY, why should the Albanians who were not Slavs be forced to remain in a loveless marriage with the Serbs, their particular nemesis? A third factor was the failure to implement the education agreement concluded in September 1996 to bring Albanians back in to the state education system. The rise of the Kosovo Liberation Army can be traced to these factors and against a background of frustration and impatience with the Gandhiesque policies of their political leaders that had brought them no concrete results.

CHAPTER 16

Final Days

While Kosovo became the new crisis point in my last few weeks as ambassador (the student demonstrations were gathering momentum and appeared likely to lead to bloody clashes on the streets of Priština), Bosnia returned sporadically to the front of the stage. In a clear attempt to destabilize Biljana Plavšić, Karadžić's successor as Bosnian Serb president, Milošević had her temporarily arrested at the Belgrade airport, a move that backfired as it drove Plavšić firmly into the pro-Dayton and anti-Pale camp. Plavšić dissolved the Bosnian Serb Assembly and called new elections. Naturally Karadžić, Krajišnik, and the rest of the Pale clique were furious and did their best to enlist Milošević's help. Milošević alternated between supporting the Pale clique indirectly and playing the great statesman who was bringing the two conflicting sides in the Republika Srpska together.

Richard Holbrooke arrived in Belgrade that August partly to try to persuade Milošević to agree to surrender Karadžić to the War Crimes Tribunal. We met at the U.S. chargé's residence to exchange views. Holbrooke said that he did not believe Milošević would ever hand over Karadžić. What did I think? I said that Milošević, like most Serbs, regarded the tribunal as a body set up to assuage the West's bad conscience at not having done enough to prevent or intervene in the early stages of the Bosnian War. The tribunal was viewed in Serbia as less than impartial, indeed explicitly anti-Serb. As the tribunal had so far mainly indicted Serbs, it had a credibility problem in Serbia that Milošević had cynically exploited. But, of course, Serbs were not encouraged by the state media to ask themselves whether the heavy preponderance of Serb indictees might reflect the weight of guilt.

From my experience, I told Holbrooke, Milošević would do the bare minimum to "cooperate" with the tribunal. A few months previously during a call on Milošević, he mentioned to me that he had received a request from the tribunal to open an office in Belgrade. I told him to agree immediately. When he began talking about constitutional bans on extradition, I reminded him that all countries were obliged by the relevant Security Council Resolution to amend their constitutional arrangements or legislation to comply. Handing over a suspect was in any case legally different from extradition. But difficulties in accepting the full extent of the court's jurisdiction was no reason to delay the tribunal's opening an office in Belgrade. Indeed for Serbs who had themselves suffered at the hands of war criminals, a tribunal office would give them a chance to lodge their complaints and hand over evidence in security. Milošević was taken aback; he hadn't thought of that. Somewhat to my surprise, he then promptly agreed and instructed Milutinović, his foreign minister, to write back to the tribunal's president agreeing to his request to open an office in Belgrade.

I had no confidence, however, that this modest first step would lead to other than a cosmetic change in his attitude toward the tribunal. References to war criminals were only marginally less neuralgic points for him than talking about Kosovo. His favored line was that atrocities were invariably carried out by a small group of paramilitaries (but who sent, armed, trained, and provisioned the paramilitaries?). Any references to Karadžić's role in war crimes were always matched by suggestions that Bosnian president Izetbegović was equally guilty of the events of the war. Either both should be indicted or neither. There was never any suggestion that he shared in any way in the guilt for having started the war. He effectively suggested, and expected others to believe, that political leaders knew nothing of the activities of individual soldiers or paramilitaries and would certainly not condone war crimes.

My final obvious point in response to Holbrooke's question was that the strongest reason for noncooperation was Milošević's fear that the trail of responsibility would lead directly to him. His hope and belief was that public interest would eventually wane, and the tribunal would run out of steam and resources. He would have taken some perverse comfort from the fact that two years after the Croatian Operation Storm and the killing of so many civilians in and around Knin, nobody had yet been indicted by the tribunal despite Carl Bildt's clear attribution of responsibility to Tudjman.

A few weeks later, on my last full day in Belgrade, I took a visiting Foreign Office minister, Tony Lloyd, to meet Milošević. The conversation was almost exclusively on Kosovo. After listening with feigned interest to Lloyd's presentation and expressions of concern, Milošević told him that he had been misinformed. The situation in Kosovo when he had come to power had been very bad, with frequent riots and demonstrations and brutal ill-treatment of one community by the other. He had restored order to Kosovo, which was now quiet. If third parties did not meddle, it would remain so. Recent student protests had been fanned by international intervention, which had raised unreasonable expectations among the Albanian students. He hoped that the education agreement he had signed with Rugova would swiftly be implemented; he was working closely with the Sant'Egidio community to that effect.

I intervened to say that if Tony Lloyd had been misinformed, that was my responsibility. But speaking as someone who had visited Kosovo about twenty times in the last two or three years, compared to Milošević's own two (public) visits, I wondered whether it was possible that he had been misinformed. Certainly the Utopian picture he had described to Lloyd was light years away from my experience. The two communities in Kosovo lived depressingly parallel lives with no interaction. If there was no violence, it was because of the exemplary restraint shown by Rugova and his lieutenants in the face of an oppressive Serb presence. The Albanians' sullen resentment of the Serb state threatened to break out into something more violent if their reasonable grievances were not met. I urged him again to declare a political amnesty and to offer meaningful autonomy to the Albanians, as Lloyd had advocated. Milošević brushed all this aside. International interference was the root cause of tension in the province. He would implement political reforms in Kosovo in his own good time. In the meantime he would continue to work with Monsignor Paglia to promote the education agreement. Milošević was in his unflappable, patronizing "I know best" mood, brooking no contradiction from a newly arrived minister nor from a shortly-to-be-departing ambassador. After a couple of hours we broke off, having made little or no impression on him.

Lloyd continued on to Montenegro without me as I was in my last stages of packing. But having been summoned back for a farewell call on Milošević, I found myself, less than half an hour after the minister's departure, back in Milošević's presidential villa for a final tête-à-tête.

I found him busily engaged, as though he were the butler, in opening windows on the ground floor to dispel the clouds of cigar smoke he had created during the previous two-hour discussion. Having exhausted the topic of Kosovo, we spoke briefly about events in Montenegro.

Milošević's reference to Montenegro was surprising. It was the first time in our conversations that he had ever raised the situation in the sister republic. I assumed it had been prompted by Lloyd's imminent visit there. But it reflected a growing unease on his part at what he saw as the brash and arrogant behavior of the new Montenegrin president, the former prime minister Milo Djukanović. While Momir Bulatović (the Milošević placeman who had been installed at the time of the antibureaucratic revolution) was president, Milošević had a ready ally willing to accommodate him in all major and most minor questions. Bulatović had had one heady rush of independence in 1991,[1] but he had otherwise obeyed his master's voice with little or no protest.

A dissenting voice was occasionally heard from the Montenegrin foreign minister, Miodrag Lekić. I had previously met him in London in October 1993, where we hoped to engage his liberal views in a dialogue on how to promote a peace settlement and how to persuade Milošević and Serbia to play their full part in ending the war. Lekić, although only in his early forties, was a rare survivor of the pre-antibureaucratic revolution government. A nonparty man, he was seen at the green end of the spectrum of Montenegrin politics. "Green" in

Montenegro is not an ecological expression. "Green" and "white" refer to the pro-independent Montenegro and pro-Serbian positions taken by different factions in Montenegro's political life. The colors refer to the voting slips at the ballot in 1918 at which Montenegro was deprived of its independence, submitting itself to the Serbian monarch and subsuming itself into the Kingdom of Serbs, Croats, and Slovenes.

Lekić's views in private were highly critical of the war, particularly of the brutal manner of its prosecution, and of the absence of normal civic life in Yugoslavia. Having served as a diplomat in Italy previously, he was well aware of how a normal democracy functioned. While avoiding specific references to personalities, Lekić was sufficiently outspoken as to cause serious irritation to Milošević and in particular his wife. Bulatović initially protected him from the Serbian president's wrath, perhaps enjoying the idea of a licensed critic within the establishment. Milošević's wife, Mira Marković, however, took no pleasure at such indiscipline, which went against her every Communist instinct. As Lekić was extremely popular in Montenegro, particularly on the coast and in Bar, where he came from, a way had to be found to transform him to a suitably dignified position. He became Yugoslav chargé d'affaires, subsequently ambassador, to Italy.

His successor, sometime musician, sometime commercial consul in Milan, Janko Jeknić, was far more circumspect. Entertaining and liberal in his views in private, he gave neither Milošević nor his wife any cause to complain. But two years after taking office, he died in a typically dramatic Montenegrin car accident, driving at great speed around mountain roads in the middle of the night only to hit a lorry. His passenger, a young woman—not his wife—was seriously injured. Jeknić died instantly.

Yet it was at his funeral in January 1997 that the first stirrings of tension between Serbs and Montenegrins came to the surface. During that winter of discontent and demonstrations, Prime Minister Djukanović and some of his young ministerial colleagues were openly critical of what had happened in Serbia and of the needless crisis that had been precipitated.

To register their displeasure, the Serbian government boycotted the funeral, a petty, mean-spirited gesture viewed with disgust even by Montenegrins who regarded themselves as particularly close to Serbia. Together with a handful of Western colleagues, I had flown down to Montenegro for the funeral and was surprised at the Serbian no-show.

The situation deteriorated. Through Bulatović, Milošević pressured the Montenegrin government to discipline the recalcitrants. Djukanović reluctantly sacrificed one of his lieutenants to buy more time and to regroup. In April that year, the Yugoslav federal president gave a party to celebrate the new FRY constitution, which brought together the main political leadership from both republics and the federal government. Djukanović and Milošević met and, according to another witness (although I was an eyewitness, I was out of earshot), Milošević said to Djukanović, "So you're the one who wants to overthrow me," an outburst perhaps prompted by a Djukanović interview a few weeks earlier in which he had said, "I am convinced that it would be completely politically wrong for Slobodan Milošević to continue to occupy any post in Yugoslavia's political life. . . . Today Milošević is a man of obsolete political ideas who is not capable of strategically assessing the challenges that stand in front of our state." Unambiguous and blunt.

The conflict continued throughout the summer and culminated in Djukanović's challenge for the Montenegrin presidency in the autumn. In the first round, Bulatović narrowly led the field, with Djukanović a close second. In the deciding round, a loose alliance of anti-Bulatović/anti-Milošević forces including Sandžak Muslims and Albanians joined together to support Djukanović and edge out Bulatović. The OSCE who oversaw both rounds criticized the voting lists in the first round but endorsed the second round as being broadly fair. Milošević was disappointed and furious by turn with the endorsement for the person he was coming increasingly to regard as a menace.

During my farewell call, Milošević wanted, he said, my frank opinion of the recent presidential elections. I told him that I had been surprised that Bulatović, the former president, had led the field in the first round. The overwhelming impression I had received from visits to Montenegro over the summer had been of strong support for Djukanović. I had, however, seen them both between the two rounds and met a range of other political figures whose views had led me to expect a narrow Djukanović victory, which had, in fact, materialized. Milošević looked disappointed. What, he said, did I think about the obvious electoral fraud. I said that the OSCE observers had declared the elections broadly fair. Any fraud was probably fairly evenly distributed between the two sides. If the results were acceptable to the OSCE, they were good enough for us. What was not good enough was for Bulatović and the official Belgrade media to suggest that Albanians and Muslims (without whose support Djukanović would not have won) were second-class voters. Milošević said that this was a misreading. Bulatović had not been downgrading the status of the Albanians and Muslim voters but complaining that they had voted many times, up to ten in some cases according to information he had received. I said that I stood by my belief that any electoral irregularities were evenly balanced.

In the course of a discussion of events in Bosnia, Milošević claimed to have lambasted Krajišnik over his failure to play an effective part in the central institutions and to show up at the memorial service for senior UN officials recently killed in a helicopter accident. Krajišnik had claimed lamely to have been tied up with business on that day. Milošević had pointed to the presentational damage he had done to the Bosnian Serb cause, which was incalculable. If the Americans had managed to find time to come all the way from the United States for the memorial service, it was ludicrous of Krajišnik to claim not to have had time to come down the hill from Pale. Milošević hoped that the new electoral process in Bosnia would remove the present chronically bad leaders.

When I asked him about the Serbian elections, Milošević gave a broad but elliptical hint that he ultimately envisaged a situation where the posts of republican presidents were abolished. They were a leftover relic from the days of the former Yugoslavia and served no useful purpose now. I took this to be an expression of his frustration at the likelihood of having to deal with an antagonistic and recalcitrant Montenegrin president for the foreseeable future, but I could not see how Milošević could engineer the abolition of the republican Presidencies without provoking Montenegrin secession. As we were talking about Montenegro, I asked him whether his family were from the sea or the mountains there—an important distinction in Montenegro. He replied, "The mountains, the only true Montenegrins are mountain people."

He then asked me about my future. I told him that I was going to Oxford to set down my thoughts on the Yugoslav crisis. I had my own views on where mistakes had been made. Where did he think he had gone wrong? Milošević said that he had no doubt made many mistakes, but he did not keep a catalogue. "If I have one general feeling," he continued, "it is that I trusted people too much" (*sic*). Keeping a straight face, I moved him back to his early days in office. Milošević said that he had been incredibly pro-American initially. It was the United States that had been most resolutely against the breakup of Yugoslavia. He knew the United States and Americans well from his earlier incarnation as a banker and felt at home there. It was something of a shock therefore to find the Americans turning against him.

One of his biggest personal mistakes was his feud with the last U.S. ambassador, Warren Zimmermann. On the six-hundredth anniversary of the battle of Kosovo Polje in June 1989, Milošević had organized a big rally there that was attended by the leadership of all the republics, the whole of the diplomatic corps, and representatives of the central and local governments. The only notable absentee was the newly arrived Zimmermann, plus a couple of representatives of countries whom he had pressed into boycotting the event. As a result, Milošević had decided not to receive Zimmermann, and for over a year they had not met. Milošević said that, in retrospect, he had acted like a "stupid, stubborn fool." Zimmermann's enmity was to have long-lasting consequences, and he still felt its negative influence today in the outpourings of the State Department and from people like Vice President Al Gore. This was the most self-critical comment I ever heard Milošević make.

We then turned to some of the lost opportunities for peace. Milošević recalled his conversations with Izetbegović after the Slovene and Croatian declarations of independence. Izetbegović had been deeply concerned at the possibility of international recognition of Slovenia and Croatia as it would force him to face up to the choice he had hoped to avoid. Milošević recounted one exchange after the EU had (prematurely) decided on the recognition of Slovene and Croatian independence in December 1991. He had told Izetbegović: "I know what you are afraid of. You are afraid of us, of Serb domination in a Yugoslavia deprived of the counterweight of Croatia and Slovenia." Izetbegović nodded agreement. "You can become federal prime minister, if you stay with us." said Milošević. "You will then have nothing to fear." Izetbegović, under U.S. pressure according to Milošević, declined to place his trust in Serb goodwill and opted for independence. If Izetbegović had ever been tempted to accept the offer, Milošević's active policies to undermine the federal prime minister, Ante Marković, as described by Milošević's own representative on the federal Presidency, Bora Jović, throughout his book on the last days of the SFRY, could only have reinforced his judicious unease.[2] It is worth noting that while the Serbs were busy undermining Marković, the international community and the then EU troika in particular were partly at fault in marginalizing him, choosing to deal with the republican leaders rather than with the last best representative of the central (federal) government.

Milošević then talked at some length of the failure of the Pale Assembly to accept the Vance-Owen Peace Plan (VOPP) in May 1993. Milošević recalled how Yugoslav president Dobrica Ćosić, Montenegrin president Momir Bulatović, Greek prime minister Konstantinos Mitsotakis, and he had all gone to Pale to support the plan. After Karadžić had made a particularly (and typically) weak speech in favor of accepting the plan, it had been attacked by, among others, General Mladić. Milošević then intervened, speaking strongly in favor. His contribution, as he recalled it, had been received with a round of applause from the majority of the deputies. The assembly was at this stage poised to vote on the plan when Biljana Plavšić interrupted proceedings by demanding that the SDS party deputies meet urgently in caucus in emergency session behind closed doors. Krajišnik, the then parliamentary speaker, accepted her demand, and the SDS members duly trooped upstairs to a separate room, leaving Milošević and three other presidents steaming outside, provided with the occasional refreshment by bodyguards. When the deputies returned two hours later, having been harangued by Plavšić on their duties to the motherland and the betrayal that acceptance of the plan would involve, they voted overwhelmingly to reject it.

I asked Milošević if he realized then what a calamitous decision this was. He said that he had told the Assembly at the time that it would mean a great deal more bloodshed, but he did not appreciate the magnitude of the disaster until much later. He still felt that if the international community had been solidly behind the plan, they could have steamrollered the Bosnian Serbs into accepting. They were so close to having done so just before the disastrous Plavšić intervention. The whole course of the war would have been different, and indeed it could have ended within days. Milošević added that the Americans were already unhappy with the plan as they were unwilling to deploy ground troops to implement it. If they had strongly supported it, it might have had a chance. I asked whether his dislike of Mrs. Plavšić went back to that time. He said that was partly the case. But her remarks about accepting with equanimity six million Serb deaths in the greater Serb interest were grotesque.

The last major turning point on the road to peace that we discussed was the decision of the Bosnian Serbs in August 1995 to surrender their negotiating rights to Milošević. He said he had brought the whole leadership to Belgrade, political and military, to ensure that there would be no backsliding by any one of them. He had assembled the full panoply of the Yugoslav, Serb, and Montenegrin state institutions, including all the presidents, the commander of the Yugoslav army, General Momčilo Perišić, and significantly the Serbian Orthodox patriarch Pavle. When the Bosnian Serbs had signed the document that gave Milošević the casting vote in the joint delegation, he warned them that they would be bombed the very next morning as a result of the UN's attribution of blame to them for the Sarajevo market massacre a couple of days earlier. He told them that having spoken to the UN secretary-general's special representative, Yasushi Akashi, he could assure the Bosnian Serbs that the decision on whether to bomb them had now been handed over to the NATO CINCSOUTH (commander-in-chief, Allied Forces Southern Europe), Admiral Leighton Smith. The only way they could avoid being bombed was first to announce publicly that a full investigation would be carried out and that whoever was found guilty would be heavily punished; and second to start withdrawing all heavy weaponry twenty kilometers from Sarajevo.

The Bosnian Serb leadership had scoffed at this and had refused to accept that they would be bombed. Milošević repeated his warning. They continued to be openly derisive. He was, of course, right. The bombing had started at dawn, before they had even returned to their headquarters in Pale the next morning. Thereafter, their political and military positions weakened dramatically. The American smart bombs had certainly limited casualties, said Milošević, but they had been very effective in destroying communication centers and had left the Bosnian Serb army in total disarray. In fact, he added, he had rescued large amounts of territory for them at Dayton that had been lost militarily. (While true in some parts of the Republika Srpska, Milošević failed to point out that he had been forced to concede other key areas of territory, notably the Serb suburbs of Sarajevo, which had not fallen to the Muslim-Croat army.)

With that statement, Milošević brought my farewell call to a close. He walked me to the front door and wished me well. "You are welcome to come back to see me anytime," he concluded. It was an invitation I hoped it would not be necessary to accept. A few hours later, I flew out of Belgrade with mixed emotions: relief at the end of a highly pressured and frustrating mission, but regret that I had not been able to achieve more. If I had hoped to be able to make a difference, it had only been at the margin. The objective of bringing Serbia back in to the European mainstream was in most respects as elusive as ever.

CHAPTER 17

Secret Emissary

Four months later, I was back in Belgrade with little enthusiasm and certainly no optimism. The impending clouds over Kosovo had darkened further in those few months, and I was asked by the Foreign Secretary to go to see Milošević as his secret envoy. In one of his typically self-defeating gestures, Milošević was refusing to meet ambassadors, including my successor, Brian Donnelly. The Foreign Office thought we should capitalize on Milošević's open invitation to come back and see him anytime. I wasn't so sure, and I had no wish to undercut my successor, who was doing a fine job in very difficult circumstances. But the absence of dialogue was troubling, and the situation was getting more dangerous. So I traveled to Belgrade incognito and was met by Yugoslav government officials and taken to one of their guesthouses. The next day I met Milošević for three hours. Unusually he was accompanied by Serbian president Milan Milutinović and foreign minister Vladislav Jovanović, who were present throughout but largely silent. My meeting took place between a call by the Russian deputy foreign minister, Igor Ivanov, and the French political director, Jacques Blot, who was delivering a message from President Jacques Chirac. Milošević was at his most affable (plenty of "welcome back" bonhomie, etc.), but the genial mask dropped on several occasions throughout the long meeting. He gave every impression of being deadly serious about his approach to Kosovo.

When I expressed strong concern at both the violence in Kosovo and the threat that Kosovo posed to regional peace and security, Milošević replied testily that any country faced with a terrorist threat would have reacted the same way. The police operation had lasted a couple of days and had been exaggerated beyond belief. What, I asked, about the civilians? Some, he claimed, had been killed by the terrorist themselves (I said that this stretched credibility to its limits), but where errors or excesses had been committed by the security authorities, these were now under investigation just as we were now investigating the events of Bloody Sunday (*sic*).

Milošević continued to express his amazement at the international community's double standards. The special forces had reacted to a terrorist threat and had pulled out within two and a half days. I said that this contradicted everything I had heard and that our own representatives, foreign observers, and journalists had seen.

Milošević said that we were trying to exaggerate the scope of the crisis. Of course, there was a problem in Kosovo, but to describe it as a threat to world or regional security was absurd. The Turkish foreign minister had recently taken him to task about Kosovo; Milošević had asked him in return how the Turkish government was treating the fifteen million Kurds in Turkey. The minister had gone silent. There was much more in this vein.

I suggested that, as we were not going to agree on our respective assessments, we might look forward. This was a problem that had to be solved politically, not by violent suppression of violence. On the question of international mediation, I maintained that the climate created by recent events had raised the level of distrust to the point where it was wholly unrealistic to expect to make progress without outside help. I quoted Russian foreign minister Yevgeny Primakov in support: "Although the problem was of an internal character it was, like Georgia, one which could not be solved without international cooperation." I also mentioned the example of the Mitchell Commission in Northern Ireland. We were not too proud to accept outside help.

Milošević was not impressed. We were a powerful country with a veto at the Security Council (which we very rarely used, I pointed out). Nevertheless, he said, we would not permit the dismemberment of our country to be imposed on us by a UN Security Council Resolution. I said that nobody was proposing that. Repeated Contact Group statements had spoken of the territorial integrity of the FRY. Milošević countered that recent public statements by the U.S. representative for the Balkans, Robert Gelbard, had made it clear that the U.S. agenda was different. "Serbia is not an adequate framework for Kosovo." This encouraged the Albanians in the direction of Kosovo as a third republic within the FRY as a holding operation on the way to independence. Milošević stated that even Britain's political director, Jeremy Greenstock, had been caught up in Gelbard's rhetoric, referring on Studio B to "independence not being an option, *at least for the time being.*" I said that the international community had never excluded any option that the parties freely negotiated among themselves. But equally I had never seen any suggestion that the international community itself was preparing an independence option. On the contrary, every international gathering made specifically clear that that option was not supported.

I returned to the question of international mediation. Milošević said that Serbia's experience of this was disastrous. The EC Troika's role at the meeting in Brioni in Croatia at the outset of the Yugoslav crisis had paved the way for the breakup of Yugoslavia (no acknowledgment here, of course, that his own behavior might have played a part). Similarly the Felipe González intervention during the local elections crisis in December 1996 had been a bad joke. González had obviously written his report before he came on his flying visit. Elections, however, were not so important. They could be repeated in four years' time. But recommendations to dismember a country, if approved, supported by the international community, and implemented, could not be reversed.

I said that he misunderstood the role of the international community. We wanted to facilitate dialogue between the parties, not to prescribe an outcome, nor to promote any pet solution. The local elections saga had been different: it was clear what had gone wrong. Nobody pretended that the problem of Kosovo was other than complex and sensitive for both sides. I said that Kosovo had had a miserable history since the Serbs had regained it in 1912 after five hundred years of Ottoman rule. In the intervening eighty-odd years, there had been a dreary cycle of repression by whoever happened to be in control of the region at the time.

Milošević said that the borders of Serbia and Albania had been confirmed at the London Conference in 1913 and guaranteed by the UK, among others. How was it that while the Badinter Commission had fixed the previous administrative republican borders as the international borders, now Gelbard and others were claiming that only Serbia's republican border was to be regarded as still purely administrative? I said that Badinter had fixed the international borders only for those republics that wanted to become independent. As Serbia and Montenegro had chosen to stay together, their common external border was internationally recognized.

Milošević returned time and again to Gelbard, against whom he clearly had a particular animus, comparing him unfavorably with his predecessors: "He compensates for his inadequacies by his arrogance." Milošević had no intention of receiving him again. I said that it was perverse to focus on personalities. It would be the FRY that would suffer by isolating themselves from the United States, whose importance and clout in the region could not be adequately replaced. If Gelbard continued to enjoy his government's confidence, Milošević should see him. Milošević said that the FRY foreign minister would receive him correctly, but Gelbard's manner and his clear agenda to urge the Albanians to be patient while their wishes came true made him an unacceptable interlocutor (much was made semijocularly of a widely disseminated photograph of Gelbard and Rugova kissing).

When we turned to his proposed referendum about foreign intervention (which I likened to the Pale referenda so beloved by Karadžić and his crew), Milošević reacted sharply. Unlike Karadžić's referenda, the question about foreign intervention would be neutrally phrased. I replied that it would not be neutrally presented by the state media (we then had a passage of arms about the independent media and restrictions on it in Serbia). The result was not in doubt, but it meant nothing and would leave the international community wildly unimpressed. Milošević then revealed the reason behind the referendum. Quoting another public comment by Gelbard to the effect that he knew that the Serbian people wanted a different approach to the problem but were held back by their leaders, Milošević proposed to show Gelbard whether it was the leaders who were opposed to outside involvement or the people themselves.

Even Drašković, added Milutinović, had said that he would be voting against outside interference in the Kosovo question. I said that this was a ridiculous basis on which to organize a referendum. Leaders should lead, not set up time-wasting stunts. A sensible question might have been, Does Serbia want to rejoin the mainstream of Europe and accept Western European standards of behavior? I repeated that the present referendum would be pointless. The Albanians would ignore it completely; it would sharpen the divide in Kosovo and do nothing to promote dialogue.

Milošević said that I was wrong. Agreement was closer than we thought. He had already agreed with his colleagues when he was still Serbian president in the last year to put everything on offer for the Albanians except territory (i.e., no secession) and provided that it did not infringe the rights of the minorities in Kosovo, not just Serbs but also Montenegrins, Muslim Slavs, Turks, Roma, and so forth. The relationship between the Albanians and these minorities could not be one of master and slave (rich!). The difficulty, however, would come in persuading the Albanians to accept the offer while they believed that the United States and others were willing to countenance secession (this led to a further flat contradiction by me).

I said that if fully devolved self-government were on offer, why did he not say so? Jovanović intervened to say that would be bad negotiating tactics. Milošević, ignoring him, said delphically that the Albanians knew what was on offer: "We have had our contacts." (I learned subsequently that the former Kosovar Albanian Communist Party chief Mahmut Bakalli had recently met in secret with Jovica Stanišić, the Serb security chief. This may have been the contact referred to.)

Attempting to conclude, Milošević said that he was glad I had come. Although my Foreign Secretary, Robin Cook, had made some unfriendly remarks after they had met, he hoped that they could work productively together. If we had specific ideas to inject on self-government/autonomy, the Serbian government would listen to them carefully and wherever possible adopt them. I said that a productive outcome would depend on a constructive response to the international community. We were not going to go away on this issue. The path to remove international pressure was not through devices like a referendum but through a genuine political process. We remained very concerned that without international help such a process would not get off the ground. If it would help, we could offer a discreet location for talks outside the country. And there was no shortage of models for self-government, including Alto Adige and Catalonia.

We would also be prepared to underpin any agreement with language on territorial integrity. The return of the OSCE long-term missions would help calm the atmosphere in Kosovo. I recalled that he had told me before that they had done a good job. Milošević, in turn, reminded me of his "gentlemen's agreement" with Bob Frasure in spring 1995 to invite the missions back as soon as the FRY was readmitted to the OSCE. Christopher and Holbrooke had taken the same line at Dayton. All these undertakings had been broken.

I said that readmission to the OSCE was a matter of consensus. The only way back in and indeed into other international organizations was through tangible progress on human rights and political dialogue in Kosovo. But the Albanians did not have a veto. If they refused a deal on self-government because it fell short of independence, the FRY would not be penalized. We left it there.

After a break of about two hours, I then had a five-hour meeting (including dinner) at Milutinović's request with Bojan Bugarčić, formerly his chef de cabinet and recently appointed to the new position of foreign policy adviser to Milošević. Bugarčić was a highly intelligent, sophisticated operator and a closet opposition supporter. He was also prepared to be indiscreet. He began by saying that Milutinović hoped I would stay engaged. Milošević was prepared to listen to me. I said that I had no wish to stay involved. Our current ambassador would do an excellent job. Nor was there any point in my doing so unless I was making an impression. Bugarčić said that repetition counted for a great deal. I could not expect to achieve a breakthrough in one visit. I repeated that I was unenthusiastic. Bugarčić reverted to the matter of my remaining engaged at the end of the evening, adding that Milošević was not seeing ambassadors other than on protocol occasions now that he was head of state. And he wanted to cut down on seeing foreign visitors. He had only agreed to see Jacques Blot, the French political director, because he was bringing a personal message from Chirac. Otherwise he would not have been seen.

Milutinović understood and was seriously concerned at the damage done to the country by the recent police action. He and Bugarčić had been present when the Serb interior minister Vlajko Stojilković (a dangerous buffoon in my experience) had reported to Milošević on the police action in Drenica. It had been a travesty, referring to one or two civilians unfortunately caught in the crossfire. Milošević, however, had backed Stojilković (they were from the same town—Požarevac).

When I asked whether the full extent of the police action had been ordered from above, Bugarčić said that the orders had been for a limited operation against the terrorists. The disaster had occurred because the police units were frightened and had lost their heads. Rather than risk a house-to-house operation, they had called in heavy weaponry to raze the area and avoid any risk to themselves. I said that that single action had internationalized the Kosovo issue more effectively than years of Albanian lobbying. Bugarčić repeated that Milutinović was fully conscious of this.

I asked about Šešelj's incorporation into the Serbian government, adding that nothing could send a more negative signal to the outside world than to have a primitive like Šešelj in power. Bugarčić said that Milutinović had been most unhappy. It had been a party decision reached very late in the day after Drašković had overreached himself asking for nineteen out of thirty-six ministerial slots. Moreover, Milošević's view was that if he was going to make concessions over self-government for Kosovo, he wanted Šešelj to share the blame.

We discussed the importance attached by Belgrade to keeping Kosovo part of Serbia. Was it, I asked, a Serb fear of being outvoted in a federal structure by Kosovo and Montenegro, and could not Montenegro lay at least as much claim to a part in Kosovo history and mythology as Serbia? The great Serbian epic poem "The Mountain Wreath" (fiercely anti-Muslim), which quotes the heroes of Kosovo on almost every page, was written by a Prince Bishop of Montenegro. Bugarčić said that the idea of Montenegro as a distinct entity from a Serbian state was relatively new. The old epic referred to Montenegro as a geographical unit, not a political one. The real concern was the belief sanctified in the 1974 constitution that republican status conferred the right to secede. Moreover, said Bugarčić, if Kosovo were given republican status, he was sure that Montenegro itself would secede, believing it had lost its privileged status within the federation.

We talked through internationalization at length. The Serb logic, according to Bugarčić, was that if any international mediator were approved by the Serbs and proposed solutions on status that the Serbs could not accept, the mediator would be able to seek Security Council endorsement and approval of his ideas. The Serb position would be drastically weakened in these circumstances by the fact that the mediator had been invited by the Serbs. I argued at length that this was not the role envisaged for an intermediary. Bugarčić said maybe not, but their experience with Felipe González over the disputed elections suggested otherwise. It was a slippery slope they did not intend to start down. Moreover, any international guarantee against secession would be worthless if the United States had already set its mind on it. I took issue with this again. Bugarčić said that I should read carefully recent remarks by Robert Gelbard, Strobe Talbott, and Madeleine Albright. The Serbs had done so and come to a clear conclusion. Their country was to be dismembered.

I reported back to Robin Cook with my conclusions. The Serbs found themselves in a familiar position. Excoriated on all sides for their excesses and egregiously awful behavior, threatened with sanctions, and subjected to international pressure, they nevertheless believed that they were in the right, exposed to the West's familiar double standards and hidden agenda of secession for Kosovo.

While Kosovo as a third republic within the FRY could look to outsiders as an acceptable compromise, it looked to Serbs like the antechamber to independence. Although Milošević did not say as much, I was sure that what was preying on his mind was that the Badinter Commission ruled that republican borders could become international borders for those republics that fulfilled its criteria and wished for independence. Having granted Kosovo republican status, it would be impossible to deny it the right to self-determination enjoyed by the former SFRY republics.

In those gloomy circumstances, I saw no alternative to continuing patiently to work at promoting a dialogue, without preconditions on either side and perhaps trying to bring Rugova and Milošević together in secret. Even if a summit meeting were to be achieved, I concluded, direct dialogue between parties was unlikely to succeed for all the obvious reasons that both sides lacked the necessary imagination, political sophistication, and common sense to make the appropriate concessions.

Robin Cook sent a message back to say that he was grateful for my efforts. Meanwhile I returned to Oxford and silence . . . for another three months. Again I was asked to return to see Milošević privately. The situation had deteriorated further, and the United States was warning of a bombing campaign if Serb troops were not withdrawn from the province.

I accordingly had an hour and a half with Milošević in early July in Belgrade. He was some way below par and smoked a lot. He painted a typically one-sided picture of the situation in Kosovo. Guns were endemic in the area. The security situation would be fine if the KLA had not been encouraged by outside forces who wanted to see an independent Kosovo. I said that I did not know which outside forces he was referring to. But the international community continued to reject independence as an option for Kosovo. It was the situation on the ground that was creating a new dynamic. A third of the territory of Kosovo was no longer under Serb control, and this percentage was growing.

Milošević said that the only way forward was through dialogue. If he wished he could reverse the position on the ground in a week, leaving no KLA fighters. But he knew that would bring international condemnation. I said that he was absolutely right. Moreover, it would lead inevitably to the use of force against him by the international community. Many more recruits would come forward to fill the ranks of those eliminated. As he had said, the problem had to be solved politically. The United States, led by Holbrooke, was trying to fold the KLA into the political process. Milošević said that he would negotiate with Rugova, Adem Demaqi, and so on, but not with terrorists.

I reminded him that Tony Blair had shaken hands with Gerry Adams of the Irish Republican Army (IRA). But, said Milošević, he was a political leader. I said that Adams had previously been the chief of staff of the IRA. It was never comfortable to negotiate with men who had blood on their hands, but sometimes it was essential to ensure peace. If he understood my reference, he feigned not to.

On possible models for autonomy, Milošević said that he was working on a plan. But there was no point in showing it to the Albanians at this stage as they would simply denounce it as inadequate. His guiding principle was equality. "Albanians should have the same rights: no more, no less than Serbs in Kosovo." I said that this was acceptable as a proposition provided the Albanians, as the clear majority, had the right to take key decisions in matters appropriate for local self-rule. Milošević said he envisaged three "houses": one for the Albanians, one for Serbs and Montenegrins, and one for Turks, Roma, and other Kosovo minorities. Each house would decide on matters impinging only on their community. Matters common to all, such as water supply, would require consensus. At one stage Milošević referred to the Kosovars having a special status in the Upper House of the federal Parliament on a par with the Montenegrins.

I said that the three-house structure seemed cumbersome and unlikely to recommend itself to the Albanians unless their overwhelming population advantage in Kosovo was reflected in the relative weight of the houses. On reflection this looked like an elaborate way to ensure that the Serb minority could block decisions they were unhappy with.

Milošević described at some length the care his authorities had taken to avoid civilian casualties. I said that we appeared to be operating off two different scripts. I handed him a list of incidents involving excessive use of force covering the month of June only. He read it in total silence. I continued that he seemed to be badly informed by his Interior Ministry. If true, he should welcome effective international monitoring.

Milošević expounded his views on the KLA. Some were merely bandits and criminals. I said that some small number might be, but most were clearly politically motivated. Milošević did not deny this. He said that the hardest core were those organized and financed from Germany who were Marxist-Leninist erstwhile followers of Enver Hoxha. They were closely followed by the Islamic fundamentalists. Whose rise you have prompted, I interjected, not only in Kosovo but in Bosnia.

Continuing, I turned to the core Contact Group demand, the withdrawal of security forces from Kosovo. This led to a circular discussion: as the situation calmed down, so he would withdraw. I said that he had to take the first step. Without withdrawal of forces, Rugova and his negotiators would not have the necessary political backing to engage in the dialogue. They had already taken a substantial physical and political risk in meeting Milošević. Milošević made positive noises about the meeting and mentioned Veton Surroi (editor of the leading Kosovo newspaper) in particular as a future prime minister instead of Bujar Bukoshi. I urged him again to withdraw forces. Milošević asked who was going to protect the Serbs if he withdrew. Already many had been killed by snipers and over fifty kidnapped. How could he justify withdrawal at this stage?

I said that we did not expect him to leave the Serbs defenseless, but the security forces involved in excessive use of force should be withdrawn. He promised to consider whether some might be pulled out in the interests of kick-starting the dialogue. He then went on to refer to the NATO threats that he said were encouraging the KLA to believe that NATO would do its job for them. I said that the threat was very real and was still out there. But its aim was not to tilt the playing field in the KLA's direction but to prevent a humanitarian/refugee catastrophe. The international community did not support independence, but it was increasingly clear that international involvement was going to be necessary to bring about an agreement and to implement it. Bosnia was not Kosovo, but there would be considerable merit in an implementation force led by NATO. Milošević, after some thought, said that he did not need NATO to implement an agreement. I asked whether he was saying that he would not accept such a force. He repeated that it was not needed. Milošević concluded by saying that he hoped to see me again soon. I said that I would return only if there was something useful for me to do. He believed there was. I repeated the need for maximum restraint, particularly in Kijevo southwest of Priština. He said that he had been exercising great restraint there and would continue to do so. It was to be our last meeting.

Milošević had been less self-confident and sure footed than of old. He had been obdurate on withdrawal of forces, not surprising given his real domestic problem with the Radical leader Šešelj, who was always threatening to outflank him on the ultranationalist right. I believed he had taken on board the reality of the NATO threat, and there was just the chance that, as he thought more about a NATO implementation force, he might recognize that it could help pacify the region and act as a guarantor for both the Serb minority and for his borders. Having left Milošević in his palace, I went to have lunch with Serbian president Milutinović. Milutinović was frank, and what he said would have been treasonable to Milošević's ears. He favored partition as a solution to the Kosovo problem. The difficulty as he saw it was how to draw the map. There were more than a thousand orthodox monasteries and churches in Kosovo, which contributed greatly to the problem. He failed to mention the substantial mineral deposits and coal mines. I asked whether Milošević shared his view. Not surprisingly, Milutinović said that he didn't.

Milutinović claimed to be close to resigning, as he found himself virtually alone in the government in arguing for serious reform. I asked how he saw the situation on the ground. He gave me a readout similar to Milošević's. I gave him the list of incidents involving excessive use of force, which he read with animation. He said that he would go through them one by one with the Serbian interior minister Stojilković. I shared with Milutinović my low opinion of the interior minister. Milutinović disloyally agreed. It was a key position and ought to be filled by one of the ablest ministers, not the stupidest.

I said that there had been deep disappointment in London with the reply to Tony Blair's letter to Milošević. Milutinović was unsighted. I gave him copies of both. I said that I understood the reply had been drafted by Foreign Minister Jovanović. It was empty of content and bureaucratic in the extreme. Moreover, it took us no further forward. Milutinović agreed that it was a poor letter. He was clearly put out that he had not been consulted about it.

I reported Milošević's reaction on a NATO implementation force in Kosovo to Milutinović, who said that on this he agreed with Milošević's line. He then went on to ask why the FRY had not been asked to join Partnership for Peace. I said that the answer was simple. The FRY was seen as an aggressive force that was the source of a good deal of instability in the region. This did not make for a natural partner for peace. Milutinović said that if only the FRY were admitted to international organizations, it would have to clean up its act. I said that with the exception of OSCE, it was exactly the other way round. First you proved your peaceful and democratic credentials; then you were allowed to join. Milutinović asked what we wanted from the FRY. I said that it was spelled out in the prime minister's letter. We wanted peace in the region, the democratic deficit removed. On that basis we looked forward to the FRY's incorporation into the international community as Tony Blair had said. Unfortunately, we were a long way from that at present. Milutinović ruefully took this in good part.

I again returned to Oxford. Robin Cook seemed less interested in my report: I got no feedback, and there was no suggestion that he might find it helpful to meet.

CHAPTER 18

Aftermath

I had met with Milošević for the last time some eight months before the NATO bombing campaign. The campaign itself and the Rambouillet conference that preceded it have proved controversial. For supporters of the Blair doctrine of military intervention (Kosovo, Sierra Leone, Afghanistan, Iraq), Kosovo was the template. For others it was another example of a military intervention undertaken without an explicit Security Council Resolution. The Kosovo Liberation Army, described by the U.S. presidential envoy to the Balkans, Bob Gelbard, only months before the bombing campaign as "without any questions a terrorist group,"[1] had since the mid-1990s pursued a straightforward strategy toward their aim of independence. They would attack Serbs, particularly in the security forces, in Kosovo and Albanians working for the Serb state with the aim of provoking disproportionate Serb responses, ideally against Kosovo Albanian civilians, and thus prompting humanitarian intervention on the Kosovan Albanians' side. The KLA's military commander, Hashim Thaçi, made no bones about the KLA's aim to get the world's attention and internationalize the case for independence. Milošević duly obliged. After a massacre of some forty-five civilians at Račak, with its pale shades of Srebrenica, it was decided to convene a conference at Rambouillet to resolve the conflict.

Was the Rambouillet conference called with any other purpose than to provide an excuse to bomb Serbia? It depends on whom you ask. Certainly for Madeleine Albright and her close team, the aim was to hold a gun at Milošević's head. Richard Holbrooke in an interview said that Rambouillet was "doomed from the outset."[2] The Europeans once again were divided over their approach. Some, but not the British, were unhappy at the prospect of the use of force, and even the British Foreign Office lawyers argued that a specific UN Security Council resolution was required to mandate the use of force. Albright's response to Robin Cook was straightforward. "Robin, in that case get yourself some new lawyers."[3] Unlike the Europeans in some disarray, the U.S. team led by Albright had already decided what they wanted: a robust NATO presence in Kosovo. They also knew that it would take bombing to get Milošević to accept this. As Albright herself put it, "We always were clear that we were going to have to use military force in order to make Milošević think again."[4] Bill Clinton has underlined how Madeleine Albright pushed and pushed for the use of force against Serbia. An unconscious echo perhaps of Conrad von Hötzendorff, the Austrian chief of the general staff at the time of the First World War, who between January 1, 1913, and January 1, 1914, "proposed a Serbian war twenty-five times."[5]

Perhaps the most controversial aspect of the Rambouillet conference, and the one that led to accusations of a "setup," was the military annex that set out the terms for NATO's presence in Yugoslavia and Kosovo. It was presented toward the end of the conference, but there is still debate over whether it was negotiable or not. Its "silver bullet" clause granting NATO "free and unrestricted passage and unimpeded access throughout the FRY" has been criticized as opening the way to NATO occupation of all the FRY. Lord John Gilbert, a former British defense minister, in evidence to the British Parliament on November 18, 1999, said the terms put to Milošević at Rambouillet were "absolutely intolerable; how could he possibly accept them; it was quite deliberate." The Foreign Affairs Committee of the British House of Commons concluded that "whatever the actual impact of the military annex of the Rambouillet proposals on the negotiations, NATO was guilty of a serious blunder in allowing a Status of Forces agreement into the package which would never have been acceptable to the Yugoslav side, since it was a significant infringement of its sovereignty."[6] Historian Christopher Clark, contrasting the NATO ultimatum with that presented by Austria to Serbia after the assassination of Archduke Franz-Ferdinand in summer 1914, says, "The Austrian note was a great deal milder."[7] The Austrian note, incidentally, was so mild that Churchill described it as "the most insolent document of its kind ever devised." What he would have made of the NATO document, therefore, can only be a matter of conjecture. But if, as James Rubin (Albright's right-hand man and press spokesman at the State Department) stated, "Rambouillet was about getting clarity as to which side NATO should defend and which side NATO should oppose and that meant the Kosovar Albanians agreeing to the package and the Serbs not agreeing to the package," then it was not a NATO blunder at all but a deliberate decision to ensure that the Serbs played their allotted role and declined to sign.

Henry Kissinger put it more succinctly and to the point in describing the Rambouillet text as "a provocation, an excuse to start bombing. Rambouillet is not a document that an angelic Serb could have accepted. It was a terrible diplomatic document which should never have been presented in that form."[8] As Christopher Clark says, "The demands of the Austrian note [of 1914] pale by comparison."[9]

So Milošević realized that, short of allowing NATO forces to march freely over Serbia, he would be bombed, and he drew the dark conclusions. In retaliation, he "ordered Serb forces to step up their operations against the Kosovo Albanian population. In the weeks that followed, approximately 850,000 Albanians fled Kosovo before Milošević's forces."[10] And according to statisticians working for the ICTY prosecutors, some ten thousand Albanian civilians were killed by them.

It is, of course, the case that the Serb regime had behaved egregiously badly toward the Albanian majority in Kosovo, but presenting them with an ultimatum that was drafted to be rejected was to place diplomatic efforts on the back burner and convince Milošević, as he had made clear to me in our two conversations in 1998, that he saw the United States and NATO as being determined to dismember Serbia. So was it this threat to national sovereignty that stopped Milošević from signing? In part yes. But there was a personal motive too. With NATO troops free to roam around Serbia, he feared for his own skin: he might be overthrown or arrested for war crimes.

If he was being cornered, he could conveniently wrap himself again in the cloak of nationalism, if not to survive, then at least to go down as a great leader in the Prince Lazar/Nikola Pašić mold (both were defeated in battles 530 years apart). To go down fighting in what he hoped would be seen in Serbian eyes as a *Götterdämmerung* had its perverse attractions. And if we did bomb Serbia, he believed the resentment would linger down the decades. Centuries didn't follow each other in the Balkans: they coexisted.

Why did he give up, just when NATO was running out of legitimate targets? Now that Milošević is dead, we shall probably never know for sure. There are many theories, and obviously a combination of factors may have played their part. The key factor for me was the Russian decision conveyed by Yeltsin to Clinton on April 25, 1999, to work with the West to find a negotiated solution and to send former prime minister Viktor Chernomyrdin as his personal envoy to help in the process. Once Milošević realized that he had no vestige of international support, he decided to give in. All other factors—the effects of the strategic bombing campaign, Milošević's indictment for war crimes on May 27, the prospects of a ground war—were converging pressure points, but without Russian intervention on the West's side, they would have been unlikely to bring about a capitulation easily. It might well have taken a full-scale ground invasion to achieve that.

Milošević's downfall relatively soon after his capitulation marked the end of the worst period for Serbia since the Axis bombing of April 1941. But the prospects of a bright new dawn for Serbia proved and have continued to prove elusive. So many of the worst criminal elements of the Milošević period remained in positions of power and influence that it proved difficult initially to believe that any real improvement had taken place. One of the most depressing events was the assassination of Prime Minister Zoran Djindjić in 2003. When he became mayor of Belgrade in 1998, we arranged for him to receive English lessons from one of the British embassy wives. As prime minister he had made many enemies as a result of his reformist economic policies, his clampdown on organized crime, and his pro-Western stance (illustrated by his willingness to hand over Milošević to the ICTY). The relative ease with which Prime Minister Djindjić was assassinated was ominous and brought universal international condemnation. But it also brought an element of Western weariness with Serbia and the problems of Yugoslavia, a sense that, far from beginning a fresh chapter in Serbia's relations with the West, the ingrained criminality and corruption were too endemic to be extirpated.

Djindjić's assassin claimed that he was killed because he was a traitor to Serbia. But it is the criminal gangs who flourished in and were spawned by the Milošević era who are the real traitors. They may have played a part also in the yet unsolved mystery of how Serb war criminals evaded arrest for so many years. Supporters within the governments and military of the early post-Milošević years may have given tip-offs, funded or organized support networks, or generally proved reluctant or positively hostile to removing protectors of Radovan Karadžić and Ratko Mladić from key positions.

Continuous pressure to yield up the remaining war criminals on Serb soil finally proved successful, but the expectations raised, that compliance in this area would yield early and substantial benefits, have been disappointed. The path to EU membership, for so many Serb liberals the Holy Grail, looks long and tortuous. And the recent travails of the eurozone, including the Greek crisis, have in any event tarnished the EU's image as an economic beacon.

To look from the other end of the telescope, it is becoming clearer by the year that the West is losing interest in the internal affairs of Serbia. The problem of Kosovo is one the West wishes to see off the table as soon as possible, but if it continues to fester in a low-key way, provided the violence level is equally low key, then it will not engage the West's attention. Serbia's inability to achieve more in the fifteen years since Milošević was removed is a source of frustration and irritation to many in the West. But Serbia would be ill-advised to assume that because it was able to capture the West's attention for so long (for all the wrong reasons), it can continue to attract attention, sympathy, and support. The hollowing out of the middle class, the continuing high levels of corruption and clientelism, and resurgent elements of toxic nationalism combine to congeal the prospects of foreign investment without which Serbia, lacking natural resources, cannot hope to progress. EU membership looks unrealistic for the next decade. Serbia may ultimately have to settle like Turkey for a second-class status vis-à-vis the EU. It certainly doesn't help the case for membership of European clubs when the supporters of newly elected president Tomislav Nikolić in 2012 demonstrated outside the Democratic Party headquarters, celebrating the election win of their candidate by chanting: "We'll give you back Tadić [the pro-Western previous president]; you give us back Mladić."

If real progress on the arrest and transfer of war criminals was a benchmark by which progress toward EU membership was judged, and no country was more exigent than the Netherlands (racked perhaps by a bad conscience over

Srebrenica and the Dutch contingent's inglorious role), a fresh obstacle looks set to be placed in the shape of the recognition of Kosovo's independence. "It is hard to explain to Serbs why, when Milošević was still in power, a settlement was imposed which left Kosovo legally and formally part of Serbia. But having overthrown Milošević and lived according to the rules of the international community for the last seven years, the Serbs now face being punished by losing nearly 20% of their territory."[11] Previous concern that this might cause a read-across to Bosnia was dismissed ("a one-off case creating no precedents, with no application to Bosnia or to other 'frozen' disputes"). Nor would partition be allowed, as though recognizing the secession of Kosovo was not itself the partition of Serbia. Nor would Albania and Kosovo be allowed to unite, though this would make perfect sense. Why have two overwhelmingly Albanian states rather than one?

And why punish the liberals in Serbia, who were willing to put themselves in harm's way to get rid of Milošević, on the specious grounds that, seven years after his fall, Serbia had, through the sins of the Milošević period, lost the moral right to rule Kosovo? What about Russia in Chechnya or China in Tibet or the Spain of the Franco period in the Basque country? The answer lies in the events of March 2004 in Kosovo, which were described by Serb foreign minister Vuk Jeremić in 2011 in Chicago graphically thus: "In less than 72 hours, 35 churches and monasteries were set on fire, many of which date back to the 14th century or even further away in history, which represents an irretrievable loss for mankind. Dozens of people were killed. Several thousand were wounded. Thousands of houses and shops were levelled to the ground. More than 4,000 Kosovo Serbs were expelled from their homes."[12] While all or most of this was undoubtedly the case, it pales beside the thousands of Kosovars killed and hundreds of thousands expelled in 1999, which appeared to have been conveniently forgotten on the Serb side. But if the Serbs were hoping that the violence against them in 2004 was going to work in their favor, the opposite proved to be the case.

While the violence created consternation in the international community, it led the United States and the UK to be convinced that the status quo was becoming too dangerous. The eruption of Albanian frustration at the failure to achieve independence and at the NATO troops in the Kosovo Force (KFOR) persuaded British and American diplomats that a military force sent to interpose themselves between Serbs and Albanians risked becoming the object of hostility from the Albanian Kosovars. It was all too redolent of the experience of the British army sent to protect Catholics in Northern Ireland in 1968, who very rapidly became the object themselves of nationalist (Catholic) hatred and antagonism there. In a U.S./UK-choreographed performance, Kosovo declared independence on February 17, 2008, and recognition followed in days from the United States, the UK, many but not all the EU and Western countries, and crucially not China and Russia. Formal UN membership is unlikely, therefore, without a political settlement that satisfies Kosovo and Serbia. So far around half the UN members have recognized Kosovo. Serbia, however, suffered a setback politically when it pushed for an advisory opinion from the International Court of Justice on the legality of Kosovo's declaration of independence from Serbia. The advisory opinion, which is legally nonbinding but had been expected to carry moral weight, was rendered by a majority vote on July 22, 2010, holding that Kosovo's declaration of independence was not in violation of international law.

Since EU and UN calls on both sides to engage in constructive dialogue, discussions on practical (i.e., nonstatus) questions have taken place and have yielded some positive, confidence-building results. The present generation of leaders in Belgrade and Priština have been prepared to be pragmatic, and the EU has belatedly been able to play a useful, honest broker role. But the underlying problem of status remains. Meanwhile, some European politicians have been to the fore in suggesting that Serbia should not be admitted to the EU unless and until it has "regularized" its relationship with Kosovo—that is, recognized Kosovo. It is understandable that the EU does not want to import border disputes. However, in the interests of consistency, it has to be pointed out that Britain has territorial disputes with several of its comembers of the EU: with Spain over Gibraltar; with Ireland over Northern Ireland; and with Denmark and Ireland (and Iceland) over Rockall. Cyprus has its territorial disputes with Cypriot Turks. There are other examples. It is sufficient that all concerned accept the need to resolve their disputes without recourse to violence. And it is intellectually incoherent (and in some cases highly insensitive) for any country to lay down the resolution of territorial disputes as a precondition for membership.

CONCLUSIONS

In looking back on the disastrous course Yugoslavia and those who interacted with it took over the best part of a decade, it is depressing to see how few lessons have been learned. Many Western politicians who favor robust intervention believe that Yugoslavia proves their point: bombing opponents to the negotiating table was a strategy that should have been executed earlier and more often. Any other approach smacks of appeasement, runs the argument. While Frederick the Great may have talked about diplomacy without arms being like an orchestra without instruments, he wasn't suggesting that diplomacy should not be tested to its limits. If we have learned any lesson of the last decade or so of disastrous wars in Afghanistan and Iraq, it is that force should be the very last option when all diplomatic options have been exhausted; when the possible gains clearly outweigh the downsides; when there is full international legal backing through UN Security Council resolutions; where there is a clear sense of proportionality and a likelihood of a successful outcome. It goes without saying that there should be a clear plan for postconflict scenarios.

To the hawks who see diplomacy and negotiation as appeasement, I would argue with Churchill (no appeaser he) that "jaw jaw is better than war war." To insist on one's own position, however strongly felt, with no willingness to concede that others may have arguments of some merit and with no capacity for maneuver is to give up on diplomacy with usually dire results. The Athenians tried this on the hapless Melians nearly two and a half thousand years ago during the Peloponnesian war. It is not a precedent to be followed.[1] It was, as the political scientist Alan Ryan wrote, "famous as the worst atrocity committed by a usually decent society, but even more as one of the most famous assertions in history of the rights of unbridled power."[2]

Diplomacy and its concomitant, negotiation, are not to be dismissed lightly even if at times progress can be painfully slow. The clue lies in the etymology of the word "negotiation": *nec otio* = "not leisure or inactivity." In other words, it calls for persistence and iteration and is not to be denigrated for that.

Diplomacy is not, of course, guaranteed to get it right. We need to recognize that however extensively the problems of Yugoslavia were domestically generated and aggravated, the international community's diplomatic actions on many occasions were culpable in making a bad situation worse. In particular, opportunities for an earlier conclusion to the Bosnian war, the various rejected peace plans, were missed with consequences that were in many respects calamitous and led to much greater loss of life. Srebrenica, that darkest page, would never have occurred, which carries with it a wider import. For today's jihadis, Srebrenica and the prolonged agony of Bosnia are, together with the Soviet invasion of Afghanistan, the early exemplars of how the Islamic nation or *ummah* have been attacked and oppressed by nonbelievers: thus is their hatred fueled.

Traditional allies in the Yugoslav crisis were frequently at odds, a factor exploited by the actors on the ground. Nor was it helpful to take a Manichaean line and maintain that the Europeans made a hash of it and required the United States to intervene on the ground to sort out the mess the Europeans had left behind. It is the case, frequently forgotten, that the United States under Bush Sr. had abandoned the field to the Europeans in the early stages of the crisis. A less confrontational approach across the Atlantic would have yielded greater dividends.

We also need to remind ourselves that the Dayton Agreement was not negotiated from a blank sheet of paper. It owed much to mapmaking begun by David Owen and carried on by Carl Bildt through the Contact Group of diplomats largely from the European Union but also, of course, from the United States and Russia. And the decision to engage Milošević as part of the solution, not just as the originator of the problem, was finally adopted by the United States nearly two years after the British and French had done so.

As for Kosovo, here again the accepted wisdom needs to be challenged. The narrative that Kosovo is a Western success story, ignoring the country's huge social and economic problems, may be convenient for the purposes of the narrative but doesn't correspond to the reality of Kosovo as an at least partly dysfunctional state propped up by international aid and support. There are wider ramifications, of course. The recognition of Kosovo, in direct disregard of a UN Security Council Resolution (UNSCR 1244) guaranteeing Yugoslavia's territorial integrity, set a damaging precedent for Crimea to be incorporated into Russia and for the latter's recognition of South Ossetia and Abkhazia as independent states. Self-determination in Kosovo justifies self-determination in Crimea if internationally recognized borders are going to be flouted. And it is no argument to say that Kosovo is sui generis. All such cases are sui generis. You cannot persuade would-be secessionists to give up their cause by saying that none of these cases provides a precedent. Once again the West's thinking has proved muddled and incoherent and its approach to international law cavalier and selective. In an imperfect world, consistency is an invaluable virtue; however distasteful it may be to negotiate with those whose morals we abhor, we make our strategic goals far harder to secure if we fail to acknowledge the interdependence of principles (including self-determination), regime change, borders, and the inevitable tension between human rights and state security.

This brings to the fore the question of forcible regime change. Was the unspoken aim of Rambouillet and the Kosovo bombing campaign to remove a bad man from power, to remove a thorn in the flesh and someone who failed to conform to Western liberal democratic norms? The press secretary of foreign policy analyst Strobe Talbott was quite explicit: "It was Yugoslavia's resistance to the broader trends of political and economic reform—not the plight of Kosovars Albanians—which best explains NATO's war."[3]

In other words, Kosovo was not to be seen as "an operation with singularly humanitarian objectives, but as a regime change operation with geopolitical purposes and implications."[4]

We need to be wary of going down the road of regime change for a variety of reasons. Doubtful legality is the prime one. And the caveat "be careful of what you wish for" is clearly another. Western support for the so-called color revolutions and the awakenings, springs, and uprisings has not always, indeed rarely if at all, ushered in a neo-Kantian world of Perpetual Peace, a world where democracy breaks out everywhere and war is relegated to history, so the neoconservative theory goes, because democracies don't fight each other. External actors in seeking to impose such regimes often find that not only is their own presence inimical to their own interests but they also have a tendency to bring to the fore those who talk the right "Western" talk but are unsuited to running their own country. Iraq and Afghanistan are merely the most egregious examples of this.

It might be argued that humanitarian intervention, the Responsibility to Protect (R2P) doctrine,[5] needs to aim at regime change to achieve its objectives, but regime change does not occur in a vacuum. Unless the interveners plan to occupy and run the country for themselves, there has to be an alternative regime to put in place, elected or not. The dire lessons from Iraq demonstrate the folly of dismantling the organizational vertebrae of a country without any viable alternative plan. In the case of Iraq, the consequences are particularly severe as the forces of the Islamic State of Iraq and Syria or the Islamic State of Iraq and the Levant (ISIS/ISIL) have at their core former (Sunni) members of Saddam Hussein's army.

We also need to bear in mind the copycat effect of intervention for whatever motive, regime change or not, without proper sanction under international law. Where one state is seen to act with high-handed disregard for international law, others may be emboldened to follow a similar illegal path. Changes of borders without mutual consent must be wrong whether undertaken in Kosovo, Crimea, or Eastern Ukraine.

It follows, therefore, that to lance this boil we should make a real effort to redraw the borders by agreement with all concerned. Both sides will have to accept painful compromises. Redrawing the borders between Serbia and Kosovo is the only sensible solution. Kosovo north of the Ibar River should be incorporated into Serbia proper, and Albanian parts of Serbia's Preševo valley, the municipalities of Preševo and Bujanovac, should become parts of Kosovo. Serbia should agree to recognize Kosovo within these newly agreed borders and should urge China and Russia to lift their veto on Kosovo's UN membership. To those who argue that many Serbs would be "trapped" in enclaves outside the area north of the Ibar, the response should be that they either accept their lot and stay, or move.

It was one of the international community's major failures, once the SFRY's dissolution became inevitable, not to use the opportunity to revisit the whole question of borders. This was often ruled out, quoting one of the principles of the Helsinki agreement, the inviolability of borders. What the agreement actually provided for was the inviolability of borders without mutual consent for change. But the international community was itself flexible enough to adapt its own rules to the peculiar circumstances of the Yugoslav crisis, relying on the advice of the Badinter Commission that, since Yugoslavia was in the process of dissolution, the new international borders should be the old republican administrative borders.

As we have seen, these frontiers failed to correct the errors so palpably committed at the time of the Balkan Wars, the London Conference of 1913, and at the Versailles Peace Conference of 1919. In particular, they took no account of the difficulties faced by minorities trapped within these new borders. Dutch political director Peter van Walsum in July 1991 (a time when Netherlands held the EC presidency) had argued in a telegram circulated to all EC capitals that as it was "difficult to imagine that Yugoslavia could peacefully dissolve into six independent republics within their present borders," it would seem sensible to look "in the direction of a voluntary redrawing of internal borders."[6] Incredibly, this proposal received no support from any of the other eleven EC countries. It was a tragic missed opportunity. With sufficient political will and imagination and with Western military backing to enforce a cease-fire and provide a peacekeeping force, it should have been possible to redraw the borders in ways that would have laid the basis for a comprehensive and stable settlement and, of course, avoided the bloody conflict, the massacres and atrocities, and the vast movements of hundreds of thousands of refugees that have been the most disastrous consequence of the latest episode of the Eastern Question. Perhaps we have come full circle. Should we not reexamine an expanded Eastern Question, taking in the events in Crimea, Eastern Ukraine, and in other "frozen" conflicts? If it is not now time for a new Congress of Berlin or of Vienna, perhaps it is time for a summit-level continental conference based neither on stable borders nor balance of power? It should be a broad security conference with European civilizational outcomes (shades of President Mikhail Gorbachev's concept of a Common European Home)[7] and with interdependence and mutual solidarity as core elements. Such a congress might be unpalatable to some but may ultimately prove the only realistic long-term solution not only to Southeast Europe but also to Eastern Ukraine and other problematic areas of the former Soviet Union. Better for everyone if this were recognized sooner rather than reluctantly conceded after another ten to fifteen years of stasis and friction. Borders may, in an ideal world, become marks more of distinction than division, but as we have seen over the Syrian refugee crisis in Europe, we are still light years away from that.

NOTES

Introduction

1. Isaiah Berlin, *The Proper Study of Mankind* (New York: Random House, 1997), 1.
2. Badinter Arbitration Committee, "Opinion No. 1, November 29, 1991," *European Journal of International Law* 3, no. 1 (1992): 182.
3. Susan L. Woodward, "The West and the International Organisations," in *Yugoslavia and After: A Study in Fragmentation, Despair and Rebirth*, ed. David A. Dyker and Ivan Vejvoda (London: Longman, 1996), 156.
4. Richard Holbrooke, *To End a War* (New York: Random House, 1998), 23-24.
5. E. H. Carr, *What Is History?* (New York: Penguin, 1990), 45, 49.
6. A. J. P. Taylor, *From Napoleon to Stalin: Comments on European History* (Brooklyn: AMS Press, 1950), 74.
7. Ian Kershaw, *Hitler, 1889-1936: Hubris* (London: Allen Lane, 1998), xx.
8. Stevan Pavlowitch, *Yugoslavia* (New York: Praeger, 1971), 21, quoted by Ivan Vejvoda, "Yugoslavia, 1945-91: From Decentralization without Democracy to Dissolution," in Dyker and Vejvoda, *Yugoslavia and After*, 9.
9. Woodward, "West and the International Organisations," 158.
10. Arnold J. Zurcher, *The Experiment with Democracy in Central Europe* (New York: Oxford University Press, 1933), 274.
11. Mirko Tepavac, "Tito, 1945-80," in *Burn This House: The Making and Unmaking of Yugoslavia*, ed. Jasminka Udovički and James Ridgeway (Durham, N.C.: Duke University Press), 1997, 74.
12. Vejvoda, "Yugoslavia," 16.
13. Susan L. Woodward, *Balkan Tragedy: Chaos and Dissolution after the Cold War* (Washington, D.C.: Brookings Institution, 1995), 75.
14. Woodward, "West and the International Organisations," 162.
15. Ray Stannard Baker and William E. Dodds, eds., *The Public Papers of Woodrow Wilson: The New Democracy*, 2 vols. (New York: Harper, 1926), 2:351.
16. Delors, cited in Owen Harries, "The Collapse of the West," *Foreign Affairs* 72, no. 4 (September/October 1993): 49. For the quote from Poos, see Timothy Garton Ash, *History of the Present: Essays, Sketches and Despatches from Europe in the 1990s* (London: Penguin, 1999), 211.
17. Woodward, "West and the International Organisations," 166.
18. David Owen, *Balkan Odyssey* (New York: Harcourt Brace, 1995), 344.
19. Ibid., 343.
20. Ibid., 344.
21. Milovan Djilas, *Wartime* (New York: Harvest/HBJ), 1977.
22. Noel Malcolm, *Bosnia: A Short History* (New York: New York University Press, 1994), 252.

23. Samuel P. Huntington, *The Clash of Civilizations and the Remaking of World Order* (New York: Simon Schuster, 1996).

24. Jasminka Udovićki, "The Bonds and the Fault Lines," in Udovićki and Ridgeway, *Burn This House*, 17.

25. Ostrozinski, quoted in Branka Prpa-Jovanović, "The Making of Yugoslavia," in Udovićki and Ridgeway, *Burn This House*, 43.

26. Prpa-Jovanović, "Making of Yugoslavia," 45.

27. Udovićki, "Bonds and the Fault Lines," 20.

28. The relations between the communities and their Turkish overlords are evoked in pointillist detail in Ivo Andrić's chronicles of the Bosnian town of Travnik. See Ivo Andrić, *The Days of the Consuls*, trans. Celia Hawkesworth (London: Forest Books, 1996).

29. Udovićki, "Bonds and the Fault Lines," 28.

30. Quoted in Michael Ignatieff, *The Warrior's Honour: Ethnic War and the Modern Conscience* (London: Chatto & Windus/Random House, 1998), 48.

31. Ignatieff, *Warrior's Honour*, 50–51.

32. Joseph Goebbels, *The Goebbels Diaries, 1939–1941*, ed. Fred Taylor (London: Hamish Hamilton, 1982), 285; Galeazzo Ciano, *The Ciano Diaries, 1939–1943* (London: Heinemann, 1947), 93.

33. Wayne S. Vucinich, *The Ottoman Empire: Its Record and Legacy* (Princeton, N.J.: Van Nostrand, 1965), 120.

34. Secretary of State Warren Christopher, "New Steps toward Conflict Resolution in the Former Yugoslavia," opening statement at a news conference, Washington, D.C., February 10, 1993; published in *U.S. Department of State Dispatch* 4, no. 7 (February 15, 1993), 81.

Chapter 1. The Pyromaniac Fireman

1. Aleksa Djilas, "A Profile of Slobodan Milošević," *Foreign Affairs*, July–August 1993.

2. Stambolić, quoted in Laura Silber and Allan Little, *The Death of Yugoslavia* (London: Penguin, 1996), 45.

3. David Owen, *Balkan Odyssey* (New York: Harcourt Brace, 1995), 271–72.

4. Marković, quoted by Slavoljub Djukić in *Milošević and Marković*, (Montreal: McGill-Queen's University Press, 2001), 174.

5. Ekmečić, qtd. in Slavoljub Djukić, *Milosević and Marković: A Lust for Power*, trans. Alex Dubinsky (Montreal: McGill-Queen's University Press, 2001), 162.

6. Slavoljub Djukić, *On, Ona i Mi* (Belgrade: B92, 1997), 31.

7. Borislav Jović, *Poslednji Dani SFRJa* (Belgrade: Politika, 1995).

8. Silber and Little, *Death of Yugoslavia*, 96.

9. Adam Roberts, "Communal Conflict and Challenge," in *Peacemaking and Peacekeeping for the New Century*, ed. Olara A. Otunnu and Michael W. Doyle (Lanham, Md.: Rowman and Littlefield, 1998), 35.

Chapter 2. Early Belgrade Days

1. Slavoljub Djukić, *Nova srpska politicka misao*, 17 September 2006, 115.

2. The acronym of *Antifašističko Vijeće Narodnog Oslobođenja Jugoslavije*, the Anti-Fascist Council of the People's Liberation of Yugoslavia, was the political umbrella organization for

the national liberation councils of the Yugoslav resistance against the World War II Axis occupation. The AVNOJ was established on November 26, 1942, to administer territories under the Partisans' control.

3. On November 20, 1991, Lord Carrington asked: "Can the internal boundaries between Croatia and Serbia and between Bosnia and Herzegovina and Serbia be regarded as frontiers in terms of public international law?" Applying the principle of *uti possidetis*, the commission concluded on January 11, 1992, "The boundaries between Croatia and Serbia, between Bosnia and Herzegovina and Serbia, and possibly other adjacent independent states may not be altered except by agreement freely arrived at"; and "Except where otherwise agreed, the former boundaries become frontiers protected by international law." Peter Radan, an Australian legal academic, has criticised the Badinter Commission's interpretation of the SFRY Constitution. Apart from principles of international law, the Badinter Commission sought to justify the relevance of the Badinter Borders Principle by reference to Article 5 of the 1974 Constitution of Yugoslavia. The commission said that the Badinter Borders Principle applies all the more readily to the Republics since the second and fourth paragraphs of Article 5 of the Constitution of the SFRY stipulated that the Republics' territories and boundaries could not be altered without their consent.

Article 5 stipulates:

(1) The territory of the SFRY is indivisible and consists of the territories of its socialist republics.
(2) A republic's territory cannot be altered without the consent of that republic, and the territory of an autonomous province—without the consent of that autonomous province.
(3) A border of the SFRY cannot be altered without the concurrence of all republics and autonomous provinces.
(4) A border between republics can only be altered on the basis of their agreement, and in the case of a border of an autonomous province—on the basis of its concurrence.

In referring to Article 5, Radan's criticism is that the Badinter Commission was guilty of selective quoting.

The reason for this opinion is that in relying on paragraphs 2 and 4 of Article 5, the Badinter Commission ignored the provisions of paragraphs 1 and 3. In doing so it was justifying the division of the SFRY and the alteration of its international borders in violation of paragraphs 1 and 3. Furthermore, it can be argued that the territorial integrity of republics and the sanctity of their borders referred to in paragraphs 2 and 4 of Article 5 only applied in the context of the Yugoslav state whose own territorial integrity and borders remained in place. A republic seeking to violate the provisions of paragraphs 1 and 3 of Article 5 could hardly reap the guarantees contained within paragraphs 2 and 4. Consequently, Peter Radan argues that Article 5 provides no support for the application of the Badinter Borders Principle to the fragmentation of the SFRY.

Based on the above analysis of the reasoning of the Badinter Commission, Peter Radan concludes that neither the international law principles of respect for the territorial status quo and *uti possidetis* nor the provisions of Article 5 of the Constitution of the SFRY of 1974 provides any justification for the Badinter Borders Principle (Opinion No. 3 of the Badinter Commission: January 11, 1992).

4. Milovan Djilas, *Wartime* (New York: Harvest/HBJ, 1977), 356.
5. Ibid.

Chapter 3. Close Encounter with the Bosnian Serbs

1. Ian Traynor, *Guardian*, March 13, 2006.
2. "You can always tell an article of Jaurès' because every verb is in the future tense." Quote attributed to the French statesman Georges Clemenceau. J. Hampden Jackson, *Clemenceau and the Third Republic* (London: Hodder and Stoughton, 1948), 139.

Chapter 4. A First Private Meeting with Milošević

1. I am indebted to Aleksa Djilas for the information in this note. In the run-up to the first multiparty elections in Bosnia, Fikret Abdić had just been released from prison. He had been incarcerated during the last period of the Communist era, reemerging into a very different political environment, seemingly a victim of a repressive regime and power-hungry party officials. The political parties that were being hastily assembled prior to the first free elections all sought Abdić's endorsement, as his popularity in Bosanska krajina (the Bosnian frontier) had remained huge. He was assiduously courted by Ante Marković's Reformists but decided to cast his lot with Izetbegović and the SDA (Muslim nationalist party). He was universally known, and of the candidates on the Muslim list, he was the most acceptable to members of other ethnic groups, regardless of political affiliation. Abdić had been prosecuted by the Communists, and Communists were beaten very badly in the Bosnian elections, winning a little over 10 percent. (The Communist defeat in Bosnia is in itself proof of the strength of nationalism, since Bosnia had a strong Partisan and Communist tradition, and it could have been expected that Communists would do well. But in Bosnia Communists could not become nationalists as in other republics, since the party itself was multinational. Simply, they could not adapt to the new situation.)

It's important to understand that Abdić was a candidate of the SDA, that he ran on the party ticket, and that the party had announced it would form a ruling coalition with the Serb and Croat ethnic parties, SDS and HDZ. Politically and ideologically, Fikret Abdić was largely an unknown ideological quantity at the time: the Serbs and the Croats had struck their deal with Izetbegović, whereas Abdić was a latecomer to the game. It was a well-known fact that he had seriously considered going with Ante Marković's lot. He made up his mind at the last minute, and no one knew exactly what had prevailed.

The ethnic parties were anti-Communist, but Abdić, widely perceived as a victim of communism and also Belgrade, was not known for being either anti-Communist or anti-Serb. At the time, he was less trusted by both the SDS and the HDZ than Alija Izetbegović. Were they afraid that he might take some of their votes? No Serb or Croat would vote for Alija, but might for Fikret.

The Bosnia-Herzegovina (BH) constitution did not include a provision on how to elect the person who would preside over the seven-member Presidency of BH (two candidates were elected from the Serb, Croat, and Muslim lists of candidates on the ballot, and one from the "other groups" list, and every voter listed his or her preference on each of the lists). The issue of who would become the first "predsednik Predsedništva" (president of the Presidency) was settled by an internal vote of the seven members. So, even though he won the most votes of all seven candidates, Fikret Abdić was never in a position to "take" the presidency.

In the first live TV interview of the newly elected Serb member of the Presidency, Nikola Koljević, he was asked whether the candidate with the most votes would become president, as the public widely expected at the time. Koljević was emphatic that this was up to the whole

Presidency and that the newly elected members had already agreed among themselves that Alija Izetbegović would become the first president. "We, the Serb members, will certainly cast our votes for him," said Koljević. Soon thereafter, Izetbegović was duly elected.

2. Richard Holbrooke, *To End a War* (New York: Random House, 1998), 160, 166.

Chapter 6. Point Man for the Contact Group

1. In fact, Milošević finally sacked Perišić in November 1998, probably as a result of Perišić's resistance to pressurizing the reformist government in Montenegro of President Djukanović.

2. I was once the victim. When tasked with writing a paper on reform of the Common Agricultural Policy of the EEC, I produced a substantial effort, having consulted experts, practitioners, and academics, only to have David Owen write on it in his illegible scrawl in red felt-tip ink "good on analysis; short on solutions."

3. In fact, the U.S. treatment of Bildt was extraordinary. Bildt had real concerns over the future of the deal because of what was emerging about the massacres at Srebrenica (see chapter 7) and expressed his worries to the administration. The U.S. reaction was to urge Bildt to conclude the deal all the more quickly. When he did so, Madeleine Albright vetoed the deal at a Contact Group Ministerial in London, quoting Srebrenica as her justification.

Chapter 8. Srebrenica

1. Jan Willem Honig and Norbert Both, *Srebrenica: Record of a War Crime* (London: Penguin, 1996), 78.

2. Laura Silber and Allan Little, *The Death of Yugoslavia* (London: Penguin, 1996), 346.

3. "Radovan Karadzic and Ratko Mladic accused of genocide following the take-over of Srebrenica," ICTY Press release, November 16, 1995, http://www.icty.org/sid/7221.

4. The court concluded in February 2007 "that the acts committed at Srebrenica . . . were committed with the specific intent to destroy in part the group of the Muslims of Bosnia and Herzegovina as such; and accordingly that these were acts of genocide, committed by members of the VRS [the Bosnian Serb army] in and around Srebrenica from about 13 July 1995."

Chapter 9. The End of the Krajina Serbs and NATO bombing

1. Laura Silber and Allan Little, *The Death of Yugoslavia* (London: Penguin, 1996), 355.

Chapter 10. Dayton from the Sidelines

1. Richard Holbrooke, *To End a War* (New York: Random House, 1998), 199.

2. Ibid., 110.

3. Rebecca West, *Black Lamb and Grey Falcon* (New York: Viking Press, 1941), 1:22.

4. To be fair to Holbrooke, he accepted his mistake. My copy of his book is inscribed by him, "To Ivor Roberts, who deserved better from me in this book—with admiration, affection and warm regard. Richard H."

Chapter 11. Independent Media and the Opposition

1. In late February 2003, Šešelj surrendered to the International Criminal Tribunal for the Former Yugoslavia (ICTY) after being indicted on eight counts of crimes against humanity and six counts of violations of the laws or customs of war for his alleged participation in a joint criminal enterprise. The closing arguments were heard in March 2012, but judgment is still pending as of February 2016. On November 6, 2014, the Trial Chamber ordered the provisional release of Šešelj on humanitarian grounds due to the deterioration of his health. He was transferred to Serbia on 12 November 12, 2014.

Chapter 13. The Winter of Discontent

1. See the discussion of Milošević's treatment of Warren Zimmerman on page 132.
2. It is to me one of the remarkable facets of modern Serbia that the Socialist Party (SPS) is a major power broker, and that its leader, Milošević's former spokesman, is a senior minister.

Chapter 14. Bildt's Farewell and the B92 Saga

1. Jan Willem Honig and Norbert Both, *Srebrenica: Record of a War Crime* (London: Penguin, 1996), 179.

Chapter 15. Kosovo

1. Noel Malcolm, *Kosovo: A Short History* (New York: Harper Perennial, 1998), 58.
2. Ibid.
3. Irena Kostić and Slobodan Vuksanović, eds., *Pesma o Kosovu, savremena srpska poezija* (Belgrade: 1991, Vidici SKZ, Jedinstvo, 1991), 12.
4. Roy Foster, "Anglo-Irish Relations and Northern Ireland: Historical Perspectives," in *Northern Ireland and the Politics of Reconciliation*, ed. Dermot Keogh and Michael H. Haltzel (Washington, D.C.: Woodrow Wilson Center Press, 1993), 13–14.
5. Leon Trotsky, *The Balkan Wars, 1912–1913*, trans. Brian Pearce (Atlanta: Pathfinder Press, 1980), 267–68.
6. Carnegie International Commission on the Balkans, *Report of the International Commission to Inquire into the Causes and Conduct of the Balkan Wars* (Washington, D.C.: Carnegie Endowment for International Peace, 1914), 151.
7. Paulin Kola, *The Search for Greater Albania* (London: Hurst, 2003), 1.
8. Malcolm, *Kosovo*, 273.
9. Vladimir Dedijer, *Yugoslav-Albanian Relations* (Ljubljana: CCM Information Corporation, 1949), 126–27.
10. Enver Hoxha, *With Stalin* (Tirana: 8 Nëntori Pub. House, 1979), 137–138.
11. Dedijer, *Yugoslav-Albanian Relations*, 67.
12. Malcolm, *Kosovo*, 319.
13. Milovan Djilas, *Conversations with Stalin* (New York: Harcourt Brace and World, 1962), 143.
14. Ibid., 177.
15. Malcolm, *Kosovo*, 314.

16. Milovan Djilas, *Wartime* (New York: Harvest/HBJ, 1977), 356.
17. Malcolm, *Kosovo*, p. 335.

Chapter 16. Final Days

1. See the discussion of Bulatović's rebellion on page 22.
2. Borislav Jović, *Poslednji Dani SFRJa* (Belgrade: Politika, 1995).

Chapter 18. Aftermath

1. Council on Foreign Relations, "Terrorist Groups and Political Legitimacy," March 16, 2006 http://www.cfr.org/terrorism/terrorist-groups-political-legitimacy/p10159.
2. Liddell Hart Centre for Military Archives (LHCMA), *Fall of Milošević* (Brook Lapping Productions, 2001), VHS, file 5/8, questions 11–12.
3. Madeleine Albright, *Madam Secretary: A Memoir* (New York: Macmillan, 2003), p.384.
4. LHCMA, *Fall of Milošević*, file 5/1, question 8.
5. Vladimir Dedijer, *The Road to Sarajevo* (New York: Simon and Schuster, 1966), 145.
6. *Kosovo*, Select Committee on Foreign Affairs House of Commons 4th Report, Session 1999–2000, para. 65.
7. Christopher Clark, *The Sleepwalkers* (New York: Penguin, 2012), 456.
8. *Daily Telegraph*, June 28, 1999.
9. Clark, *Sleepwalkers*, 457.
10. James Ker-Lindsay, *Kosovo: The Path to Contested Statehood in the Balkans* (London: Palgrave Macmillan, 2009), 15.
11. Ivor Roberts, "Partition Is the Best Answer to the Kosovo Question," *Independent* (London), December 5, 2007.
12. Vuk Jeremić, speech at Wheaton College, Chicago, March 17, 2011.

Conclusions

1. The Athenians demanded that the small state of Melos surrender the city or face its destruction. The Melians claimed their right to remain neutral (although this wasn't strictly true as they had been allied with Sparta), asserted that it would be shameful and cowardly of them to submit without a fight, and stated that they had potential allies. The Athenians retorted that the strong do what they can while the weak suffer what they must. They then starved the city into submission, killed the adult males, and enslaved the women and children.
2. Alan Ryan, *On Politics: A History of Political Thought from Herodotus to the Present* (New York: Liveright, 2012), 1:23.
3. John Norris, *Collision Course: NATO, Russia, and Kosovo* (New York: Praeger, 2005), xxiii.
4. Rein Müllerson, *Regime Change: From Democratic Peace Theories to Forcible Regime Change* (Leiden: Brill, 2013).
5. R2P is a doctrine, developed at the UN since 2000 and endorsed unanimously by heads of state and government at the 2005 World Summit, that asserts states have an obligation to protect their populations from genocide, crimes against humanity, war crimes, and ethnic

cleansing, and that failure to do so can lead to a state forfeiting its sovereignty. The corollary is that the international community, in that case, has the responsibility to intervene with coercive measures and ultimately through military means to protect that state's citizens. Military intervention can only be authorized by the UN Security Council.

6. Van Walsum, quoted by Lord David Owen, Archive Document 45, *Balkan Odyssey* (CD Rom), academic ed., vol. 1 (London: Electric Company, 1995).

7. Launched in 1987, the idea was most clearly articulated by Gorbachev in front of the Council of Europe on July 6, 1989. "The philosophy of the 'Common European Home' concept rules out the probability of an armed clash and the very possibility of the use of force or threat of force—alliance against alliance, inside the alliances, wherever. This philosophy suggests that a doctrine of restraint should take the place of the doctrine of deterrence. This is not just a play on words but the logic of European development prompted by life itself."

SUGGESTED FURTHER READING

Banac, Ivo. *The National Question in Yugoslavia: Origins, History, Politics.* Ithaca: Cornell University Press, 1984.
Bildt, Carl. *Peace Journey: The Struggle for Peace in Bosnia.* London: Weidenfeld and Nicholson, 1998.
Clark, Christopher. *The Sleepwalkers: How Europe Went to War in 1914.* London: Allen Lane, 2012.
Crampton, Richard. *The Balkans since the Second World War.* London: Longman, 2002.
Djilas, Aleksa. *The Contested Country: Yugoslav Unity and Communist Revolution, 1919–53.* Cambridge, Mass.: Harvard University Press. 1991.
———. "A Profile of Slobodan Milošević." *Foreign Affairs*, July–August 1993.
Djilas, Milovan. *Wartime.* New York: Harvest/HBJ, 1977.
Djukić, Slavoljub. *Milošević and Marković: A Lust for Power.* Trans. A Dubinsky. Montreal: McGill-Queen's University Press, 2001.
Doder, Duško, and Branson Louise. *Milošević: Portrait of a Tyrant.* New York: Free Press, 1999.
Glenny, Misha. *The Balkans: Nationalism, War, and the Great Powers, 1804–2012.* London: Granta, 2012.
———. *The Fall of Yugoslavia: The Third Balkan War.* 3rd rev. ed. New York: Penguin Books, 1996.
Gow, James. *Triumph of the Lack of Will: International Diplomacy and the Yugoslav War.* New York: Columbia University Press, 1997.
Holbrooke, Richard. *To End a War.* New York: Random House, 1998.
Honig, Jan Willem, and Norbert Both. *Srebrenica: Record of a War Crime.* London: Penguin, 1996.
International Commission on the Balkans. *Unfinished Peace: A Report.* Foreword by Leo Tindemans. Washington, D.C.: Carnegie Endowment for International Peace, 1996.
Judah, Tim. *Kosovo: War and Revenge.* New Haven, Conn.: Yale University Press, 2002.
———. *The Serbs: History, Myth, and the Destruction of Yugoslavia.* New Haven, Conn.: Yale University Press, 1997.
Kaplan, Robert. *Balkan Ghosts: A Journey through History.* New York: Vintage Books, 1993.
Ker-Lindsay, James. *Kosovo: The Path to Contested Statehood in the Balkans.* London: I. B. Taurus, 2009.
Lampe, John R. *Yugoslavia as History: Twice There Was a Country.* Cambridge: Cambridge University Press, 1996.
Malcolm, Noel. *Bosnia: A Short History.* New York: New York University Press, 1994.
———. *Kosovo: A Short History.* London: Pan, 2002.
Morrison, Kenneth, *Montenegro: A Modern History.* London: I. B. Tauris 2009.
Müllerson, Rein. *Regime Change: From Democratic Peace Theories to Forcible Regime Change.* Leiden: Brill, 2013.
Neville-Jones, Pauline. "Dayton, IFOR, and Alliance Relations in Bosnia." *Survival* 38, no. 4 (Winter 1996–97): 45–65.

Owen, David. *Balkan Odyssey*. New York: Harcourt Brace, 1995.
——. *Balkan Odyssey* (CD Rom). Academic ed., vo1. 1. London: Electric Company, 1995.
Ridley, Jasper. *Tito: A Biography*. London: Constable, 1994.
Roberts, Elizabeth. *Realm of the Black Mountain: A History of Montenegro*. London: Hurst, 2007.
Silber, Laura, and Allan Little. *The Death of Yugoslavia*. Rev. ed. London: Penguin Books/BBC Books, 1996.
Tanner, Marcus. *Croatia: A Nation Forged in War*. New Haven, Conn.: Yale University Press, 1997.
Thompson, Mark. *A Paper House: The Ending of Yugoslavia*. New York: Pantheon Books, 1992.
West, Rebecca. *Black Lamb and Grey Falcon: A Journey through Yugoslavia*. New York: Penguin Books, 1982.
Woodward, Susan L. *Balkan Tragedy: Chaos and Dissolution after the Cold War*. Washington, D.C.: Brookings Institution, 1995.

INDEX

Note: Milošević, other than at main heading level, is usually shortened to "M." "IR" refers to the author, Ivor Roberts.

Abdić, Fikret, xv, 49
Akashi, Yasushi, xv, 134
Albania: collapse of Berisha government (1997), 125; Kingdom of Serbs, Croats, and Slovenes and, 4; as "nationality," 7–8; sinecure to, 31–32; UK relations with, 31–32; union with Kosovo, 116–17, 150. *See also* Kosovo / Kosovo Albanians; Macedonia
Albright, Madeleine, xv, 63, 107, 141, 146–47, 161n3 (ch. 6)
Annan, Kofi, xv
Arkan (Željko Ražnatović), xv, 43–44
Ashdown, Paddy, 21
Austin, David, xv, 28, 69, 87
Austria, 11, 12, 146–47
Austria-Hungary, 4, 114–15
AVNOJ/Jajce borders, 36–37
Avramović, Dragoslav, xv, 34–35, 86, 95

Babić, Milan, 61–62, 76
Badinter Commission / Robert Badinter: AVNOJ/Jajce borders as basis of task, 36–37; Badinter Borders Principle (Opinion 3), 159n3; Badinter's credentials, xvi, 37; confused opinions, 15; "in the process of dissolution" status of Yugoslavia, 2, 155; international status of republican administrative borders, 138, 142; self-determination and, 142
Baker, James, xv, 12, 30
Balkan Odyssey (Owen), 14–15, 27, 42–43
Berlin, Isaiah, 1
Bihać, attacks on, 47, 50–51
Bildt, Carl: arrival as EU representative/ICFY cochair, 63, 64, 68; B92 incident, 103; career, xv; evaluation of, 64, 91; farewell call, 110; as High Representative for Bosnia, 88, 91, 103; on Karadžić, 88, 91–92, 110; lifting of sanctions, 93–94; and M, 68–69, 70; mapmaking, 153; on Srebrenica atrocities, 110; and Tudjman, 76, 128; U.S. attitude toward, 64, 79, 87
Blot, Jacques, xv, 136, 140
B92 incident. *See* Radio B92
Bone, Roger, 39
borders: administrative versus international (AVNOJ), 36–37; Badinter Borders Principle (Opinion 3), 159n3. *See also* Badinter Commission / Robert Badinter; territorial integrity / inviolability of borders
Bosnia: as autonomous province (Jajce discussions), 37; human rights in, 18; independence (*see* independence: Bosnia); London Conference on (1996), 74, 96; multiethnic character, 8, 30, 81; no-fly zone, 29; recognition (1992), consequences of, 15, 132–33; SFRY break-up, effect of, 12–13; Turkish/Ottoman rule and, 18; UN membership, xxiv
—elections (September 2006): lifting of sanctions, dependence on, 93–94; M's determination to capitalize on, 94; OSCE certification as free and fair, 93; SDS participation in / success, 92; SPS failure, 92
—peace plans/agreements: Cutileiro plan (1992), xxiv, 30; Invincible plan (1993), 30, 41, 42, 49, 55–56, 79; land swaps, 48, 53–54, 55; Vance-Owen Peace Plan (1993), xxiv, 30–31, 34, 44, 61, 63–64, 81, 133; Washington Agreement (1994), xxv, 31, 54, 55. *See also* Contact Group plan; Muslim-Croat Federation; Vance-Owen Peace Plan

Bosnian Muslims: Abdić's role, 49; Bosnian Croats and, 30; early days, 19; *Mladi Muslimani* (young Muslims), 22; Sandžak, 13, 83, 131; SDA (Muslim nationalist party), xvii, 22, 83, 160n1 (ch. 4); Vance-Owen plan, 30–31. *See also* Izetbegović, Alija; Muslim-Croat Federation; Srebrenica

Bosnian Serbs / Republika Srpska (RS) (1992–): army's dependence on FRY government / JNA, xxiv, 61; attribution of responsibility for atrocities, 48–49, 128; blockade of border (1994), xxv, 44, 47, 52, 55; boycott of Bosnian independence referendum, 15, 29; Churkin-brokered Sarajevo exclusion zone, 33–34; as country bumpkins, 20; direct negotiation with versus M as interlocutor, 33–34, 42, 52, 56, 133; effect of sanctions, 52, 55; establishment, xxiv; guardians of gate, 43, 57; Holbrooke's advice to Croats to take control of Serb-held territory, 50, 79–80; lifting of arms embargo / air strikes, 30, 31, 33, 37–38, 49, 69, 94; loss of territory, xxv, 76; M's hostility toward leaders, 27–28; M's relations with, 33–34; M's willingness to recognize, 58; Muslim-Croat Federation, possibility of union with, 58; NATO bombing of army headquarters / destruction of communications, 77–78; negotiating objectives / RS as *sine qua non*, 42; negotiating rights, surrender to M, 77–78, 134; occupation of large part of Bosnia, 29; Plavšić as successor to Karadžić as president/leader of SDS, 91–92; rejection of Vance-Owen plan, xxiv, 30, 34; risk of collapse following NATO bombing, 78; Serbian Democratic Party (SDS), 48, 92, 133; Serbs-Croat Federation (Clinton initiative), 53–54, 55. *See also* Karadžić, Radovan; Krajina Serbs / RSK; Sarajevo, siege of

Boutros-Ghali, Boutros, xv
Božić, Milan, 95–96
Braithwaite, Julian, xv, 103, 111
Bugarčić, Bojan, xv, 140–41
Buha, Aleksa, xv
Bulatović, Momir, xv, 22, 29, 129, 130–31, 133
Busby, George, xv, 57
Bush, George H. W., 29–30

Čanak, Nenad, xvi
Carr, E. H., 2
Carrington, Lord Peter, xvi, 14–15, 22, 79
Carter, Jimmy / Carter initiative, 52–54
ceasefires: Carter initiative (December 1994), 53, 54, 60, 65; post-Sarajevo shelling (September 1995), xxv
Ceaușescu, Nicolae, 31
Chernomyrdin, Viktor, xvi, 148
Christopher, Warren, xvi, 23, 63, 93
chronology, xxiii–xxvii
Churkin, Vitaly, xvi, 33, 34, 43
Ciano, Galeazzo, 19
civil war (Partisans/Chetniks/Ustasha) (1941–44), 5, 16, 19, 36–37
Clark, Wesley, xvi
Clinton, Bill, xvi, 29–30, 77, 125, 146–47, 148
communism: in Albania, 115–16; AVNOJ/Jajce border proposals (1943), 37; in Kosovo, 117; legacy / democratic deficit, 3–4, 16, 20; of M, 1, 20–21, 24–26, 36, 46, 47, 82, 83, 86, 108; post-1974 nomenklaturas, 7; in Slovenia, 21; under Tito, 5–6. *See also* League of Communists
confidence-building measures, 88, 128–29, 151
constitution (SFRY) (1974): criticisms of, 6–7; history of, 6; "nations"/"nationalities," 7–8; quasi-republic status of autonomous provinces, 118, 119–20; republics as "states based on popular sovereignty," 6, 8; summary of provisions, 6–7; Tito's biggest mistake, 6, 119. *See also* SFRY
Contact Group plan: Bosnian Serb rejection of, 42–44; Carter initiative and, 53–54; Ćosić and, 41–42; Dayton Agreement, dependence on, 79, 153; establishment/membership of group, 31, 49; 51/49 percent division as *acquis*, 41, 42, 55–56; Holbrooke's takeover of negotiations, xxv, 62–63, 77, 79–80; Karadžić alternative, 41; Karadžić's attitude toward, 53–56; Koljević and, 41, 42; Mladić and, 56–57; M's role, 43–44, 47, 48–49, 50–54, 56–64, 68–69, 143–44; natural gas episode and group's credibility, 56; Owen's role/departure, 63–64, 68–69; Plan B (Bosnia-FRY mutual recognition), 52, 56, 58–62; secretive working of group,

42; as starting point, 53–54, 55; twin-track approach (mutual recognition / sanction relief), 49, 52, 56, 58–62; U.S. role, 42–43, 56, 58, 62–63
Conversations with Stalin (Djilas), xii, 116
Cook, Robin, xvi, 73, 139, 141–42, 145, 146
Ćosić, Dobrica, xvi, 42, 47, 120, 133
Croatia: cession of Serbs and Serb territories as M's condition for secession, 13–14; Croats' propaganda victory over Serbs and Montenegrins, 14; ethnic cleansing, 21; human rights in, 72; in Kingdom of Serbs, Croats, and Slovenes, 4–5; mono-ethnic character, 21; Serbs' territorial gains, 14; UN membership, xxiv; UNPA truce (1991), 14; Ustasha regime, 5, 16, 19. *See also* independence: Croatia and Slovenia; Krajina Serbs / RSK; Muslim-Croat Federation
Crombie, Tony, xvi, 67
CSCE, 11–12. *See also* OSCE
Cutileiro plan (1992), xxiv, 30
Czechoslovakia, 7, 11, 20, 118

Dayton Agreement (1995): best available, 81; despondency of Bosnian Serbs, 81; FRY, Western neglect following, 86–87; FRY–Republika Srpska bilateral agreements, incompatibility with, 91; High Representative for Bosnia, creation of, 88, 91, 103; Holbrooke as only begetter, xxv, 79–81; Izetbegović's post-Dayton unhelpfulness, 22; Koljević and, 46; Kosovo and, 86, 87; making it work, 81; M's attitude toward, 81, 108, 109; NATO bombing, contribution to success of, 78; sidelining of Europeans, 80–81; violations / failure to implement by Republika Srpska, 91–92, 110
de la Presle, Bertrand, xvi
Dejammet, Alain, 58
Delić, Rasim, 70
Delors, Jacques, 12
Demaqi, Adem, xvi, 123, 142
democratic deficit, 3–4, 82; suggestions for making good / benefits of, 86–88
Djilas, Aleksa, xii, 3, 19, 25–26, 160n1 (ch. 4)
Djilas, Milovan, 5, 16, 36–37, 85; *Conversations with Stalin*, xii, 116
Djindjić, Zoran, 84–85, 102, 107, 148–49

Djukanović, Milo, xvi, xxvi, 130–31, 161n1 (ch. 6)
Djukić, Slavoljub, 28, 35
Dolanc, Stane, 10
Drašković, Danica, 35–36
Drašković, Vuk: candidacy for Serbian presidency, 107; coalition relations, 107; insuperable obstacles, 83–84; M's attitude to, 35–36, 89–90, 93, 139; overreaches himself, 36, 141; peacenik, 35–36; referendum on foreign intervention, 139; Studio B and, 84–85

EC policy: deafness to federal government, 11; German role, 14, 33; information office in Kosovo, possibility of, 109; neutral mediation, 12; support for Croatia and Slovenia, 11; troika visit (1991), 11–12; unity at any cost, 13–15
economic/debt crises, 9–10
EC-U.S. relations, 11–12, 56
education agreement (Kosovo Albanians) (September 1996): failure to implement, 97, 124–26, 128–29; M's intentions, 88, 128–29; Paglia's role, xix, xxvi, 92–93, 97, 124–25, 129; signature, 92–93
Ekmečić, Milorad, 28
enclaves, Muslim: Bosnian Serb stranglehold/vulnerability, 68, 69, 70; as burden, 70–71; territorial exchanges as solution, 47, 69; U.S. attitude toward, 71
enclaves, Serb. *See* Bosnian Serbs / Republika Srpska; Krajina Serbs / RSK
ethnic cleansing, 21, 80, 82–83; R2P doctrine, 154
ethnic divisions, 2, 15–16, 17–19, 21, 22–23
European common foreign and security policy problems, 2

Frasure, Robert, xvi, 63, 64, 65, 67, 77, 140; Karadjordjevo meeting with M, 62–63, 65
freedom of press (Serbia): *Borba*, 85, 89; elections (1996), 96–97, 101–2, 103–4; ill-conceived support schemes, 84; M's attitude toward, 84–85, 89; Ottoman legacy, 18; Radio B92 (*see* Radio B92); Radio Brod, 84; radio/TV stations, stifling of, 85–86; Soros Foundation, 89; Studio B, 84–85, 89
Frowick, Robert, xvi

FRY (1992–2002): establishment, xxiv; federal elections (November 1996), 94–97, 98; presidency elections (2000), xxvi–xxvii; proposed abolition of republican presidents, 132; sanctions against/lifting, xxvii, 29; Western neglect post-Dayton, 86–87. *See also* Montenegro; Serbia
—local elections (1996) / demonstrations: JUL's lowered profile, 108; M's cave-in / *lex specialis*, 106–7; M's views on, 101–3, 104–5; opposition success, 84, 98; overturn of results / as electoral fraud, xxvi, 98–101; press restrictions, 101–2, 103–4; Zajedno's fractured unity, 107

Galbraith, Peter, 76
Ganić, Ejup, xvii
Gelbard, Robert, xvii, 125, 137, 138–39, 141, 146
Genscher, Hans Dietrich, xvii
Gligorov, Kiro, xvii, 22
Goebbels, Joseph, 19
González, Felipe, 106, 137, 141
Goražde: Bosnian Serbs' shelling of, 39, 40–41, 43, 46, 47; as burden on Muslim leadership, 70; demilitarization, 72
Gotovina, Ante (ICTY indictment), 77
Granić, Mate, xvii
Greenstock, Jeremy, xvii, 137
Gvero, Milan, xvii, 57

Helsinki Final Act (1975), 12, 155
Hogg, Douglas, xvii, 39–41, 55
Holbrooke, Richard: brio and panache, 79; career, xvii; Croatia offensives on Serb-held territory in Bosnia, encouragement of, 50, 79–80; Dayton role, xxv, 79–81 (*see also* Dayton Agreement); Europeans, suspiciousness/sidelining of, 56, 62–63, 77, 80–81; Karadžić, pressure for removal as president / surrender to ICTY, 92, 127–28; Kosovo and, 142, 146; M's gripes, 109, 142; NATO bombing of Bosnian Serb army headquarters and, 78, 79; snubbing of Owen/Stoltenberg, 30–31, 79, 153; *To End a War*, xi, 2, 50; on wicked leaders, 2–3. *See also* Holbrooke/Frasure plan
Holbrooke/Frasure plan, 62–63, 77, 78. *See also* Frasure, Robert; Holbrooke, Richard

Howard, Michael, 34
Hoxha, Enver, xvii, 115–18, 143
human rights: in Bosnia, 18; in Croatia, 72; in Kosovo, 10–11, 88, 108, 140
Hungary, 10, 11, 12; Hungarians in Vojvodina, 13, 119
Hurd, Douglas, xvii, 33–34, 35, 74

ICFY (International Conference on Former Yugoslavia): Cutileiro plan, xxiv, 30; establishment, 30. *See also* Vance-Owen Peace Plan
ICTY indictments: examples of, xviii, xix, xx, 71, 77, 148 (*see also under individuals*); failure to indict / slowness, 75, 76–77, 82–83, 127, 128
Ignatieff, Michael, 19
Ilić, Mile, xvii, 98–99, 100–101, 102, 103
Illyrian movement, 17–18
independence
—Bosnia: failure to arrange UN prevention force, 15; Izetbegović's options/decision, 15; referendum, EC requirement, 15; referendum result, xxiv; U.S. support for, 15. *See also* Bosnia
—Croatia and Slovenia: declaration of independence (June 25, 1991), xxiv, 11–12, 13; elections / independence referenda, 13; international line-up, 11–12; JNA intervention, 13–14; jumping ship, 11; M's attitude toward secession, 13–14; self-interest versus interests of rest of Yugoslavia, 12–13, 21; Serb statelets in Bosnia as common goal, 13. *See also* Croatia; Slovenia
intervention in internal affairs, justifiability, 2
Invincible plan, 30
Ischinger, Wolfgang, xvii
Italy, 4, 5, 11, 19, 116
Ivanov, Igor, xvii, 136
Izetbegović, Alija: career, 22; M, meetings with, 59; opposition to recognition of Croatia and Slovenia, 15, 29, 132–33; unhelpfulness post-Dayton, 22; withdrawal of support for Cutileiro plan, xxiv, 30

Janvier, Bernard, xvii, 78
Jeknić, Janko, xvii, 130
Jeremić, Vuk, xvii, 150

JNA (Yugoslav People's Army): intervention in Slovenia, 13–14; links with Bosnian Serb army, 61; as seventh republic, 7, 61; as unifying force, 7
Jovanović, Vladislav, xvii, 136, 139, 145
Jović, Borislav, xviii, 28–29, 133
JUL (Yugoslav United Left), 27, 108
Juppé, Alain, xviii

Karadjordjević dynasty, 4–5
Karadžić, Radovan: big talker, 41; Bosnian Serb Assembly's attitude toward, 48; Carter initiative and, 52–54; character, 55; Dayton agreement, responsibility for delays in implementing, 110; Goražde and, 39; ICTY indictment / evasion attempts, xviii, 59–60, 71, 127; Invincible/Contact Group plan (51/49 percent division) and, 41, 43, 55; Koljević and, 39, 41, 46–47, 54–55, 66, 77, 81; Mladić and, 48, 51; M's attitude toward, 28, 54, 59; M's pressure on / desirability of, 43–44, 48, 88, 89, 91–92; Plavšić's role in removal of, 89, 91–92; removal as president of Republika Srpska, 88–89, 91–92, 110; Sarajevo post-Dayton and, 22; Vance-Owen Peace Plan and, 30
Kardelj, Edvard, xviii, 5, 6–7, 36–37, 116–17
Kershaw, Ian, 3
Kertes, Mihail, 52
KFOR, xxvi, 150
Kinkel, Klaus, xviii
KLA (Kosovo Liberation Army): end to peaceful solution, xxvi, 123, 125; gaining world's attention, 146; M as recruiting agent for, 19–20; M's views on, 142, 143, 144
Kohl, Helmut, xviii
Koljević, Nikola: character, 39, 41; Dayton agreement and, 81; on Goražde, 39, 47; Krajišnik and, 39, 41, 54–55, 66, 77, 81; Mladić and, 78; M's views on, 47; on Patriarch's Meeting, 77; as regular interlocutor, 41, 42, 46–47; on Sarajevo market bombing, 45, 77–78; on Srebrenica, 73; suicide, xviii; weak link, 35, 46–47, 78, 81
Kornblum, John, xviii
Kosovo, Serb nationalism in: M's exploitation/encouragement of, 19–20, 25–26, 120–21; M's Kosovo Polje rallies (1987/89), 120, 132; M's placemen, 26, 121; M's threat to use Kosovo Serbs to crush postelection demonstrations, 104; post-1981 upsurge, 119–20; Ranković's role, 117–18; SANU draft Memorandum (1986), 8, 120
Kosovo / Kosovo Albanians
—history (in chronological order), 113–26; Kosovo Polje, impact, 113; Balkan War atrocities (1912) / Serb reconquest / occupation (1912), 18, 113–14; London Conference (1912–13), 114; World War I peace treaties, 115; harassment of / pressure on Albanians to emigrate (1920–40s), 118; World War I exacerbation of problem, 114–15; World War II Italian occupation / collaboration with Italians and Germans, 115; mass emigration of Serbs and Montenegrins, 116; post–World War II sticks and carrots, 117–18; Tito's proposals for Balkan federation including unification of Albania and Kosovo (1948), 116–17; anti-Axis Albanians' reluctance to join Partisans, 116; harassment of / pressure on Albanians to emigrate (1950s–60s), 118; Albanian protests / escalation of Albanian/Serb tensions (1968/1981), 118, 119–20; harassment of / pressure on Albanians to emigrate (1980s–90s), 121; Dayton treatment of, 86, 87; education agreement (see education agreement); fighting between KLA and Serbian security forces, xxv; escalation of violence, xxvi; mass exodus/killing of Albanians, 147–48; Račak massacre / Rambouillet conference, xi–xii, xxvi, 146–47, 154; declaration of independence / recognition (2008), xxvii, 150–51
—personalities/institutions: Demaqi ("Kosovo Mandela"), xvi, 123, 142; Democratic League of Kosovo (LDK), 121–22; Hoxha, 39–41, 55; KLA (Kosovo Liberation Army), xxvi, 19–20, 123, 125, 142–44, 146. *See also* Rugova, Ibrahim
—status: as autonomous province (1945–63), 6, 117; as autonomous province (1968–74), 6, 117; as autonomous province / quasi-republic (1974 constitution), 118, 119–20; autonomous status for Albanians, refusal of, 12–13; autonomy / enhanced status terminology, 122; autonomy /

Kosovo / Kosovo Albanians (*continued*)
republic status as Albanian objective, 118, 119–20; as "dagger pointed at Belgrade," 19; independence, declaration of / recognition of (2008), xxvii, 150–51; M as mischief maker, 86–87; M's plan for autonomy (1998), 139, 143; M's secessionist anxieties, 82, 121, 139, 141–42, 150; as socio-political community within Serbia (1963–68), 118; union with Albania, 116–17, 150; voting rights on federal presidency, 26
—treatment of Albanians: confidence-building measures, 88, 128–29, 151; economic and social problems, 119–20; human rights, 10–11, 88, 108, 140; pressure to emigrate, 118; purges/persecution, 117–18; representation in state and security structure, 117, 118–19, 120
—United States and: New York lobby, 86; Priština Information Office, 87, 109; reluctance to become involved, 87
—why no solution: failure to implement education agreement, 124–26; Kosovo's disappointment with Dayton, 125–26; law-and-order problems in Albania, 125; loss of Western interest in, 149–51; mounting KLA attacks / Serb overreaction, 125, 140–41; M's rejection of international mediation, 134–41; M's unwillingness to acknowledge reality, 128–29; M's unwillingness to negotiate, 86–87, 123–24; U.S./EU failure to provide M with clear road map, 86–87

Koštunica, Vojislav, xviii, xxvi

Krajina Serbs / RSK (1991–95): arrival of dispossessed colonists from Serbia, 17; attacks on Zagreb, 75; Belgrade's efforts to support, 75–76; Bosnian Serbs, possibility of union with, 61–62; fall of Knin / exodus of Serbs, 76; federal attempts to reduce conflict, 11; Holbrooke's advice to Croats to take control of Serb-held territory, 50; ICTY's failure/slowness to indict, 76–77; loss of Croatian territories, 50, 76; M's attitude toward, 58; Operation Flash, 72–73, 75–76; Operation Storm, 75, 76, 128; rumors of Croatian offensives, 49–50; Tudjman's cleansing of, 21; Z-4 plan, 75, 76

Krajišnik, Momčilo: career, xviii; character / negotiating tactics, 54–55; Contact Group peace plan and, 41, 54–56; Dayton agreement, pathetic figure in, 81; Dayton agreement, responsibility for delays in implementing, 110; Karadžić and, 55; M's attitude toward / pressure on, 28, 81, 110, 131–32; Sarajevo post-Dayton and, 22

Kučan, Milan, xviii, 13, 21

Lake, Tony, 77
League of Communists: Kosovo, 119; Serbia, 24, 26, 120; Yugoslavia (LCY), xxiii, 5, 9, 27, 29, 108. *See also* communism
Lekić, Miodrag, xviii, 129–30
Licht, Sonja, 89
Lilić, Zoran, xviii, 87–88
Little, Alan, 70
Ljajić, Rasim, xvii, 83
Lloyd, Tony, xvii, 128–29
London Conference (1912–13), 114
London Conference on Bosnia (1996), 74, 96

Macedonia: Albanians in, 118, 119; exit from SFRY / recognition as FYROM, xxiii, 22, 29, 87, 125–26
Major, John, xviii, 30
Malcolm, Noel, 16
Marković, Ante, xviii, 8, 11, 13, 133
Marković, Mihailo, xviii, 7, 42
Marković, Mirjana (Mira): downfall, 103; influence on M, 27, 28, 62, 86, 105–6, 107, 124; JUL, 27, 108; Lekić and, 130; life / career / political views, xviii, 24, 27; M's only friend, 27, 48
Martić, Milan, xix, 61–62, 75; ICTY indictment, xviii, 75
Matić, Veran, xix, 103, 110–11
Mesić, Stipe, xix
MFN stabilization programme (1982), 9, 10
Mihailović, Draža, 5, 35, 115
Miles, Dick, xix, 94, 95
Milinović, Goran, 40
Milošević, Slobodan
—character: as autocrat, 27–28; as Balkan butcher, 27; charm, 28, 41; as "cold narcissus," 28; communist schooling, 36, 47, 82; as conundrum / flawed personality, 1–2, 27, 107–8; crowd-shy, 27, 35; as economic wizard, 99–100; friendlessness,

27; as "genius of petty manoeuvring," 28; handling of meetings, 40–41, 47–48; as listener, 62; as manipulator, 23, 42, 50, 51, 62; as "most dangerous man in Europe," 40–41; as nationalist, communist, or chance-taker, 1, 20–21, 24–26, 36, 46, 83, 86, 108; negotiating skills, 62; as political cannibalist, 25–26; as procrastinator, 97; thirst for power, 27, 107
—politics / political role / career: in balance post-1996 local elections, 98–108; blockade of Bosnia-Serbia border (1994), xxv, 44, 47, 52, 55; Bosnian Serbs and, 27–28, 33–34, 48, 58, 77–78, 134; as conspirator, 27–28; Contact Group plan, 43–44, 47, 48–49, 50–54, 56–64, 68–69, 143–44; Dayton Agreement, attitude toward, 81, 108, 109; death (March 11, 2001), xxvii; dominance, 2–3; election as FRY president (1997), xxvi; election of FRY president (2000), loss to Koštunica, xxvi–xxvii; ICTY, cooperation with, 127–28; ICTY indictment, xix, xxvii, 148; Kosovo Serbs and, 25–26, 104; Montenegro and, 26, 121, 129–31; M's assessment of achievements/failures, 132–34; overview, xix, 24–27; post-Dayton elections, 91–97, 98–107; rescued by opposition, 107; responsibility for crisis, 2–3, 19–20, 27, 128; secession of Croatia, Slovenia, and Bosnia, different approaches to, 13–14; Serb nationalism, approach to, 11, 19–20, 21, 25–26, 29; short-changed by Dayton, 86–87; SPD as M's creature, 92, 98, 108; Srebrenica, 72–73, 110; Stambolić and, xxiii, 24–26; on UNPROFOR, 49, 65–69, 72; Vance-Owen plan and, 133–34; wife (Mira Marković), importance, 27, 28, 48, 62, 86, 105–6, 107, 124; as wounded animal, 106. *See also* Marković, Mirjana

Milutinović, Milan: B92 crisis and, 103; career, xix; at odds with M, 99, 106, 140–41, 144–45

Mirković, Saša, xix, 103, 110–11

Mladić, Ratko: Bihać attacks, 47, 50–51; character, 57; ICTY indictment, xix, 57, 71; IR's meeting with, 57; Karadžić and, 51; Milošević and, 1–2, 48, 50–51, 61–62, 68, 89; as replacement for Karadžić, 61; strutting on Belgrade stage, 89; on UNPROFOR, 68; Vance-Owen Peace Plan, opposition to, 30, 61

Montenegro: leaves State Union of Serbia and Montenegro, xxvii; Lekić's views on, 129–30; M plans abolition of republican presidents, 133; M shows unease, 129–31; M's placemen, 26, 121, 129; Muslims in, 130, 131; presidential elections (1997) / fraud, 130–31; tensions with Serbia, 130–31. *See also* FRY

Muslim-Croat Federation: army's role in Srebrenica, 70; Carter initiative and, 53; ceasefire (1994), 53, 54, 60, 65; enclaves as burden, 70–71; establishment (Washington Agreement [1994]), xxv, 31, 54, 55; Koljević's support for, 46; military strength / U.S. and German support, 30–31; M's attitude toward, 58; Republika Srpska (RS), possibility of union with, 58; Sarajevo, failure to break siege, 70, 134; support of NATO forces, 53; support of United States and Germany, 30–31. *See also* Srebrenica

nationalism, as effect and cause: centrifugal tendencies, role, 8, 16, 19; collapse of communism, 16, 19; Croatian/Slovenian nationalism, 18–19, 37, 80; as driving force, 1; how much of a cause, 19; M's role, 11, 19–20, 21, 25–26; Serb nationalism (*see* Kosovo, Serb nationalism in); Tudjman as nationalist, 1, 21

"nations"/"nationalities," 7–8

NATO bombing: Bosnian Serb army headquarters / destruction of communications (1995), xxv, 77–78, 134; Kosovo/FRY (post-Rambouillet) (1999), xi–xii, xxvi, 144, 146–48

natural gas episode, 56

Neville-Jones, Dame Pauline, xix, 58

Operation Flash, 72–73, 75–76

Operation Storm, xxv, 75, 76, 128

Orić, Naser, xix, 70; ICTY indictment, xix

OSCE: González mission, 106, 137, 141; Montenegrin elections (1997), 131; M's attitude toward, 106, 109, 140; readmission of FRY, 140, 145; return to Kosovo, 140

Ostrozinski, Ognjeslav Utjesenović, 17

Owen, Lord David: *Balkan Odyssey*, 14–15, 27, 42–43; character, 63–64; Holbrooke's snub of, 79; as ICFY cochairman, xix, 30; M as key to resolution of crisis, 33–34, 40; M's views on, 68–69; resignation / evaluation of work, 63–64, 68–69; seizing his chance, 44. *See also* Vance-Owen Peace Plan

Paglia, Don Vincenzo, xix, xxvi, 92–93, 97, 124–25, 129
Panić, Milan, xix
Patriarch's meeting (August 25/28, 1995), xxv, 77, 134
Pavelić, Ante, 21
Pavlović, Dragiša, 26, 120
Pavlowitch, Stevan, 3
Pellnas, Bo, xix, 44, 52
Perišić, Momčilo, xix, 53, 61, 134; ICTY indictment, xix
Pešić, Vesna, xx, 107
Pijade, Moša, 37
Plavšić, Biljana: as best Western hope, 30, 127; falling out with M and Pale colleagues / creation of Serbian People's Alliance Party (1977), xx, 127, 133–34; ICTY indictment, xx, 30; as successor to Karadžić as president / leader of SDS, 89, 91–92; Vance-Owen plan, rejection of, 133–34
Poland, 10, 11
Poos, Jacques, 12
Primakov, Yevgeny, 137
protected areas. *See* UNPROFOR/UNPA
Proudhom, P. J., 7

Radio B92: announcement of decision to annul Belgrade election results, 99; attempts to shut down, thwarting of, 103–4, 110–12; Bildt and, 103; finessing diplomatic privilege, 111–12; independence of, 85–86; UK/British embassy support for, 85–86, 110–11
Rambouillet conference, xxvi, 146–47, 154
Ranković, Aleksandar, 36–37, 117–19
Ražnatović, Željko (Arkan), xv, 43–44
recognition
—between former SFRY republics as mutual act: M's objections to, 58–60; triple recognition (FRY/Bosnia/Croatia) (Holbrooke/Frasure), 77; twin-track approach (Plan B), 49, 52, 56, 58–62
—of former SFRY republics, 87; by FRY (1996), xxv; Kosovo and, 125–26, 150–51; recognition of facts and approval distinguished, 87
—as premature act (Bosnia) (1992), 15, 132–33
—as premature act (Croatia and Slovenia) (1991): as death knell for comprehensive settlement, 14–15; German role, 14; opposition to (including Izetbegović), 14, 29, 132–33
Redmond, Charles, 42–43
religious factor, 1, 2, 4, 11, 18, 19, 22
Republika Srpska (RS). *See* Bosnian Serbs / Republika Srpska
Republika Srpska Krajina (RSK) (1991–95). *See* Krajina Serbs / RSK
Rifkind, Malcolm, xx, 6, 72, 74, 119, 124
Romania, 31
Rose, Sir Michael, xx, 33, 48
R2P doctrine (Responsibility to Protect), 154
Rugova, Ibrahim (LDK leader): attempts to arrange meeting with M, 142–44; character / as Kosovo Ghandi, 121–23, 129; education agreement (1996), role, xxvi, 92–93, 97, 124, 128; negotiating tactics / limitations, 121–23

Sachs, Lyndall, 39
Sacirbey, Muhamed (previously Muhamed Šaćirbegović), xx, 22
sanctions against FRY: double-crossing, 109; effects of / effectiveness, xxiv, 27, 35, 36, 39, 55; effects of lifting, 44–45; imposition (1992) / tightening (1993), xxiv, 29; lifting following "free and fair" elections (1996), 93–94; lifting following "free and fair" elections (2000), xxvii; lifting of natural gas sanction, United States as obstacle to, 56; lifting (partial) following blockade of Bosnia-Serbia border (1994), xxv; M's capitalization on lifting, 94; M's determination to secure lifting, 34, 40–41, 49–50, 51, 56, 58–63; as negotiating lever, 14, 34, 43, 47, 108; reimposition issues, 63, 89

INDEX [175]

Sandžak Muslims, 13, 131; SDA, 83
Sarajevo, siege of (1992–96), 22, 42; exclusion zone, 33–34; Koljević's attitude to, 46; marketplace shelling (February 1994), xxv, 33, 77–78; National Library attack (1992), 46
SDA (Muslim nationalist party) (Bosnia), 22, 160n1 (ch. 4); Izetbegović's role, xvii, 22; Sandžak branch, 83
self-determination: Badinter Commission and, 142; domino effect, 153; Helsinki Final Act, 12; Kingdom of Serbs, Croats, and Slovenes and, 4; Partisan Communist movement and, 116; recognition of republics and, 15. *See also* territorial integrity / inviolability of borders
Serb nationalism. *See* Kosovo, Serb nationalism in
Serbia: blockade of border with Bosnia, xxv, 44, 47, 52, 55; EU membership, 149–50, 151; ICTY indictments, impediments to, 148–50; loss of Western interest in, 149–51; media (*see* freedom of press); obstructionism, 8; post-M's downfall, 148–49; status under 1974 SFRY constitution, 6; unity myth, 20
Serbian Democratic Party (SDS), 48, 92, 133
Serbian opposition, as disappointment, 82–84
Serbs, Croats, and Slovenes, Kingdom of (1918–41): Albania, absence of, 4; as compromise between national self-determination and balance of power principle, 4; constitution, suspension of (1929), 4; as fatally flawed romantic dream, 4–5; more to divide than unite, 4; 1941 carve-up, 4–5; Serb dominance, 4; violent chaos and collapse, 4–5
Šešelj, Vojislav, xx, 42, 82–83, 95, 141; ICTY indictment, xx, 82
SFRY (1945–92): Axis invasion (1941) / war of liberation, 5; collapse of special relationship with the West, 10–11; devolved powers / as de facto confederation, 6–7; economic/debt crises, 8, 9–10; federal power in thrall to republics/provinces, 7–8; federal versus republic elections, 8; interrepublic infighting, 28–29; Kosovo/Vojvodina as autonomous province, 6; North-South divide, 9; republics' refusal to transfer taxes to federal government, 10. *See also* constitution; JNA
Silajdžić, Haris, xx, 22, 54
Silber, Laura, 70
Slovenia: communism in, 21; confederation of sovereign republics proposal (1985), 9–10; constitution (1974) and, 9–10; JNA intervention in, 13–14; mono-ethnic nature, 21; M's encouragement of secession, 13–14; obstructionism, 8; recognition, consequences of, 14–15, 132–33; UN membership, xxiv. *See also* independence: Croatia and Slovenia
Smith, Leighton, xx, 134
Smith, Sir Rupert, xx, 65, 68, 73, 78
Socialist Party of Serbia (SPS): as M's creature, 108; post-Dayton elections, poor performance / vote rigging, 92, 98
Srebrenica, 70–78; acts of genocide (ICJ: *Application of the Genocide Convention*), 71–72; Bosnian Muslim army's role, 70, 71; Dutch air attacks, 70; exodus of Serbs / Muslim attacks on, 70; fall of / massacres, 71; jihadism and, 70, 153; Mladić's motivation / hostility to Dutch peacekeepers, 73; M's reaction to, 72–73, 110; war crime, xxv, 71–72
Stambolić, Ivan, xx, xxiii, 24–27, 84, 85, 120
Stanišić, Jovica, xx, 65, 66, 139; ICTY indictment, xx
Stojanović, Svetozar, 42
Stoltenberg, Thorvald: Contact Group cochairman, xx, 44, 63; Invincible plan, 30; Kosovo and, 123–24; Krajina Serbs and, 75–76; M's meetings with, 44, 68; U.S./Holbrooke's snub of, 30–31, 79, 153. *See also* Contact Group plan
Stranka Prava, 17–18
Strossmeyer, Josip, 17–18
Surroi, Veton, xx, 143

Tadić, Ljubomir, 27
Taylor, A. J. P., 2–3, 36

Tepavac, Mirko, 6
territorial integrity / inviolability of borders (Helsinki Final Act), 12, 155; Badinter Borders Principle (Opinion 3), 159n3; "no force" to preserve, 10–11, 14, 29–30; self-determination principle, conflict with, 12; territorial exchanges, acceptability of, 48, 53–54, 55
Thaçi, Hashim, xx, 146
Tito, Josip Broz, Yugoslavia under: break with Moscow, 5–6, 19, 117; constitutional changes, 6; economic success, 5–6; as expensive Western asset, 8–9; as haven of peace, 6; as "only effectively functioning institution," 6–7; purges, 5; responsibility for crisis, 3, 19; Third Way / Non-Aligned Movement, 9
To End a War (Holbrooke), xi, 2, 50
Trebjesanin, Žarko, 28
Trevisan, Dessa, xx, 50
Trotsky, Leon, 113–14
Tudjman, Franjo: Bildt and, 76, 128; Bosnian carve-up, 13, 21; career, xx; ethnic cleansing, 21; "Father of the Nation," 35; ICTY indictment, 76–77, 128; M's meetings with, 59; as nationalist, 1, 21; responsibility for crisis, 2–3, 23
Turkish/Ottoman rule, xxiv, 4, 16–18, 20, 113–14, 138

Ugljanin, Sulejman, xxi, 83
UN hostage crisis, 65–69; Greek intervention, 67–68; IR delivers formal written warning to Bosnian Serbs, 66; M's response, 65; release of hostages, 66–68; trigger, 65
UNHCR, 39, 49, 72
UNPROFOR/UNPA: Bihać, attacks on, 47, 50–51; Bosnian Muslims' attitude toward, 69, 70; creation (1991 truce), xxiv, 14; as flawed concept, 69, 71–72; mandate (UNSCR 743 of February 21, 1992), 71–72; M's attitude toward, 49, 65–69, 72; Operation Storm, xxv; Rapid Reaction Force proposal, 74; threatened withdrawal of UK contingent, 49; UN hostage crisis, 65–69; UNHCR criticism of, 39. *See also* Srebrenica; UN hostage crisis

U.S. policy: Contact Group and, 42–43, 56, 60–63; lift and strike, 30–31; M's assessment of, 132; natural gas episode, 56; "no dog in this fight," 12, 29–30; reassessment of Yugoslavia's role, 10–11; recognition U-turn, 15. *See also* Holbrooke, Richard
Ustasha regime, 5, 16, 19
uti possidetis. See territorial integrity / inviolability of borders

Van den Broek, Hans, xxi
Vance, Cyrus, xxi, 14, 30
Vance Plan (UNPA). *See* UNPROFOR/UNPA
Vance-Owen Peace Plan (VOPP) (1993): as best chance for multiethnic Bosnia, 63–64, 81; Mladić and, 30, 61; M's role / rejection by Bosnian Serbs, xxiv, 34, 44, 133; summary of provisions, 30; U.S. hostility to, 30–31
Vatican: Serbian Church and, 124; support for Croatia and Slovenia, 11
Vejvoda, Ivan, 7, 16
Versailles, Treaty of (1918), 3, 155
Vllasi, Azem, xxi, 119, 121
Vojvodina: as autonomous province, 6, 117, 118, 119; Hungarians in, 13, 119; IR's contacts with leaders, 82; M's placemen, 26, 121; secessionism, 82; UN hostages in Novi Sad, 66–67; voting rights on federal presidency, 26
von Hötzendorff, Conrad, 146–47
Vucinich, Wayne, 20
Vukmanović-Tempo, Svetozar, xxi, 116

Walsum, Peter van, xxi, 155
Washington Agreement (1994), xxv, 31, 54, 55
West, Rebecca, 1, 34, 80
Woodward, Susan, 2, 4, 10, 12

Yeltsin, Boris, xxi, 148
Yugoslav crisis, contributory factors / overview, 1–23; centrifugal internal structures, 3, 6–8, 16, 19, 22–23; collapse of special relationship with West, 10–11, 19, 24–25; communist heritage, 16; democratic deficit / absence of civic society, 3–4; economic/debt crises, 8, 9–10; ethnic

divisions, 2, 15–16, 17–19, 22–23; fault lines, 15–16, 17; hatreds, 2, 3, 16–17, 49, 57; international factors, 3, 8, 10–15; North-South divide, 9; religious divisions, 1, 2, 4, 11, 17, 19; Tito's settling of scores, 19; villain-led or inevitable, 1–3; "Wild East" stereotype, 16–17; World War II / post–World War II violence, 16. *See also* nationalism, as effect and cause

Zajedno: attempt to set up meeting with M, 102–3; Avramović as short-lived leader, xv, 95; fractured unity, 107; rumor mongering, 95–96; success in 1996 local elections, 98

Zametica, Jovan, xxi, 66

Žepa, 70, 72–73

Zimmermann, Warren, xxi, xxiv, 3, 10–11, 28, 30, 132

Zurcher, A. J., 4

www.ingramcontent.com/pod-product-compliance
Lightning Source LLC
Chambersburg PA
CBHW012231230426
43666CB00040B/2899